# FIRE
# WITHOUT
# WITNESS

**BRITISH AMERICAN PUBLISHING**

*Also by Mark Nepo*

GOD, THE MAKER OF THE BED, AND THE PAINTER

**Plan of
Sistine Chapel**

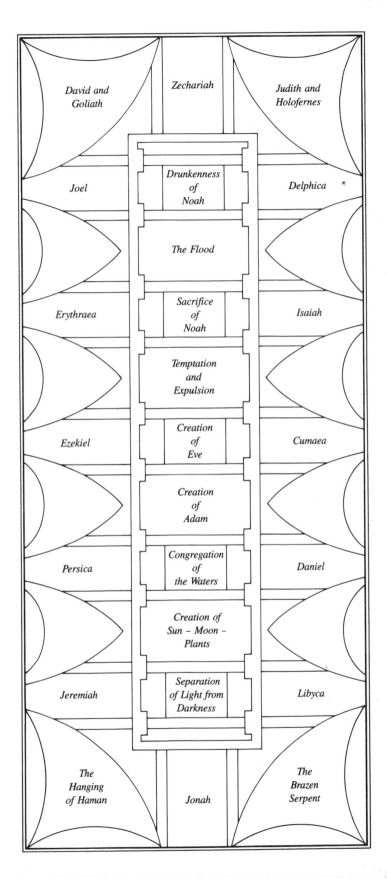

David and
Goliath

Zechariah

Judith and
Holofernes

Joel

Drunkenness
of
Noah

Delphica

Erythraea

The Flood

Sacrifice
of
Noah

Isaiah

Ezekiel

Temptation
and
Expulsion

Creation
of
Eve

Cumaea

Persica

Creation
of
Adam

Congregation
of
the Waters

Daniel

Jeremiah

Creation of
Sun – Moon –
Plants

Separation
of Light from
Darkness

Libyca

The
Hanging
of Haman

Jonah

The
Brazen
Serpent

MARK NEPO

# FIRE
# WITHOUT
# WITNESS

BRITISH AMERICAN PUBLISHING

1988

Portions of this poem appeared in the
following periodicals:

*Chelsea:* The five "Hidden Angel/Pico" passages from
"God Separates Light and Dark"
*Confrontation:* The final two passages in Ezekiel's voice
*The Dalhousie Review:* "Vestments Lie" from "The Libyan Sibyl"
*The Kansas Quarterly:* Three Michelangelo narratives
from "God Separates Light and Dark"
*The Kenyon Review:* The opening and closing sections
of "The Punishment of Haman"
*The Massachusetts Review:* "Lorenzo and the Pazzi Conspiracy"
from "God Separates Light and Dark"
and "Moses Has Trouble With God's Instructions" from
"The Brazen Serpent"
*The Mid-American Review:* The Parables of Isaiah

Published by British American Publishing
3 Cornell Road
Latham, NY 12110
Manufactured in the United States of America

93 92 91 90 89 5 4 3 2 1

Library of Congress Cataloging in Publication Data

Nepo, Mark, 1951—
Fire without witness: Michelangelo in the
Sistine Chapel/Mark Nepo.
p. cm.
ISBN 0-945167-06-7 : $19.95
1. Michelangelo Buonarroti, 1475-
1564—Poetry 2. Vatican Palace (Vatican
City)—Sistine Chapel—Poetry. 3. Bible—
History of Biblical events—Poetry.
I. Title
PS3564.E6F5 1988
811'.54—dc19                          88-17726
                                       CIP

# CONTENTS

List of Illustrations
Preface

## 1509

## 1510

# 1511

APPENDICES

# ILLUSTRATIONS

*Unless otherwise noted, all prints are of The Sistine Ceiling and all work is by Michelangelo. Photographic credits are as follows: color prints–SCALA/Art Resource; black and white–ALINARI/Art Resource; numbers 29 and 35–The Clark Art Institute.*

*So, waiting, I have won from you the end:*
*God's presence in each element.*

—GOETHE

# ACKNOWLEDGMENTS

When you spend almost a decade of your life wrestling with something you can't really see or put your hands on, you continue living through the grace of those who truly love you. And I would like to thank Robert Mason for his tireless, relentless care and for all his astute and crucial suggestions which can be found across the entire book. And Odette Meyers for sharing her impeccable knowledge of Biblical folklore and mirrors. And Judith Johnson whose selfless support is only matched by her openness of mind. And Paul and Anne Bowler for the ease of sanctuary their friendship provides. And Cindy Winter and Diane Cornell for their constant encouragement. They gave me the book in which I wrote this. And Alan Ledet for his abiding belief in what it means to be alive. And John and Linanne Sackett for their unending generosity. And I can never repay the tender unflinching honesty and faith with which my wife, Anne Myers Nepo, has kept herself between me and the world when I've needed to work, which has been often, and how she's dragged me back when I've avoided life. Her spirit informs this poem thoroughly. Nor can I sufficiently praise the integrity and precise commitment of my editor, Susanne Dumbleton, without whom these pages would have yellowed.

I want to express a special thanks to Yaddo, where most of this poem was finally written. The place is an invaluable crucible. And appreciation to the following editors for such clear support in their journals: Paul Jenkins, Carol Fetler, Philip Church, Galbraith Crump, Sonia Raiziss, Martin Tucker, Alan Johnson, Sally Kraine, Harold Schneider, Andrew Wainwright, and Alan Andrews. And to *The Massachusetts Review* for nominating pieces from the book for the GE Younger Writers Award.

I am indebted to dozens for the canon of Michelangelo source material, including Umberto Baldini, Luciano Berti, Georg Brandes, Robert J. Clements, Ascanio Condivi, Charles De Tolnay, Frederick Hartt, Howard Hibbard, Paul James Lebrooy, Giovanni Papini, E.H. Ramsden, Franco Russoli, Roberto Salvini, Charles Seymour, Jr., John Addington Symonds, and Giorgio Vasari. For the Biblical side, I relied mostly on the Old Testament.

In addition, I would like to extend my appreciation to Dustin Wees and The Clark Art Institute in Williamstown, Massachusetts for their careful assistance in securing the fine reproductions of Michelangelo's work which appear throughout the book.

To all, I say what Pico said, "Friendship is the end of all Philosophy." I thank you for your gift of light.

# PREFACE

FIRE WITHOUT WITNESS centers on the world of Michelangelo as revealed through his painting of The Sistine Ceiling. While painting the different panels, he reveals stories of his time, his life, and through his dreams, the future. As the panels are painted, the prophets and sibyls and objects of Creation come alive, unknown to Michelangelo, and tell their stories. The poem presents two skewed realities. And while at times the Biblical and Mythic voices see Michelangelo, they never reach his awareness. They barely interact, in brushing contacts we alone witness.

The poem follows, in sequence, the way Michelangelo actually painted the frescos on the Ceiling. The order of painting here is what I see as most logical. Other suggested sequences exist, due to the uneven progression of his work, but it is clear he painted the story of Creation in reverse order, moving from Noah to Adam to God creating the elements, winding his way back to the beginning. It took him three years to paint the Ceiling, not including the border of lunettes, and the poem is broken into three parts or movements, 1509, 1510, and 1511, each part into sections representing the panels painted during those years—25 sections in all.

I was born to write this poem, to use it as a phoenix, a clear fire for issues as old as they are immediate, as deep as they are contemporary. It seems, now, a painting itself, a vision of that rim between the human and the infinite, where our body of sense almost leaves us, then settles and hardens into what we are. And when dealing with the infinite, all comes down to one encompassing, unnameable source, one fire without witness. As Michelangelo himself put it, "What is in the very center is always free."

MARK NEPO

# 1509

*Dearest father*

*I myself am quite concerned, for this Pope hasn't given me a single grosso for a whole year, and I am not asking for any, for my work is not progressing in such a way as to make me think I deserve anything. This is due to the difficulty of the work, and to the fact that this painting is not my profession. I am wasting my time fruitlessly. God help me.*

*Your Michelangelo,*
*Sculptor in Rome*

# I. ZECHARIAH

*In 1508, in Florence, Michelangelo Buonarroti, already having designed and begun a tomb for Pope Julius, already having fled Rome once after Julius aborted the project; Michelangelo is summoned to Rome again. This time to paint, of all things, the ceiling of a chapel. It seems an odd choice with the remarkable gifts of the older Leonardo and the younger Raphael within reach of the powerful Pope. Nonetheless, the ceiling is a burden the sculptor undertakes begrudgingly with virtually no experience at painting frescos. It is a political maneuver orchestrated by Bramante the Architect to get Michelangelo out of the way, to mire him in an impossible task.*

*And Michelangelo, a chronic complainer who wants nothing but to sculpt, a compulsive worker who forges his own tools, trudges off to Rome to begin the Sistine Ceiling. A small band of willing Florentines follow. They begin working on The Flood. But after several months, in 1509, not liking what his assistants have done, and not able to tell them, the moody loner arrives early one morning and locks them out, refuses to answer, and begins again, alone—while they knock and call to him—begins again, mixing paints, cleaning brushes, up and down the scaffold, incessantly, by himself. Alone again, he moans for the wondrous safety of his youth in the Medici Garden, where he felt the love of the patron of the age, Lorenzo the Magnificent.*

MICHELANGELO: God, how do I come to this?!
It was Bramante! *He* brought me here!
He prods the Pope! Always the whisper
like a leash. Now I scratch scratch
*scratch* the vault. And the damp plaster
soaks up my bodies. And the colors
go where they will. Look! The stone
is skinned! No bone at all! All tattoo!

Lorenzo always said the life is spilled by events,
not mapped or drawn, "And you'd better land feet first
Buonarroti. Yours is to continue, chisel in hand,
searching for the *right* stone, the *live* stone.
That the life leaves the stone before you're done
is not your affair."

I'd rather be working the mouth of the faun
when Lorenzo himself rapped the teeth,
"Too many for a faun, I think."
And how I stood where he stood when he left,
chipped one tooth, looked again,
chiselled out another.

Eh! Why not Leonardo, or the boy, Raffaello?

*Days pass. The sculptor, having scraped off what the others had done, has almost repainted The Flood, when the colors start to mildew and blister severely. As Michelangelo's frustration mounts, Zechariah, unpainted, lingers over the entrance, formless and out of view. He is an unwilling prophet whose name means "God Remembers." His whole life is agitated by unexpected visions he cannot understand though he's compelled to proclaim them. Ever restless, the prophet hovers, out of breath, alarmed by yet another unwanted vision.*

ZECHARIAH: Up! Up! Flee from the land of the North!
Up! O Scion! Escape! You who dwell with Babylon!
It was the second year of Darius, I had a vision
like this vision. A terror deep among the myrtles.

And black as it was, behind it, a stallion,
the color of fired blood. It crazed me, and then,
I whinnied in a pitch which rose like surf and
hot as the terror made my lungs, I entered
the shade of the myrtle where wolves were
prowling, and the terror rushed me, a black shadow
owning my mind, till I whinnied like a bludgeoned horse,
and I'm an old man now, haunted into service.

I tell you what followed has cost me
a life's serenity: visions pressed in the brain
like wax sealed to vellum. No matter how I've tried
to keep it to myself, I've told everyone
of the stallion and the terror, and then, they wait,
quizzical, for some explanation.

The dark Lord visits like flint on stone
and Oh the itch, the rub, the scar!
Wanting for a spark that's passed.

*As Zechariah spreads like ether along the vault, Michelangelo contemplates his form till the prophet recognizes his agitation in this strange man trying to paint a dim and arched ceiling.*

ZECHARIAH: He sweats and squints, grunts and squints,
complains and squints, and the wood jiggles
and creaks. This Buonarroti is possessed.
His eyes flare amber, amber of the stricken.
He swipes at the stone as if it were
the hole left by his birth. He swings
the brush like a torch. Set me aflame,
Buonarroti! Stroke on stroke from out
the living rock, lose your peace too.

*Startled by a flare of voice, the seer skims away, as Sangallo arrives to inspect the ruined fresco and discovers that the plaster was applied too wet.*

*Michelangelo throws his brushes and abandons The Flood. It is then he is drawn to begin, yet again, over the entrance by drafting the image of Zechariah. Weeks pass and the Chapel turns a honeycomb barely waxed at its mouth by one frantic bee; his buzzing, his scratching, his shifting weight. The scaffold gains its creaking patterns. Here he stops. He thinks someone's there and dreads the appearance of his theological consultant, as he tries to feel his way through the half-finished prophet.*

MICHELANGELO: The place is wrong!
    The vault—grainy and warped!
    And the Cardinal leans over my sketches
    and yaps like a dog, "Zechariah *must*
    be over the entrance, he *must!*"
    He's driven me up the scaffold
    more than once. When I hear him
    enter the Chapel, I swing open
    to my Ceiling, sweep a thick brush
    on nothing till the paint sprays
    and the scaffold trembles.
    He backs away gingerly. He can't
    stand blue spots on his robe
    and the dust aggravates his sinus.
    He yaps his way out. I rock
    and tell him I'll be down shortly.

    The light has sifted, has bleached
    this prophet's eyes.

    I dislike painting:
    to deepen, you darken
    and too much vanishes the face.
    By the time my stroke is clean,
    my knuckles go numb, my forearm
    quivers. I pull in to rest,
    the bristles split. Paint streams
    the handle, fills my palm. It runs
    my wrist. It is useless.

*Being worked into view by the artist's strokes, Zechariah squirms at a buried vision, resurrected by Michelangelo's filling of his eye.*

ZECHARIAH: The lead cover was lifted, and there, a girl,
    naked in the bushel, all steamed and whiny.
    She pawed her own chest and I ran shouting:
    "Wail! You cypress trees! For the cedars
    are fallen! The mighty have been despoiled!"
    Then I raised my eyes and saw two primal Queens,
    wet linens to their full manilla breasts
    and they moaned, a hot wind peeling my robe,
    and I wanted them, their wet nipples pronounced.
    I wanted their softness to soothe my tense mouth!

    When I came to, I was holding a lizard
    to a stone.

    I've taken to books. They are safer.
    They are there when you look again.

*In order to paint the Ceiling, the previous depiction, a panorama of stars, a
planetarium of sorts painted by d'Amelia, has to be covered with plaster.
This is done in stages, and though the work being covered is not extraordi-
nary, the process annoys Michelangelo. As he settles into his new creative
prison, he sadly realizes he must plaster and paint his way out and can't help
but stall; distrustful of all but his impulse to sculpt, which nags him with the
image of a Colossus he saw fixed inside a mountain while in a quarry at
Carrara.*

MICHELANGELO: How the plaster gobs and
    spreads, sticking to everything like teeth
    to prey. Today's blood, tomorrow's paint.
    Before I start, I'm done. And d'Amelia will haunt me
    beneath this white hood. Only a thug or Emperor
    could ruin another and not see himself levelled
    for the new. Oh, Julius has an appetite for art,
    but he thinks, like meat, it's a matter of cutlery.
    And Bramante's worse. He knows the pain. Yet it was he
    who screwed the hooks into the Ceiling, and the scaffold
    swung like a hammock, "And how, Your Holiness, am I to fill
    the holes when this hammock is dismantled, when the painting

is complete? Am I to leave the plaster holes
like pus marks in my work?"

Lately, in the grey before dawn, I wake,
forgetting I'm in Rome. The light clouds my room
and I'm a child, my hand cold about the chisel;
my palm, after hammering, warm and chafed. And there,
the vibration in the stone, the chisel, my hand sore,
the dust of hammered marble floating in the sun;
the stonecutter's yard, ancient and charged;
the stone flat out, both hands learning
how the blow travels. And here I crush the brushes
light as twigs. But in the Apuanes, beyond the quarry,
I saw a mountain jut over the sea, saw dusk splinter
its horizon! And in the peak, pulsed and waiting,
Godlike Hands worn Sheer to Cliffs! Arms Wide
to the Heavens! 1000 Feet High!

It always calls, not in words,
but pulsing off the dark as I let go,
orange and pulsing, reaching for the lowest stars
or putting them back! I burn to set it free! Always!
The mind skips in panoramas! The hands crawl!
And we grow thin as clothesline
stretched between.

# II. JUDITH AND THE HEAD OF HOLOFERNES

Judith, whose name means "Jewess," is the widow of Manasses, a gentle soul who died of a fever while working his fields. Hardened by her loss, she is tender only at the core. As a widow, her deep grief makes her more willing to face danger. This leads her to encounter Holofernes, the Assyrian general, who has taken the Jews of Bethulia under siege because they refuse to send troops to support Nebuchadnezzar's attack on Media. Holofernes has an appetite for domination and wants the Jews to worship Nebuchadnezzar. He circles the town and cuts off their water supply. Judith evolves through a curious inner storm, finding God in her grief. It brings her to an unexpected destiny. She is sent by the elders to foil Holofernes with no question of her plan. As Judith sinks into her fate, Michelangelo is drawn to contemplate his own sense of grief.

*Judith's thoughts—of her dead husband Manasses, and of God's presence—
wash together unclearly.*

JUDITH: One firm within me,
     like a pellet of heat.
     Now, my life's a glove for thunder.
     Now, the life of night destroys
     and the bluest things make me weep.
     I ache for him
     to brush this grief
     from my taste.

     I've cupped the dirt
     where he fell,
     and he is there,
     between the dust
     and my fingers.

     I now believe in voices
     which disguise themselves
     as queer untimely passions.

*Michelangelo, in considering the accuracy of Judith's neck, recalls his first
attempts at dissection.*

MICHELANGELO: I'd take my stepmother's meat knife
     with its nicked blade, and a clean pair
     of scissors, and after twelve, the tubby Prior,
     with ice burning in his eyes, would lead me
     to the dead room.

     That first cut from sternum to belly
     parted like a bloodless tent, and the lungs,
     the dried fruit pressed, bulged between
     the bluish ribs and felt like hardened
     sponge.

How sad and pulled I was at first,
peeling back a sheet of skin
from an arm like green bark
from a stump. The illusion
of strength was gone
forever.

Once, near dawn,
the tubby burning Prior
fell asleep. I hauled out a boy.
His muscles had not rigored yet.
I worked his arms like clay in a pouch.
I flipped his head, gently, but quickly
like a sack of grain, and watched
the young skin drag his throat.
He had a mole beneath his collarbone
and it was warm. I put him back
to finish passing.


*Judith speaks of fear and grief and God's will as rings.*

JUDITH: I squeezed the towel and the bead bled to a ring
and the ring to a ripple, again to a wave. Only
when first a ring was the circle confining.
It was then I knew I would still Holofernes.
God was the wave, the horizon
the ripple, and Holofernes
bled within them both.

I've learned. Inside a fear,
the ring tightens. If I can wade
past its draw, it closes to a point
and I am free.

Manasses was binding sheaves in the field,
the heat wrapped about his head.
He couldn't step past its shimmer
and the ring fisted him.

I wrung towel after towel
across his burning bone.
His eyes rolled, flared
and snuffed.

He died in Bethulia,
buried with his fathers.

I wept in warm towels
and made a Tophet of the attic,
becoming the ring of our house.

It was God's rimless breath that broke me;
sheer moisture on a sweltered urn
that pushed me from my grief.

To disembody fear,
rush the ring.

*Unexpectedly, the head of Holofernes seems unpaintable, as Michelangelo relives a dream about Piero de Medici, Lorenzo's eldest son, who drowned at the age of 34 in the river Garigliano, a month before the sculptor finished his David in 1504.*

MICHELANGELO: He was reaching over the water, up
into a tree, for fruit or something still
unseen, and then he fell. I was on the bottom
and could see his bubbled mouth turn maroon,
the water pressing at his face. He died, for sure,
but seemed content. I was there. This seems
so clear. We floated then, the body and I
as its underside, wavering down through time.
We swelled and puffed and spent eternity
tangled in a fallen limb. And then the birds
began to nip serenely.

*Holofernes encircled the city, and Judith rippled to a wave as her moment arrived. The elders themselves were astonished at her magnetism, as they authorized her to hunt the Assyrian general.*

JUDITH: I knew after I spoke to Ozias
    I must wash my thighs and fold the haircloth
    back. I anointed myself with the old linaments,
    but couldn't wash, for Holofernes had muddied
    our springs. The oils fumed about my body
    as I heard men smash urns in the night.

    As I approached the gates of Bethulia,
    I knew the Lord had made me beautiful
    for even the cattle cooed and slowed
    and I felt like a calm breezing over ponds.

    Ozias kept his word, not asking my plans
    and I left the city for the Assyrian camp.
    Descending the hill, in the thin blue
    preceding dawn, I heard stones scatter
    beneath my feet. I walked that moment
    over and over and knew the color of my soul.

*All day the left arm of Holofernes, as he paints it, is taking the shape of
Christ's arm in The Pieta. The sculptor tires and complains.*

MICHELANGELO: It takes too long to mix the pigments.
    They stick in the morning, gobs of copper
    and bronze. It takes half an hour to thin them.
    Then the swirl doesn't clear but streaks. At first,
    I wipe the spray from my face. Then it covers me
    like gilded rain. I squint in time to have it
    hit my lids. I keep painting. The Ceiling is rough
    and potted and the thick pigment soaks in fast.
    It barely covers, and when it does, patches and nicks
    stay untouched. Then I dab and press in swatches. Then
    smooth it out. Rub hard and smooth. It sticks. Then—
    out of paint. It's impossible to gain momentum. First—
    sweep the line of robe or blade, then dab rub rub.
    Just when the figure needs its blood, the brush goes dry

and splits. And I can't reach the bucket fast enough. Move
the bucket. Spill the bucket. The blood drips down my hands.
Prophetic blood spots the scaffold. It splats the Chapel
floor. It smears my palms.

I dig with the stylus, dig and paint their ridge of hide,
then fill with the left till the thick rub makes the hand,
deep beneath the palm, burn and ache. I never stop.
When the left swells, I fill with the right. I *refuse*
to stop. My back tightens as I rub the potted stone.
My sore hands puff. My numb back drains.
It snags a rib. It forms a bunch.
I *have* to stop.

They swell and puff, the hands, and late
at night, I try to sleep, as they throb and burn,
twin suns pulsing beneath my palms like the spiked holes
in Christ. His blood, puddles of sore light. And I stare
into the faithless dark, spread on my bed like a cross,
palms up to the leeching night. I pulse and glow
and imagine His molten pain burning out my hands.

*Judith relives how she rode a heated moment which Holofernes could neither*
*resist nor break, and how she, as a ring in God's burning sea, beheaded*
*Holofernes without thought, regret, or strain.*

JUDITH: He had me dine in his tent.
There was a chill between my legs
where the haircloth had been. I felt sheer.
He raised my skirt with his eyes several times.
O Manasses, what leads me on comes not from me!
This general's skin was thick as hemp and he thought
it made him powerful. The ring tightened. He drank
and I ate my figs. It grew late and he passed out.

His chest heaved like a slumbering bull,
his sword strapped to his waist, dull brass
and heavy in the grip. I shook it loose. He stirred.

My lips quivered. I kissed his sweating skull
and knew he would gore me, could he only wake
and mount. I knelt in prayer, "Lift me, O God
of Israel . . " Manasses, I could never have
killed—It was God—Surging
through my Entire Body!

I fisted his hair
and raised his head
like a bucket from a well
and God rose the sword before I could think
and the blade smacked his neck open like a log.
It stuck—he gagged and God rose my arms—
he gurgled—God dropped me swiftly—his neck
snapped clean with a hiss
and his head rolled free
as the bucket spilled red
and thick about the bone.

I left the Assyrian camp
with the head of the slumbering bull
on a tray. What was pain in life,
was mere heaviness in death.
I no longer felt beautiful,
rather hot and waning.

# III. DAVID SLAYING GOLIATH

The story of David begins when the great priest-judge of Israel, Samuel, becomes dissatisfied with Saul as king. Once in power, Saul seems to deteriorate under pressure, and Samuel begins to look for a likely successor. He finds David, the youngest son of Jesse, tending his father's sheep in the hills, and anoints him the king to come. As time passes, the innocent David feels stirred by this anointment, though he seems without purpose. He grows confused. It is then he is called to Saul's court, to play his lyre to soothe the king's frayed nerves. Later, of course, David meets Goliath of Geth when no one else will face the behemoth. As David grows stronger by replaying his anointment, Michelangelo grows frustrated with the repetition of his creations. It compels him to dwell on his secret, how he can see figures waiting to be taken from the uncut stone. He then admits to the unlikely way he first arrived in Rome in 1496.

*As he begins to paint David, Michelangelo can't rid himself of the figure of Holofernes he has just completed, for it has the fallen arm of Christ in his Pieta. It agitates him as he plans, but can't find David. It irritates him no end to paint what he's already sculpted; first the arm of Holofernes and now David, whom he has sculpted magnificently only five years before. But despite his aggravation, his way of seeing in the stone begins to transform into a seeing in the soul.*

MICHELANGELO: Somewhere in this wretched corner
    David swings his sling, like a conscience,
    scraping the dark stone. He spins and spins.
    I can feel it in the draft. But where?! And how
    to bring him up with these brushes?! Oh my fingers
    itch! With marble, there's a way, a pulse, the figure
    waits, and I was born with an instinct where to strike!
    But Where? To feel God's will, intact, spilling
    all its sense? Where the air to burn
    as white as purity?

    At times, the mind drains like a sink,
    a sieve, the heart's revisionist,
    draining blood to spruce.

    I feel insufficient, repetitive as Hell,
    a bird following a bird following a bird.
    Yet a conscience pours out honey in this way.

*David recalls how his brothers were refused, as he was anointed by Samuel.*

DAVID: I was tending the sheep when Samma came
    running over the hill. The sheep scattered
    and he was out of breath, sweat under his eyes.

    He took father's staff, and I climbed the hill
    to Bethlehem. A slight breeze made the grass
    feel very clean. The sky was crystal above the clouds.

    I found father surrounded by my brothers. Eliab
    saw me first. The others fell silent as the ancient Samuel

held my face in his leathered hands. He looked through me
as if to another who somehow answered him.

A stillness pricked me. I was taller, stronger
across my chest. Samuel nodded to father and Abinadab
brought a horn of oil, which Samuel took,
calling my brothers close.

Father wept as Samuel put his fingers to the oil,
chanting as he rubbed my head and when he bid me rise,
I saw myself in father's eyes: I was blue and the grass
was cool as water as he led us from Bethlehem,
arm in arm, back to Samma and the sheep.

*Unable to shake the fallen arm of Christ from his mind, Michelangelo stalls
on the scaffold to recall how he first saw The Pieta, complete, in the un-
quarried marble at Carrara.*

MICHELANGELO: Someday, I'll carve a Venus, bunching
      the warm breasts high, the silk legs closed,
      the most perfect virgin, with everything
      to give, and no desire.

      O what if Heaven is as cold.
      The things I love most wait hunched
      in the white Carrara grove, never
      where the workmen mutter. Like fish,
      the statues scatter from the lines.
      I hunt alone, away from the crews,
      and the statues pull back, deep
      in the thick of the mountain.
      They hold still as the stone,
      and some arch themselves
      along the inner faults,
      dreaming slowly
      not to be found.

      But a sculptor
      must know how to quarry,

32    know where in the mountain
the statue lives. The Pieta was done
when I saw her high on the east wall;
the Mother hovering, arms pleading,
a good four yards in. I went back
at dusk and there, the crumpled Jesus,
his infallible arm dangling in the ocean
of stone, and as the sky deepened,
the body flared orange. It found
the Mother's arms
and vanished.

In the morning,
the statue slept,
the veins glossed blue.
They cursed me for wanting it.

I insisted, began to move their ropes myself.
It was yards higher than they were working.
It took four days. No one believed me.
The son had drowned and the Mother was floating.

*As David's sense of what would come inflamed his unconscious, his range of
mood grew more extreme.*

DAVID: I flashed, daily, a pool rising,
        seeking to let the waters rush,
        but where, for what purpose?
        Samuel's face appeared everywhere,
        in the smell of cheese,
        in the clump of straw
        chewed by a goat.
        I grew dizzy, nightly,
        swirling back on myself.

My brothers no longer chased me.
My father no longer kissed me.
Everything had changed
and nothing had changed.

*Each day, by midafternoon, the sculptor's head begins to ache behind his eyes,*
*enough that he must count his paints, and rest.*

MICHELANGELO: This blue Buonarroto sent
    is like paste. One batch runs. One batch
    sticks and I'm a huge rag of color.

    I tend to spend all day up here.
    I dread the descent.
    The scaffold creaks
    and shakes, and I am 34.

    The rooms I rent are useless
    and I go through servants
    faster than paint.

    Cramped, I'm always cramped
    wherever I live and the air
    is stale.

    Here, the space reels; enough
    to lie back and peel the Chapel
    till the Heavens float in view.

*When David was sent to calm Saul, an angel whispered between his father's*
*words.*

DAVID: I was with Samma and Eliab
    when messengers from the King
    appeared on the hill.
    We quickly found father.

    They spoke in private
    and then Eliab brought an ass
    and Abinadab dragged a goat
    while father gave me my harp, his hand
    to my cheek, "Saul is troubled.
    Go play for him." As he pulled away,
    another voice said, "Let the waters flow."

Samma fastened a bottle of wine to the ass
and gave me some bread.
He shrugged, puzzled.

There wasn't a word as we rode.
I looked back down the hill and Eliab waved
as father stood motionless, and off by himself,
among the sheep, Samma, scratching something
in the dirt with father's staff.

*Frustrated with the flatness of painting, the expanse yet to do, and the seeming
dirth of gestures to use, Michelangelo regrets how he first arrived in Rome.*

MICHELANGELO: I carved a young St. John for Pier, the
    other Lorenzo. It was not satisfying. I kept to myself
    and drifted, for weeks, till I found another piece of marble,
    old, chipped, on the bottom of a cutter's pile.
    I spent my commission for it.

    When I moved it, there was a reclining figure,
    within, close to the base. As the chips flaked off,
    I realized it was a child sleeping.

    I worked swiftly. Pier was impressed, "I say
    bury the Cupid. Let the soil fill its pores.
    It will bring a fine price,
    a marvelous antique."

    It was the end of winter and Lorenzo had been dead
    three colorless years, and Rome seemed a comet to catch.
    Nothing mattered in those days; even the chisel
    spat faults, forked tongue of a snake
    splitting stone.

    They sent the sleeping child by mule to Rome
    where Baldassare sold it to Cardinal Riario.
    Within months a burly servant was inquiring in Florence,
    wanting the sculptor who fashioned antiques.

All I could think of was the child's stained face
as we trotted the streets of Rome. I couldn't bear
what I'd always known: to hide what we must face
seals the price of the soul.

*Saul was pacified by the inaudible river frothing sweetly through David's
harp.*

DAVID: Saul rubbed his brow. His forehead was red.
He sat deep in his troubled throne, "Well?
Play! Play, blessed child. They tell me
your harp is cooling. Play!"

I shut my eyes and the wind brushed the grass.
My strings were cold, but notes echoed through the hall.
I plucked, spanning changes I'd never managed,
untying each hollow space that closed
or covered lies. My hands were afloat.
Amazing chords swept round my head:
blue chords, crystal;
they flew from my chest—

a hand lifted my chin.
I opened my eyes.

The King was standing,
peaceful. He bid me rise
and I was as tall as he.

*Pier tried to ease Michelangelo's awkward entrance into Rome with a glow-
ing letter of introduction.*

MICHELANGELO:
I delivered the letter to the Cardinal immediately.
I couldn't see the statue anywhere. He read Pier's
lines slowly. He had a silver ring on his left hand
which he rubbed back and forth with his thumb.
It caught the light, and the way his fingers

spread about the rubbing thumb sent ripples
of tension which minimized the ring.
I wanted to sketch it, but he folded
the letter, done.

"You must see the statues about Rome.
Then, I will call on you, Sunday."
His heavy robe twisted, the shape
of a rose, stem up. As I knelt,
I could hear it drag the cold floor.

On Sunday, he asked if I had the confidence
to do something beautiful. His silver hand
was limp on the chair, forefinger down.
I smiled. He laughed, "We'll buy some marble,
life-size." We agreed over wine. He held the goblet
in his right, not by its handles, but lifting
underneath. I knew already what to look for.
He nodded. We drank. Details obsessed me.
Beneath the Cardinal's robe, the swollen Bacchus:
weight on one leg, cup raised high,
silver hand limp.

I found the stone and he bought it.
And there was Baldassare in his shop.
My child faced a corner.
I offered to repay him. He rustled
his receipt, a quaking duck.
I offered again. He swung a hammer,
threatened to smash it. I left.
The child's been lost to me since.

I finished my Bacchus in less than a year
and though I hid the ring, the Cardinal
must have known. He refused it at once.

The banker Galli bought it and put it in his garden
near San Lorenzo where he kept his antiques,
and soon, I went to work for him.

DAVID: I was searching the trenches for my brothers.
   Father had sent me with loaves and cheeses
   and bags of parched corn. I had never seen
   so many tired.

   The Philistines were strung across
   the valley. Everyone was sweating
   and waiting.

   As I saw Eliab, I was swept by a crowd
   mounting like a wave.

   Then men scattered, unthinking as cattle;
   hundreds, loping in stampede.

   In the plain, a behemoth, with thighs
   thick as cedar, the staff of his spear
   like a weaver's beam.

   He spoke like an avalanche,
   "Day after Day! Is there No One?!
   Choose a Man of you, and have him Fight!
   Give me a Man!"

   Greaves of brass strapped his legs.
   "Choose!" A thin fear growled.
   I saw the horn of oil and Samuel's hands.
   "Choose!!" My head began to throb.
   I heard father chase the sheep.
   His voice rang transparent.

   My brothers found me shouting, "Is there not Cause?!"
   Eliab was angry I left father with the sheep.
   His mouth was slow and faint.

   I arced lines that weren't mine,
   "Who is this Uncircumcised Philistine?!"

I shook free from Eliab, but two guards
seized my flailing arms and I was brought to Saul.
His words were time in echo, in the past
as they were spoken.
He thought me a boy.

My head flared,
"I've killed a lion and a bear,
and this Philistine shall be as them."
Saul rubbed his brow.
Everything in the moment
had already happened.

I began to sweat
before he clothed me in mail,
felt smothered
before he fastened the helmet,
felt the weight
before the sword
was girded to my armor.

I couldn't walk,
and shed them for the brook
where the clearness rushed soft,
through and about my hand.

The clearness, where I saw my face
as a boy, as a man, as a King,
the son of Jesse. I saw my hands
ancient in the stream,
childlike in the air.

I felt many stones.
Chose one for its smoothness,
another for its age,
a third for its weight.
The fourth was severe.
The last, a blue vein.

I put them in my scrip
and unwound my sling
and felt a hundred Davids
in a hundred nations, unborn
and long gone, do the same.
I had the strength of civilizations.
I felt a breeze off the water, then
heard his scales jingle in the valley.

The lines in his shins were wide
like cracks in bark; his face, bearded,
a thick bough of leaves.

I set the blue stone in the cloth
and swung wide at a scooping angle, swung
and circled, swung and pulled, around
and again. And each time he passed in glimpse,
he grew smaller, and the sound of the pouch
whipped in a winded rhythm that opened Time.
I'd already seen him dead. The thin fear
growled and I let go. Time left my hand
with the whir of an arrow.

There was fast daylight and noise
and through the glare, Goliath of Geth,
his brass and leaves spread in the dirt;
blue stone sprouting from his head.

IOEL

# IV. JOEL

Joel, whose name means "Jahweh is God," is the son of Pethuel. He is a guarded visionary who lives in Jerusalem around 400–350 B.C. Often quoted as saying, "Rend your hearts and not your garments," Joel is a sharp but minor prophet who views his calling more as a superior isolation than an ineffable drive. He simply can't stand to share the light. He finds Michelangelo's power audacious and uses his Godly vision to demean the sculptor's sexual confusion and curse his knotted days.

JOEL: How dare you conjure the dead?
Your flapping heart will stick and end,
your stiff mind shut down, cast out its dream,
and I will never let you rest.

If you were set to work by God,
why haven't you appeared to me?
Why didn't I see you coming,
your fingers, streaks of grey,
teasing my hair white?

But I know you Michelangelo.
The more the marble wastes,
the more the statue grows.
You took a boy against a gate,
took a girl and wouldn't take her.

Hordes will swarm your head,
will blight your eye, a sea of locusts
preying on your mind, and as you age,
Things Will Blaze!

Buonarroti! Whose teeth
are lion, whose tongue
is lioness! Who dared
to leave me barefoot!
You will hunt while keen
and grope while kind.

Along porch and altar,
let the priests weep.
You are only of God
if touched where none
can reach you.

# V. THE INTOXICATION OF NOAH

After enduring the Flood, God establishes a covenant with Noah never again to destroy the earth by water. Burning His light through the Flood's moisture in the air, He creates a rainbow that envelops the earth as a sign of that covenant. The colors that saturate the sky wash through Noah till days later they glow in the ground he works and in the vineyard he plants. God's pigments rise in the animals grazing, the beached Ark, his sons. And when the vineyard ripens, Noah gets drunk from the exotic harvest and falls, through a ravine of sleep, into a sluiceway of the future where, through a series of visions, he glimpses across 4000 years; each glimpse filtered through a hue of the spectrum. His hypnotic sleep sweeps him by Moses and the burning bush, Buddha and Channa and the dead man on the sandy river, Plato blooming at Socrates' death, Shi-Hwang-Ti overseeing the Great Wall of China, Caesar and Cleopatra, Mani and the Persian Monarch, Attila and his concubine Honoria, Muhammad at Ibrahim's sandy grave, Marco Polo returning with coal to Venice, and Michelangelo painting him sadly, resigned to his thin painterly mood.

46    NOAH: I feel myself bobbing, face down, ears afloat.
        I can't lift my head, and there are my sons, Sem
        and Japheth, rustling a robe about me. I can't reach
        Sem's hand. The bobbing sinks to black. I spin slowly
        and launch from a bluff, to a cliff where the ground
        feels stony and porous. Ahead, bleached funnels
        of light steaming from below. Their brightness
        dims and blisters. I begin to float. A current
        sweeps me through: everything is crimson.
        A blood-red scrub ignites. It whips
        as in a gale. The hillside flares.
        A man before the bush, broken
        by an echo of red. The fire
        snaps. He drops his staff.
        The knotted end unfolds
        to the head of a snake.
        It slithers in the sand.
        It arches its belly. The man,
        frightened and willing, lifts it
        by its throat. A ruby-shimmered gust
        sends me slipping through another:
        the air is soft maroon. Two men
        stare at a swollen body as pink
        birds nip, gulping shreds.
        The smaller man shrugs.
        The birds tear away.
        A sandy river appears.
        The same man cuts his hair
        and the undertow eats his curls.
        He drops his sword in the burgundy river
        and removes his rings. His voice is nearly sweet,
        "The disorder that prevails requires my efforts."
        The maroon loosens and billows. I spin twice,
        slide to my right. A third hole puffs up
        orange rings: below, a pillared garden

lined with tangerines. A silvered man
unties his tunic, joyous as he sips
and waits. The goblet splinters as he falls
and of his mourners, one grows old. He shouts
in amber shrill, "Take hold of your lives!
These things that dominate you, you can
Overthrow!" His face flies to slivers.
I swivel on my back and tumble along.
Another draft: the land is cracked
beige and men labor to the horizon
hauling rocks to a wall which flares
ocher; the sky, deep flame. Men sweat
in apricot. A lord is fanned beneath his
canopy, "Nothing weighs one down like stone."
I hear my own breathing bob. Another shaft and I,
blown through: a man bleeding on a statue, his wounds
dripping gold, groans steeped in yellow while others
raise daggers thick with his glitter, smearing their
arms with the metal of his blood. And now a siren
lifts her lace to press a wriggling saffron cord
between her milky fates. Dark whispers fade,
a creamy mist. A disfectionate maid clings
to a curtain, "You choose how you will break
by what you topple." The image grows therein.
I keep drifting, unable to weep. Each hole comes
faster: a lemon king with a lemon cape pins a dark
thinker to a lemon cross. As a hot stake sears his palm,
he claims, "I've taught nothing new." Green sears through
in bursts. A woman dressed in olive slides her legs beneath
her gown, "I will keep you hard and snug." Her man cloaked
in animal breathes, expressionless, counting jade, gulping
wine. My arms go limp. A shaft of blue: an old man kneels
in turquoise sand. His face ripples like a shawl. Lamp-
black camels slouch in squint. There are others, all
different moods of blue, and a lavender marker.
The old man spreads his hands, smoothing

the sand above the grave, "This eases
my afflicted heart." I smooth the air
and the entire scene washes. A lapping
within the next: a sackful of pebbles glisten
and a man in a ruffled shirt speaks of a black
stone which burns, while lazy boats with the lean
of a stick slip indigo depths. He sets his stone afire,
but no one watches. He throws his polished beads. They puff
through the water. I bob on with a numbness and here is one
with a violet branch, poking at my stomach. I'm hunched
in a curve and he scratches at me, pokes and scratches.
I spin into a dizzying sun and half-rise, squinting,
below Sem's shoulder. I feel him in my side,
nudging me awake.

MICHELANGELO:
For a whole week, I've tried to manage violet
in the folds of his trunk, but it doesn't fit.
Violet was my first color. Bruises turn violet
as they heal. Father, with the back of his hand,
his pointed raps across my scalp. No one wanted me
to look inside the stone. I'd close my will and shut
the pain. I've always done this, though it takes more
to close now, and even so, the judgments slip through.
I'm never as thorough as when I bleed the edge. In work
there is fevered grace and time away, from the Pope
and my rooms, and the streets of Rome. Sometimes,
I dream I am trapped within the mountain at Carrara,
paralyzed in stone, hidden in my Colossus. Then I sweat
and chip my way out. It is no comfort to wake and come here.
Noah sleeps, a giant watched by his sons, except for Ham
who scowls. There is trouble in Florence. Giovansimone
threatened father with a block of wood, and set fire
to the house and farm. I'd drag him through Pisa
and dump his life south of Rome. And father's
such a simple man, "Above all, Michelangelo,

take care of your head. Allow yourself to be rubbed, but do not wash." What lotion to soothe my brain? Be my father, Noah. I can be a good son. Be my mother, Noah, and rub the violet into scars.

# VI. THE DELPHIC SIBYL

*Sibyls are female prophets, mythic and magical sources, Greek and Roman seers whose special function is to intercede with the gods on behalf of human supplicants. Delphica is the young prophetess of Delphi, awakened into desire, emerging through her innocence on the Ceiling next to Judith, who's now widowed in the stone. They need each other to be complete: Judith's peace and Delphica's abandon. They pry at each other as Michelangelo fills the young seer with his own haunted desire till she turns to Judith as she dries. Here, Delphica, still a virgin, confuses her sense of being, touching, and loving with her want; as Judith entwines, hopelessly, her wisdom and her grief.*

DELPHICA: I want to be entered
         by something more alive than me.

JUDITH: You must accept you are alone,
     a body drifting, and in that drift,
     aloneness, no more. And when you die,
     beneath a spotted veil, the emptiness will dry
     to a flake, and a deathless wind will carry it,
     to coast the universe or land on another.

DELPHICA: But somewhere, there's this presence
     that can make me burn and light—

JUDITH: O Go! Go on! Go roll the sea!
     Go swallow its mist! Go!
     Feel quite temporary as like
     a shell you fill with wet sand—

DELPHICA: But what I feel—And seek—
     Perhaps there's someone
     who without a word—

JUDITH: You're worse than lost.

DELPHICA: I can't believe we are alone.

JUDITH: When I thought I needed Manasses,
     I sent him off.

     I ached along each darkened bone.
     We didn't speak for weeks and each time
     I saw him, the hollow would tighten.

DELPHICA: How did you know you loved him?

JUDITH: I don't remember
     the day or month.

We went to the spring, and when
he dipped his face, I thought
to myself, who is this man
I think I know, who gives me
space, but comes always closer?
And suddenly, he looked a stranger.

He raised his head
and shook the water
free. Beads ran his hair
across his cheeks, and the light
off his lips passed through me,
flooding a place that had been sad.

Some moments rise within like dawn
and simply wait for us to wake.

*Having raced through painting Delphica, Michelangelo feels heady in the
sudden calm at having finished, and is drawn to the likeness she bears for the
Bolognese woman he almost loved while finishing his ordered casting of Julius
in 1507.*

MICHELANGELO: All the madonnas, for
her. She paints herself lovely.
Her arms lead the brush swiftly.
I scarcely had to decide and now
she's done. She stares like that woman in Bologna,
the same wide eyes which came late to watch me work
my clay into Julius. It was the week I let Lapo go.
She wore a garland in her hair and sauntered
till her dress would cling, pressing her nipple,
then bunching loose. We spent the nights together,
but I couldn't. It was hot in Bologna and the wine
was bad. We seldom spoke. Then she wanted picnics
and daytime, but my statue was going poorly.

Bernardino came from Florence
to manage the casting. He didn't found

the metal well, and Julius came out only to the waist.
I had to dismantle the furnace to retrieve what was left.
It was then she appeared, puppy-eyed, as the unfused bronze
simmered, the furnace strewn in pieces, my statue ruined.
There was no time for anyone. The next week we poured
from the top and the statue came out whole,
but not clean. She never came back.

I had to wait a month for them
to set the bronze in San Petronio.
I would see her often, sauntering, her dress
pressing, then loose. There's enough of her here
to make me limp. I lost her to the firing of the bronze
and since, I've learned—to love is to give up something
forever. O God, I've put it here, the mouth I should've kissed.
What am I doing? Fifty-nine feet up, pressed to the arch
of this vault? To love anything heightens
a lover's greed.

# VII. THE FLOOD

Noah, whose name means "Rest," is the son of Lamech. In the midst of a corrupt world he finds favor with God because he is a righteous man, "blameless in his generation." Therefore, at the age of 600, Noah is commanded to build an Ark of "gopher wood," in which he must enlist his family and two "of every living thing," to ride out the Flood which will rage for 40 days and nights, obliterating the world. After 150 days, the waters recede and the Ark comes to rest on Mount Ararat, from which Noah begins the world again. Noah lives another 350 years beyond the Flood and dies at the age of 950. Here, as the Flood is finally brought to life by Michelangelo, Noah, a man simplified by hard and swift reality, speaks from an elemental solitude rinsed through his mind by his rising with the water, while Michelangelo is swept under in turbulent recollection of the flood of 1500, which devastated Rome at dawn, as he was finishing his Pieta.

NOAH: I told my wife first.
She said nothing. She looked out of breath.
Ham was the only one who felt cheated.
He grew bitter as we built the Ark.

It was difficult to cover the bottom with pitch.
We spoke to no one. I would wake smelling
the water in the air. When alone,
I pushed myself, not asking why.

As animals filled the Ark, it grew heavy.
I had no idea how to reach the sea. My last chance
alone, I went deep into the desert, stove both hands
in sand up to the wrist, and wept.

There was a calm for several days, and then
I heard more birds sing than I can remember.
A massive grey, pitted with black, whirled,
rumbled and a horrific wind drove us to the Ark.

Soon, everything was mud and people were running,
crying, calling out, not sure where to go.
Within an hour, the streets were covered
with a murky film.

By nightfall, the lapping was halfway up the wood
and men were pounding, splashing, shouting.
The Ark shook at both ends.

By morning, there were no sounds apart from us,
just the ruffled whistle of trees on mountains.
Below the surface, branches wavered,
scraping the hull.

As the Ark began to drift free, I worried
it would sink or tip as hundreds of animals
shuffled and whinnied and growled.

After several days, there was a veil of wet
loneliness: no birds across the grey sun,

no land against the dull sky. We were tired
of wind pushing rain, driving us ever back
through the water.

MICHELANGELO:
The clay slopes, in the autumn rains, turn to sop
which pastes and skirts the olive trees far north of Rome.
And quietly the mud and root choke the gravelled earth,
the throat of flow where Tiber, Arno, Sieve begin. And
all we knew in Rome was pelt of rain three days long
which made the altars creak and sway, and soon
puddles were ditches no one walked through.
I was depressed. My broken Jesus, almost done,
rain streaming his ribs despite the tent. The sludge
mounted in the Tuscan hills, the brown back of the Tiber
gaining hips, thick watery hips that pasted every stump
and stone, ingesting fences, buckets, ancient sows and
lemons waiting for the dew. I was rubbing strokemarks
from his slope of throat, rubbing Christ's last swallow,
the lump Mary couldn't free; rubbing, rubbing
in the lashing three-day rain, the breath of flood
already trickling, soaking through the basements, staining
with a chill. As I rubbed into dawn, the cats slipped on,
their dirty pads slick. The Roman sewers began to bubble,
to bleed thin streams. And young lovers asleep in cellars
couldn't hear the muddy water beading through the walls.
Sludge oozed around the base of columns.


NOAH: My son Ham and I grew apart.
He paced the Ark with a heart of sulphur,
"What am I to Do with my life?
There is Nothing, just space and rain.
Everyone is dead! Dead, father!"

The animals mostly managed themselves,
creating networks of territory

across the bottom of the Ark.
We scattered food at midday and sunset.

Sem fed the largest ram
and Japheth befriended the male swan.

The rain eased to a steady mist.
I began to enjoy the feel of it. Late,
under the stars, I would lie on deck,
naked, feeling a star myself.
I became a peaceful man.


MICHELANGELO: Some say the animals knew.
   They say no birds flew the day before.
   I was with my Jesus in my tent, rubbing his throat
   and his Mother's palm. Well north of Rome, trees cracked,
   a splitting funnelled roar, slapping banks; the goring flow
   exploding cellar homes, wrenching doors, chewing roots,
   as if flood alone could make the dead cry from below.
   This breakneck tide, this battered voice beneath all
   tongues, was coming for my Jesus, pumping unknown tons.
   The endless rain began to hum and suddenly, my Christ
   was real, all wet and bleached of blood; I, dabbing
   his throat in the rain, the storm across my back.
   We'd brought him down. Mary and I
   were kneeling in the slime.


NOAH: Thirty-four days past the last mountain,
   the rain stopped. I wondered if we were still rising.
   The deep green swelled into white, swayed back
   into green. I found the rhythm of this life
   relaxing and it was hard to remember
   when there was land and why.

   I had little to say to anyone.
   I kept to myself and watched the sea.
   Ham scratched the rail for each day adrift.

I'd wake with the same meditation.
Straddling the bow, I'd pick a far-off glimmer
and let it roll till I felt cleansed.

I had stopped feeling restless. Even the lion
had learned to spread his weight
when the Ark pitched.

MICHELANGELO:
It ran deeper into Rome; a brown sea rushing,
breaking, slicing up the arched and vaulted stone,
pounding cattle, barrels, tiles, tables into sludge.
I ran like Peter denying Christ, leaving him wounded
in his Mother's torrential arms; and now, waist-deep,
the rushing scoured out the hives, the groggy
unexpected drones racing to their roofs.
The river poured its carrion, its tools,
its instruments; a spinet, a cittern,
a marbled tub, a lute. And bluish Saints!
And Angels with water in their lungs!
And Virgins slipping through the waves!
My Christ, all drowned, sinking back
to worm and rock and silt! I stumbled on,
shins splashing free, and bumped a whitened man
carting his grown, unconscious son. I ran beyond
and ducked into a whirlpooled, siphoned shop.
The floor began to crack, explode and geyser up!

NOAH: On the 190th day, we hit a pocket of heat.
There was no wind and the waves spread flat.
The sun had back its mirror.

I was convinced the soul was made of water,
certain time was made of wood.
The wind took up the other way.

On the 17th day of the seventh month,
we ran aground, jamming upon a huge stone.

The breeze continued and within 30 days,
the rock spread to a jutting piece of land.

By the first of the tenth month, sandbars
were visible and we were perched on the side
of a hill. I let no one leave the Ark.

MICHELANGELO:
  Buckling, mounting,
  the furied basin rose!
  My legs were swept along.
  I fell and managed up. It
  slapped me forth. I swivelled
  to a church where priests were
  rapping frantic hands to free
  the gilded door. I made it
  through. A pistonned stream
  shot five feet in the nave,
  rafting pews like broken gifts.
  They bolted the doors. The old doors
  groaned. I thought it was my Christ!
  He'd come for me! The iron snapped!
  It savaged through! I plunged and struggled
  toward the source, was driven back, numbed,
  slapped blue. The goring flow dug at my knees.
  It dragged me down.

NOAH: I waited 40 days and then, without looking,
  let a raven fly. I imagine he circled strangely
  above the rocks.

  Then, a dove, and I felt melodious
  as the white glided in semicircles away.
  But the dove returned in two days, aflutter,
  her belly and chest wet.

I sat in the bow for seven dawns
and prayed in the new quiet way. I dreamt
of soil and grass and children. The waves
came to me and washed my mind.

I took the dove, her feathers fluffed,
and tossed her up. As she circled the Ark,
I knew we were safe.

She hovered the deck that night,
an olive leaf freshening her mouth.

The next time I let her fly,
she didn't return. We waited and then,
there was the smell of wet soil and ferns.

Ham and Japheth pulled back the cover
and I helped my wife touch down upon the mount.

My lungs grew long and pure
when the dove stayed in flight.

ERITHRAEA

# VIII. THE ERITREAN SIBYL

As she's created, Eritrea hovers on the other side of the Ceiling like a dirty gull over stagnant water, trying to sight the painter who surfaces like a tired fish forced from the depths by his own hunger. The sibyl lifts and swoops, playing with her human catch, before making her dive. The two tug, each thinking the other a stubborn piece of meat. As they pull each other in, Michelangelo finds his concentration mitigated. Her fluttering stirs him into uncomfortable considerations of his sexual initiations. He loses grip. His quarrelsome sexuality continues to intrude till he slaps the surface long enough to paint her in. And there she wins, nibbling him into a lonely confusion where the pain of the work and the fear of falling oscillate into a brief and terrible longing for death.

66    ERITREA: Why have you given me no breasts?
          Why have you crossed and covered my legs?

MICHELANGELO:
    A sweat beads the Ceiling this early in the day.
    The light barely floods the lunettes. The paints
    have dried overnight, as usual, and the scaffold
    is cold. The plaster's been dead a thousand years
    and I can't call up what I was to paint.
    Cracks run the Ceiling, irregular as
    trickles through the streets of Rome.
    So much undone. There's no one in the Chapel.
    There never is. I lie on my stomach.
    Can feel the boards breathe.
    What moves this lump of flesh
    to slap wood against the stone?
    What squints to rearrange the sky
    as if it were important? The height sways
    and dizzies today and this melancholy sinks.
    I glimpse beneath the scaffold.
    I must shake these chills.

ERITREA: He moves his lips, but says nothing.
          His breath falls off. No breasts. No milk.
          No soothing of the burning hole.

*Michelangelo goes deeper and pulls out of view.*

MICHELANGELO:
    There was a boy in a sheet in the dead room
    at Santo Spirito. He'd drowned that day
    and was still wet between his legs.
    His wet skin turning blue was lovely,
    drying and wilting in the night.

I felt between his legs and sketched
the grain of wrinkles in his sac.
I felt my own and sketched myself.
I had no longing, only amazement
at how the trunk ran into pelvis,
the sac into leg.

ERITREA: Stand still! You bloated bag of urge!
Stand Still! Surface!
Or go deeper!

MICHELANGELO: Sometimes I watch this girl tuck her blouse
and her bounce ignites a more pointed grace
than a doe poking bushes for food.

Last week, I sat the farthest wall and sketched her,
full and blonde, hungry to have her swift
and delicate, but her breasts came out
motherly, her arms massive.

The woman in Bologna was not the first.
There was a heavy, warm girl in Venice.
I was 19. Her eyes were far off,
her breasts everywhere.
I wanted to smother myself.
Her nipple went hard as a twig
and I flinched, in a sweat,
dressing quickly, dizzy,
afraid she would strike me.

*She soars, he surfaces.*

ERITREA: Who are you? Nudging Crab! Flesh of Straw!
Truth Governor! Where do you belong?
You've given me a book.
Are you in this book? Where are You,
Crab-Sculptor with a Brush?

MICHELANGELO: I can picture the Pope in his chambers
half-naked with his attendants, his robes fresh,
his skin fragrant. What does he think I do up here?
I don't want his Ceiling. It presses closer
every day, and the drop from the scaffold
pulls. What would he do, his Chapel half
done, my beard soaking up the floor?
I've always worked naked. But now,
it seems a trick to use models
and I'm driven to cover everything
and the plaster swallows more. The cold
is thick as I curl into myself, fixed
to my Ceiling—a whining bat, given to moan,
to stitch a nest behind the eye, to squeal;
the head, a swollen pouch.

*She flaps, about to dive.*

ERITREA: A man was given a robe
by a blind priest
and when he wore it,
he was never seen again.

MICHELANGELO: I must return to Florence.
I send my father money, and my brothers,
yet Giovansimone is a maniac and father
swindles the florins I give him.

The walk from the Chapel at dusk
embarrasses me, for I have no friends,
and my eyes stumble, away from the work.
I put off sleep and sketch when I burn.
I walk some nights till the Tiber gurgles
before dawn. Dear God, I'm dead as the plaster.
It's a race to cover the Pope's cave
before I pass out some day next winter,
stiff on a scaffold with nothing in focus.

ERITREA: A man stood before a mirror.
            He saw a woman with his face.
            The woman reached for his body.
            The man ever chased his face.

# IX. THE SACRIFICE OF NOAH

Noah, having built the Ark, accepts his destined ordeal as inescapable, while Michelangelo stubbornly refuses his own. Noah's acceptance enables him to approach the ensuing destruction of the world with an eerie calm, while Michelangelo's reluctance to comply with his creation makes him a victim of the dark chapel. With deliberation, Noah prepares a sacrifice, asking God to sanction their survival. But Michelangelo, undermined further by Noah's serenity, questions the nature of his love for God and the nature of his own sacrifice. While Noah's faith affords him the mystery of unity, Michelangelo's doubt separates his mind severely into pledges of despair.

*After planing the Ark smooth and pulling the timbers away, Noah offers the blood of his animals to God.*

NOAH: We all would change, and I had thanked God many times
      without words. There was a seepage of peace
      which flowed from earth to air to Ark.

*Michelangelo can't paint fast enough, and prays to be able to see in the dark, but only sinks into his entanglements with Julius.*

MICHELANGELO:
      It is my God, or some pure rod of vision repeated
      forever, that burns, and yet I can't burn up. It
      *burns*, and yet it will not light. And still, I
      love my God. Before Lorenzo died, he scoffed,
      as if chiding eternity, "God must be a woman
      to make me want Him so." And God has wormed
      inside the stone, silent since. When Julius
      refused me after signing for the Tomb, I spent
      those nights brooding, believing it God's will
      I demand the money, that I continue to work. I'd
      already bought wagons of marble, barged to Rome,
      34 cartloads from Avena. And within a month, 60 more
      from Florence. I told the guard, "I demand to see him!"
      He pushed me aside. "Tell him I will see him!" A sword
      was drawn behind me. I flared, "Then we are Finished!
      Finished!" I stormed north to Florence, and within eight
      months, I was before the General Julius in Bologna.
      He rocked as he stalked me, "I think you shall be pleased
      to do it in bronze, seated, larger than life, of course.
      There's a studio behind the church. You can work there.
      Whatever it is you need, ask."

      Why has my life been stitched
      to this man's dreams?

NOAH: We built an altar and I took a hawk
    by its talons and severed its head.
    It sputtered, and instantly, its bones
    like wood the sun had dried.

*What Michelangelo has considered sacrifice, now seems no more than suffering. It sours him.*

MICHELANGELO: The brush angles like a stiff
    wing. I thrash it in the dirty water.
    Eritrea glares through her one wide eye
    as I push back the vault. I despise her.
    I created her. Perhaps God feels the same
    about winter, or me. Perhaps the sibyl
    is a mirror. Perhaps, I hate myself.
    Perhaps I am God and Eritrea,
    with her lame eye, me.

*Noah is careful to offer God something he has nurtured.*

NOAH: Sem straddled an ox he had fed
    and cut its throat. There was a sweet
    warmness in the air. It spread slowly.

*Michelangelo cannot consecrate his emptiness.*

MICHELANGELO: I left early yesterday, before sunset
    and watched the Romans wear their streets.
    I wanted to touch someone, anyone, but couldn't
    decide who and for what reason. I met the boy
    Raffaello. He glowed. I watched his hands as
    he spoke: opening, swinging, coming together.
    I watched the muscles of his young tight rump
    ripple in shadow as he walked away. I noted
    the source of light. I might use his ass.

Someone tugged my arm. It was Baldassare.
Ever since David, he bothers me constantly.
We stand. He talks. His smile flips slippery.
There were no pretty women bathing yesterday,
no children chasing each other, just vertical
figures, dry stems turning silhouette as the sun
burrowed beyond the Roman hills.

*Noah takes the sudden blur of seasons as God's blessing.*

NOAH: The animals did not
    run, but circled close
    and it began to snow.
    The spilled blood cooled.
    When I cut the bull,
    the sun went bright
    and the snow melted.
    We cleansed the altar
    and then, began to wait.

*Sad and raw, Michelangelo has flashes of his mother, who died when
he was six.*

MICHELANGELO:
    All I remember is her eyes,
    too dark, her mouth too wide.
    Eritrea reminds me of her. I
    shouldn't have made her bodice
    rose or her headdress blue. Her
    complexion is not right. I don't
    think she loved me. There's never
    enough natural light and last night
    I wept in my sleep. I dreamt my skin
    was marble and God was inside, peering
    through me. I was driving the chisel
    from within, high on my cheek, when

my face cracked, letting the slivers
fly. I was dead, and God was the light
dancing atop the slivers.

# 1510

*Dearest father*

*Nothing is new with me here, and at the end of next week I'll have finished my painting, that is to say, the part I began. After I unveil it, I think I will be paid, and I shall try to get one month's leave to come to Florence. I can't know what will happen, but I really need a leave, for I am not too well.*

*Your Michelangelo,*
*Sculptor in Rome*

ESAIAS

# X. ISAIAH

Isaiah is the son of Amoz, a man of considerable stature in Judah, and thus the prophet seems at ease with nobility and kings. He spends most of his life in Jerusalem, is often consulted by royalty on matters of state, and seems to have free access to kings. He seems content, but after a painful penetration by God, he is at heart numb, in search of some unfailing pulse that will verify what it means to be alive. His want for influence is continually deflated by his Godly knowledge that these achievements are petty. It is a quandary that parallels Michelangelo's commission to paint these traditional figures while judging them severely as an innovative sculptor. As Michelangelo is thrown into chaos repeatedly by the pandering of lesser men, the prophet's reputation is galvanized by his flair for social advantage. The two seem very distant from the lives they inhabit as their moods aggregate and their desires fragment. What they want and need merge in a province of distraction. They sputter at the center of a desert of their choosing: gifted enough to be misunderstood while shy of the self-worth necessary to understand. They squint so thoroughly that each seems a mirage to the other, an indistinct reflection of where each feels deeply broken.

80 MICHELANGELO:

I've had nightmares of prophets drowning
while I race to break the cold paints free.
I've seen Joel and Isaiah floating in the reeds
and Judith casting stones for them like fond dreams
that always sink. I've seen these hands rake a brush
like an oar scarring up the deep. And always the smell
of old fluids coursing with spite elastic veins,
the way old souls despise adaptive bodies
never letting them break free.

I've broken pieces of myself, gifts
to crippled things too ignorant to speak,
and worse than breaking is drowning
in the socket of our love.

I thought Julius cared. I knew he was shrewd,
but there was a glint that fooled me. I was certain
he would want to talk, discuss Delphica and Joel,
but he rocked his heels, swung his robe
and scanned above, "You Are quite good,
Quite good." A servant brought the money
on a silver tray.

Finishing things is tedious.
For Genius sulks in its province,
owned as the ground owns snow,
the way a woman claims beauty
as it melts into her aging skin.

*Isaiah relates how, in the courtyard of the Temple, he was brutally seared
by seraphim and branded with the word of God.*

ISAIAH: I was thinking, weaving
out a thought, watching a reef
of clouds, imaging the same clouds
as they might seem to someone half my age

reclining in Damascus, wondering, were God's ways
symmetrical? And playing with the dots of sun, I'd
shut my eyes till the spots formed wings to dizzy me.
And seeing the heat wing into thought, long after I'd
looked, seemed the root of all language. The image dizzied
out till freedom was the stillbeat of the world, in which
men think they can pluck or plant or build. I began
to sweat. The spotted wings then fanned the center,
then the fringe. Steam circled as if it had a will.
A terror seized my thoughts and words were skinless
people I had loved. I had to leave, to flee
and swim the pulsing stars. I fell and swam
the clumps of sand. There dozens of wings throttled on.
Two spun my mouth like a conscience wrapped in song.
They swooped and lit my hair, the song now fired thin.
Each time they flared, a strong pure tone flashed true.
I couldn't breathe. A fire formed behind, ahead,
the orange song shed steam. I hugged the earth,
head spinning with the planet. The Temple filled
with smoke. A live coal broke my lip into a
blistered warming flow. I remember singing
smoke and eating steam as I pressed my palms
to my useless mouth rimmed with savage light.

*When just a boy, Michelangelo drew a large cartoon of John the Baptist and
showed it to his father and his uncle.*

MICHELANGELO:
Father shrugged. Uncle leaned into my face,
"You're so young and there are other things
to do with your life." I knocked his wine,
grabbed my cartoon and ran. I'm sure he forgot
as he wiped his sleeve. I moped the narrow streets
and sat against a wall, studying my John. He
was good. He was clear, as well proportioned
as any Saint. But the robe didn't hang the way
a robe would. Perhaps Uncle caught the robe.

It swelled before me. Of course, the robe
was wrong. I kicked the wall and bruised
my foot, then buried John and trampled home.
I couldn't let it go. His face was drowning
in ample light, but the robe grew worse each time
I thought. I went back, uncovered it, changed it
several times. In a week, in a rage, I set the Baptist
on fire. The smell entranced me. The swirl of smoke
edging brown to grey. Again, I salvaged it.
Disgusted, I buried the blemish in the yard.
Months later, Uncle, working his garden,
came and pulled me by the ear, "You see,
young man! I've uncovered an antique!
You see! *This* is how to draw!"

*Feeling locked in a rigid sense of self, Isaiah fears he's lost his urge for God.
His life seems a thinning wound, bleeding out of reach, as he rubs his numbness harder and harder.*

ISAIAH: I live dying in myself.
    My mortal being's become a god to me,
    a crust keeping me unsure.

    Beyond, I find Him in camels two-thirds dry,
    in minds tired of their loaves of stone,
    in gypsies about to dream, yawning bodies
    through which the purest chance
    curls and skims.

    This urge to rise Him up, as if
    the deep can stay deep up here.
    He starts in me so far down,
    in a basin that barely holds.
    I go for Him in others.

    This urge like a splinter
    begs to be removed. My son
    calls it a taste for truth.

Yet how can I believe each want
a splinter the other must remove.

*Michelangelo, while describing how he came to carve a Hercules out of snow,
reveals his fundamental notion of history.*

MICHELANGELO: With Lorenzo gone, there was no work.
His sons were beasts with teeth for brains.
I bought a large marble for myself. It had
been exposed to wind and rain for years.
I began to search for Hercules.
No one came near. It was clear
the way they'd watch me work.
They thought me arrogant.

Piero was Lorenzo's dullest
and it was in early January
he leaned against my stone, arms
folded, hat cocked, goading me,
"Hercules is quite a venture
for one so young."

I had the left arm done
and was chipping beneath,
finding the lay of his lungs.

"We must consider ourselves *fortunate*
to have antiquity breathing before us."

I kept smacking my hammer.

"It takes the confidence of Leonardo
to go off like this. You must be *pleased*
with yourself."

He planted his hat on my statue, and left.
I threw it across the yard.

I see no reason to believe history
a ladder of shoulders we trudge.

Rather, coils of the same spiral.
Each, born as Plato, or Uncle.
Each, even Dante, the same golden
reach from center. Drawn, finally,
to center, the way a fern
or naked impulse leans.

There was an odd snowfall
packing round the Duomo
and Piero sent for me.
He was frivolous and unrelenting,
"I know how *Herculean* life is for you,
but if you might stray,
I'll pay you well."

He described a Tantalus larger than grief,
grapes above him, water swirling fast,
"I've a wager with my brother. I say
the snow is thick as clay. He claims
no sculptor alive can touch it."

I tossed him his cap
and with the oddest impulse
went outside to examine my material.

*Isaiah, with a rakish melancholy, recites the twelve parables sung by his wife
at the stillbirth of their second son.*

ISAIAH:
  1. What good the root,
     if beak breaks nest,
     if heart of rings
     goes punky
     to the worm?
     What dream is left,
     but lightning
     which may never come.

2. A hero shot a burst of future
   from his bow. It travelled
   through many lies.

   A dead woman rose,
   an arrow in her thigh.
   In dream, she smothered
   his chance to know. In life,
   he trusted none.

3. A warrior wore an anklet
   his mother left him.
   She said it would cue him
   when to be brave.

   A coward saw the warrior coming.
   He rubbed the ring left him.
   He knew it would warn him
   when to run.

   The warrior charged.
   The coward ran.

4. A man settled a theft
   between two farmers.
   The village made him a judge
   and gave him a turban.

   He wore the turban proudly
   and bought a slave to wind it.

   A man stole the turban,
   arguing he made it.

   One of the farmers came along
   and silenced the dispute.
   The village made him judge
   and gave him the turban.

5. A siren gave an amulet to a girl,
   "It will only protect what's invisibly yours."

   She hung it from her throat
   and fell in love with a voracious man
   who left her eaten and empty.

   She begged for him to eat her through. He said,
   "Give me your crystal and I will love you again."

   She gave him her secret
   and laid down like a wafer.

6. A palmist
   had a box of lilac
   and a cloth of vinegar.

   She'd let them choose
   and those who needed lilac
   could bleed the troubles from the troubled,
   but those who sucked the cloth
   would never believe in things
   that did not sting.

7. An elder had a daughter
   who thought she was small.
   Three men wanted her.

   The first offered her a palace,
   large-roofed and full of echoes.

   The second offered her nothing,
   but told her, she would blossom in time.

   The third made a pendant of small stones
   which looked most delicate when set against
   her long slender frame.

8. A captain of fifty was ordered by his king
   to retrieve a stolen shawl and behead the thief.

He found it wrapped about a starving child.

By nightfall, he tossed the bloodstained shawl
at his king's feet, and his king was pleased,
"I have no use for a bloody shawl. Remove it."

He cleansed the shawl of lamb's blood
and returned it to the mother, and the child
grew up to say, "He who seeks blood for justice
will not spare blood for mercy."

9. A nobleman asked his faithful servant
   if he would like to wear a nose ring.

   The servant always tried to please,
   so he said, yes.

   The nobleman hired a doctor, to place
   a brass ring in the servant's nose.

   The servant passed out from the pain.
   The doctor removed the ring at once.

   The servant had a fever for several days
   and the nobleman nursed him in his own bed.

   The servant woke, believed himself oppressed,
   and that night, stabbed his lord
   while he slept.

10. A lonely woman went to a why-cave.
    She said, "I want to be loved
    constantly."

    The cave asked, "Why constantly?"
    She said, "I'm afraid to sleep
    alone."

    The cave asked, "Why alone?"
    She spoke through her wounds,
    "Love is not enough."

The cave asked, "Why not enough?"
Her voice began to siphon,
"The emptiness is too vast to fill."

The cave asked, "Why fill?"

11. An illusionist changed everything
to mirrors. He sold bark to an old man,
pointing out his roughness. Sold cobwebs
to a widow as twine to her dead. Sold broken
words to generals as scraps of glory. And
sold nothing to the blind as the stuff
of dreams.

12. Let each child be as elegant when dying
as when born.

*As Isaiah dries, Michelangelo wades deeper into his sense of estrangement
from his work, his brothers, and his time.*

MICHELANGELO: He fills out slowly,
pastelike, brings me to a halt.

*He stares a while.*

MICHELANGELO: I lose my passions here.
Can't bear you looking on.

*He rubs his palm against the vault, smearing Isaiah's face.*

MICHELANGELO: I'm sick of not being understood.

*He kicks his brushes. Two flick their way about the braces to the floor.*

MICHELANGELO: I begged Buonarroto to dissuade Gismondo,
      but he came anyway while I was retouching The Flood.
      He squinted up and paced for an hour or so, barking
      questions, "Why is This, Here, so Large?!" I kicked
      a bucket. It wobbled down the Chapel, splatting
      perfectly where he had been.

      I met him in my rooms at night.
      He wanted to talk, but my eyes
      burned and I fell asleep.

      He spent most of his time in the streets
      and left forever, chilled and resolved I'd pay.
      It never would've happened in Florence.

*Thinking of home, he sits now, legs over the scaffold, and barely surfaces the chaos surrounding his first flight from Florence in 1494, at the age of 19, as Charles VIII invaded Italy.*

MICHELANGELO: Preachers had come and gone all summer.
      Thousands would gather to hear the sermons.
      There'd been a riot in the Piazza. I was there,
      was bounced about. It was September and the Friar
      Savonarola shrilled like a horn of bone
      that floods would swallow Florence
      before the French could burn Genoa.
      The crowd frothed and swayed as hundreds
      bunched in panic and still Savonarola
      arced invective above us all!

      Three days later Poliziano died.
      Poliziano, who understood the how of gift,
      who knew I only copied till I learned.
      Why Poliziano? I saw him fall!
      So many in the Garden
      were mere technicians.
      Lorenzo would've raged!

But Piero had no control.
I couldn't work the worries in the street.
And no one with any sense remains.

Come Isaiah, show your other face.
You cronies are all I have.

*Isaiah, drawn into a violent whisper, feels deeply attracted to his painterly
reflection and can't tell if it's a buried want for a male lover or a desperate
urge to love himself.*

ISAIAH: There are moments I can picture my sons,
    nude, wrestling, bent over, weight on their toes,
    sweat gleaming the backs of their thighs
    the way impulse slimes the heart.

    Since burned alive, my mind's
    a heavy lid. Go on, touch me
    where you can. I am content
    to feel you work.

    Your legs are tight.
    Stay tense. It's strain
    that makes us pop.

    Be the tongue of fire.
    I will glisten.

*Envisioning Isaiah once more, Michelangelo struggles, through a cloud of soft
denial, with his own desires.*

MICHELANGELO: His legs cross loosely at the ankles,
    his arm, about to drop, his mouth all flushed,
    flushing; again, his face seems queer, unplaced,
    impossibly strange, drawing me in.

ISAIAH: Vegetable winds control
    the uncreated spheres
    where knowledge soft
    as moss clings
    to men.

# XI. THE FALL OF MAN AND HIS EXPULSION FROM PARADISE

It is with the reach of a fallen man, no longer worried about his process or achievement, that Michelangelo boldly casts the Temptation of Adam and Eve and their Expulsion from Eden as a single event. And oddly, with this lashing portrayal, the sculptor begins to shed his despair, as if the fresco is cathartic. And while Eve is quietly stunned at how the Serpent reeled her in, Michelangelo is released to feel those perfect moments in his own creative Eden while carving his Pieta, moments gone due to his own expulsion from lighted days burned up. But hardened to his task, he begins to paint with speed and surety, and his progress now toward the Beginning, toward God unadorned by all He's created, unleashes a counterflow in which Eve and all the characters in the Ceiling know fully where they've been, but not where they come from. They ride a cross-tension of time, pioneered by Eve who, though she's already fallen, has yet to be created.

94        *Eve describes the pull that impelled her to open the core of Paradise.*

EVE: The figs were wet and huge,
        hanging, a pouch of mystery
        swelling in the grip of air,
        and all at once, to lick and swallow mystery
        seemed worth the lonely perfect path.

THE SERPENT: She swayed but wherever she looked I shook
        branch after branch. I slithered down the trunk.
        She was almost under. I knew she would feed him.

        And why not? What greater convolution
        than to feel his leg lengthen like a bull?
        I'd coil his hips and slip on bare.

EVE: She was hovering from the trunk,
        figs spilling from her slender coils,
        figs dropping everywhere, a sullen pregnant
        kind of rain, and it occurred—too clearly—
        nothing is forbidden. Her tail was sashing in
        and out along the moss, across the bulging roots.
        It stung at once—eat, take in!
        And we won't have to stay!
        The Garden will grow within.

        She kept shaking the branch.
        I went to suck the wet bulge.

        I failed. It fit my hot palm,
        magnificent as a gland, and I,
        watering for something real
        to firm up my life, I sunk
        my teeth like a cougar.

        The crunch thundered
        my soft white skull.

A draft strengthened my chest.
My hands itching, burning red.
They fingered my cooling breasts.

And there was Adam, half-erect,
reaching for a fig. His thighs
were arched. His pouch grew tight
and warm against my cheek.
My nipples welled.
I spread inside.

*As he relives carving* The Pieta, *Michelangelo revives an appetite for destiny.*

MICHELANGELO: In releasing Mary and Jesus,
    I was a fuming vein of God!

The stone was at rest in Galli's house.
I waited for a shaft of light. I waited
three days, grew semi-cankered and insecure.
But I had seen the drowning son in the mountain
at Carrara. He could not escape me. By midmorning,
on the fourth, he appeared, squirming and beaming
from within. It was never more clear where to strike,
his earthline streaming from below. Just swift, deep,
close, and his figure burst the marble like straps
of ice. And in Mary, a softness I had lost,
had never had, had never dared to open
in the world. As I polished her fingers,
they seemed to spread. I almost wept.
Her cheeks were smooth, expressionless,
the way mother loomed, her hair and eyes
fuzzy, cool, her skin calm and milky.
For hours, I rubbed the folds
along her breasts. For hours,
she arched toward me.

As I settled Jesus in her lap,
I could hear the brush of cloth.

For one year, my body was a lantern
and my spirit flickered from my hands!

I refuse to see it now,
afraid it has aged like me.

*Eve confides that, after tumbling beneath the Tree, the sense of estrangement was immediate.*

EVE: I woke, my head on his chest,
     my leg across his stomach. He stirred
     and backed away, grabbing leaves in batches.
     I went to show him we were real.
     He backed into the bushes.

     To stay now seemed impossible.
     Eden was a placid, sterile reservation.
     Even God was vaporous, a spirit holed up
     in a decanter. I felt Him spying in the leaves
     dropping after wind.

     Adam came to me clothed
     and we hid till nightfall.

     As we left, he was knotted
     and the Cherub dove about the Tree,
     flames swiping the dark behind us.

     I turned and let him trudge,
     and in a private lapse of eternity,
     saw the storm brew for our absence.

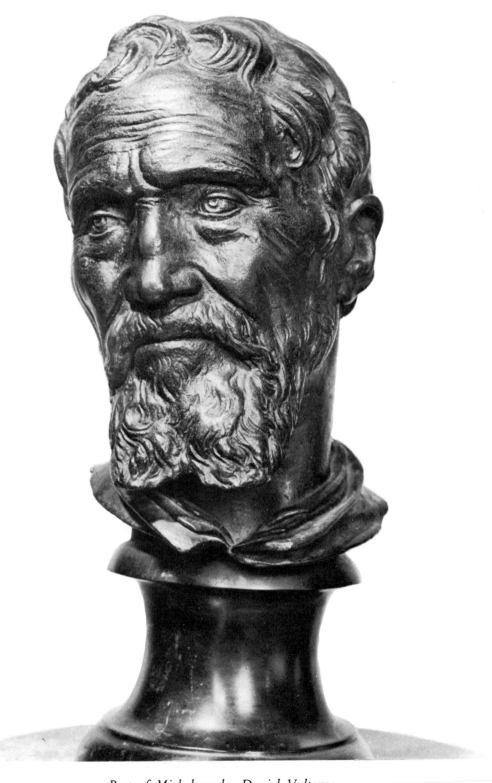

*Bust of Michelangelo, Daniel Volterra*

# XII. EZEKIEL

In Ezekiel Michelangelo finds a kindred spirit, tenacious and unwilling to loosen his grip on all he sees. Ezekiel's singularity and eccentricity reinforce the sculptor's inner perception of himself, and the prophet's political parables refract through Buonarroti's memory to energize his recollection of how he came to sculpt David in 1504. Further on, the prophet reveals his journey as a spirit through a valley of bones, while Michelangelo gripes about all that remains out of reach as he winningly portrays the stubborn exile in argument with unseen voices.

*Ezekiel is herded by four cherubim and led to the eating of the scroll.*

EZEKIEL: As I am the son of Buzi,
 I swear it was here,
 in the land of exiles
 by the river Chobar.
 A storm swept above the trees,
 foraging the tips for fuel.
 I was alone and there was the blinding shine
 of chrysolite and electrum, a clouded fury
 like sources, trapped, stirring up the world.
 I was swept into a hive of air, to squint
 the trap of wind where strange-winged
 velocities buzzed. I was delirious. Encased.
 One Veered with the Face of a Lion! Its Heat,
 a Growl of Light! One Dipped with the Snout
 of an Ox—Innately, I tell you—Pumping!
 Humping the Air! Behind! An Eagle's Beak!
 Screeching at the River! Without Sight or Mask!
 Or Skin! And Up Close, Hovering like a mirror,
 a Vacant Hood that pedalled sand. The velocities
 flocked and muscled feathers slapped.

 When I rose, they were gone,
 just an inhalation of storm
 and this cocoon of thought whistling,
 rubbing the roof of air. I walked into the gale.
 What keeps us from stripping down?! A scroll
 unraveled by. I snagged it. What keeps us
 covered and flapping?! I burrowed and peeled it
 free. My tunic snapped. The scroll had scenes
 etched in silver, maxims chalked in red.
 I couldn't understand the signs,
 but somehow know they meant:
 Life hardens to perceptions
 we must break to live again!

I tore it into equal parts
and ate the scroll which split
like a husk deep in my throat.
It had the taste of honey.

I relearned my way to Chaldea, trying
to explain these cryptic agitations,
but my tongue foamed and stuck.
You are the first. No one else.

*Michelangelo's time alone becomes a nest of confusions. He thinks irritation
is a longing, takes aching for squinting, and endures pain in hopes of seeing.
Work is slowing down. The figures tend to turn away, hide, recede. He's
forced to pin them quickly. He grows homesick and idealizes his first trip
back to Florence in 1501, five years after first arriving in Rome.*

MICHELANGELO: Savonarola had been burned at the stake,
    his hem charring up his coccyx. He smoked
    for days in the very spot he raged.
    It made the Piazza dispassionate, cold,
    made the Palazzo Vecchio a resolute, indifferent jaw.
    And three years on, I stood the spot, despite the cloud,
    till an uncertain wrongness circumscribed my thought.
    It made Florence merciless as ash or ice
    or the final wall the prehistorics couldn't scale.
    O Ageless Spy! Relentless open space, unchanged
    but stained with centuries of dextrous blood!
    O where did Dante stand and beg the Gods
    for loving caves to win?!

    I never wanted to be born,
    but since it's done, leave me there
    beneath the song that glides the Arno,
    or as a crack in that melonned cone
    of unsung light, the Duomo,
    as it lances streets alive!

I'd wear the magnitude of such a place!

Still, Leonardo beat me back by months,
after all those odd, procured Milano years.
His cartoons were on display. People flocked,
amazed, of course.

What intrigued me was his lane of depth.
The figures seemed to flee their ground.
I only had to see them once.
He never seems to let it fly.

It was all politick,
all preening for the stone.

The Cathedral Board was after a master
to down the brooding massive block
stored in the yard. Rumors
had reached me in Rome.

It was the stone spoiled by Duccio.
I knew I'd be considered, with Sansovino
and Leonardo himself.

I wanted it. My Pieta was gone
and I was hungry and strong,
a salty flood without a path.

*Ezekiel wants to make his change of life public, and winds up cutting his
hair.*

EZEKIEL: I spent weeks in the city.
    Things appeared differently to me.
    The outstretched hand seemed treacherous.
    I was too much like them, so I bought a sword
    and sharpened it for days. You can't care
    what others think or even if they understand.

    I knelt in the square and clipped my beard,
    then shaved my head. There were horsemen, warriors

and merchants who laughed, but I felt lean.
How could they know that feeling.

I gathered up my hair and found a set of scales.
By now, a small crowd rimmed me. I weighed my
fists of grey in even piles of three.

A horseman leaned with whiskey on his breath,
"You're an ass to do this in public."

I would've answered in a rage, but since Chobar
and the scroll, it seemed only whiskied air
and I was still lean, a son of Buzi,
unchanged for his words.

I poured oil on one third and set it to burn.
A man cocked his spear. I raised my sword.
He backed away.

I shrieked, "There are many ways to blind a man,
but till he feels danger, he will only dream
and wake!"

They followed me beyond the outer walls
where I dropped a trail of hair.

I was tired of pretense and punished the trail,
flashing my sword through silver hair and dirt.

Only the whiskied man and a boy remained.
I faced them both, hair in one fist, sword
in the other, head gleaming like a shield.

The liquored man spit and steamed away.
The boy came closer, "I understand.
I just keep it inside."

I groused my tight fist to the wind
and chased the ignorant air.

The boy watched me slashing and fisting
till, as a speck, I slipped from view.

I threw the sword in the grass
and waded far into the Chobar,
dipping my naked head
into the coolest of dreams.

*The prophet is difficult to capture, and Michelangelo circles the spot
methodically, still infatuated with him memory of Florence.*

MICHELANGELO:
Spring was almost gone
and still no decision.
To fill the time, I worked in Siena,
carving figures for niches in an altar.
I was sorry I took it on. What I'd learned
by freeing Christ smoldered in my palms,
and there I was, whittling stone pucks.

I left them and returned to Florence.
In mid-August, I had the commission and went
to examine the stone. Others were hovering.
It was Carrara white. No other marble could
tame that whiteness for 80 years. It was 18
feet high with a gouge in the center. No wonder
it was thought lost. Duccio must have been haunted
after ruining such a stone. I let no one see me work.
I measured the depth of the gouge, growled
at a passerby, and began to pile the wax.

When everyone had gone, I set trestles
and partitions, and the first thing I did
was free the jag binding David's chest.

*Ezekiel circles the city, repeating, through the night, the story of axes.*

EZEKIEL: Six men entered the city.
Three carried chains.
The others brandished axes.
They met another dressed in linen.

He had a writer's case at his waist.
The city was asleep.

They started waking families.
I watched how they asked questions.
Everyone stammered.

They went from house to house
and some looked away or laughed
till the one dressed in linen
opened the case at his waist.

After facile notations,
he traced an X across their foreheads
or shut his case and walked away.

If he walked away,
the chains swept the stoop
and the axes flashed silver to red.

I could see families
with bundles of clothes
leaving the city, while others
avowed allegiance to the X.

Soon, there were fewer questions.
I overheard the one in linen,
"There's no need. I can tell
by how they answer the door."

By daybreak, they had gone.
Those left wandered the streets
to bury their dead.

That night, they returned
with a new set of questions.
This time, he traced an X
on each cheek.

The next day, everyone left
but Leonard and his wife.

They came early in the evening.
Leonard was asked a new question.
He begged, "Please,
leave us alone."

The chains swept him
and he saw the silver
slash his face.

The six men chased his wife
and the one dressed in linen
shut his case and walked away.

When the axes returned,
the one in linen pulled a chain aside
and asked him a new question.

*Frustrated by Ezekiel's evasive spirit, Michelangelo hungers for more striking
visions, as when he blocked out David and was warned he was carving an
anti-Medici symbol.*

MICHELANGELO: No one saw what I saw in the stone.
From the day I scratched his belly
till his chest was worried smooth,
No one saw, No one knew.

As I chipped and freed his back,
there was a moment, a plane—a momentary
plane—where viewed from here and there
he seemed two statues.

I wiped the marble dust.
It sugared my thought:
could I carve his eye
glaring from above,
pouting from below?

And if it's so, one stare—
both moods, then there's

no salve without a wound,
no liberation without bondage,
no shaman without possession.
No good without its evil.

*With no more patience for the city, Ezekiel wades the Chobar in the heat of the day, whispering the lethal tale of Ohola and Oholiba.*

EZEKIEL: A mother bore a fitful pair:
    one in darkness, the other
    with the dawn.

    The elder was Ohola,
    the younger, Oholiba.

    They became whores
    in the land of Egypt.

    Oholiba was gentle.
    She'd do anything
    to please.

    Ohola was stern.
    She'd do anything
    to be pleased.

    Oholiba enticed governors
    in hard purple and princes
    impressed with Death
    and Assyrian warriors,
    much like her sister.

    Ohola steamed up Chaldeans
    with sashes to their waist
    and shepherds in loose tunics
    and servants, like her sister.

    Oholiba lay spotted with incense
    and oil, and nestled in her couch,

she'd imagine her insides
flushed and soused away.

Ohola ran her bedroom like a stable
with tight muscles rolled in sweat,
legs chafed and raw from jeopardies
of rocking.

Oholiba always felt she was passing
things by. She rode an undertow
of emptiness, was certain her self
was somewhere in her past.

Ohola always felt she was falling
short. She could never reach
far enough, was convinced her self
was somewhere in her future.

When their mother died, Ohola
snapped. Her sister ebbed.
The years hardened their grief
to a crust.

Jabel passed from sister to sister.
He suffered from a gust within
which made him rough his way
to fragile.

Ohola needed Jabel. She spilled
her sister's oil, "I want him!
You leave him alone!"

Oholiba, who wanted to please,
sent Jabel away. Ohola
never saw him again.

She cornered her sister,
"Where are you keeping him?"

Oholiba denied it. Ohola could
picture him, snug, rocking

in her sister's legs.

She slit the couch and lanced
her sister's arm, "Tell me!
When did you have him?!"
Oholiba shook her head
and held quite still.
"You stole him from me!"
Ohola sliced her side,
"Tell me! Tell me!"
Oholiba shivered
and finally said,
"Yes. Have it your way.
Yes." Ohola, in a rage,
beheaded her sister.

Months later, a strange
unwilling man brought red
wine and a silver bracelet
coiled like a snake.

She lathered him to ride.
They laughed and drank and
rough-housed on the floor.
She coughed and flushed
and couldn't see.

He rushed her face, "When
your sister died, he moped
for weeks."

She spun, "Who Are You?!"

"I suggested we leave.
He began to sob."

"How Dare You?!"
She threw her knife
and missed.

"Three days and I found him:
bloated, head bobbing
in a stream."

The room was a blur.
While she staggered,
he grabbed her and slipped
the silver on her arm.

Ohola scratched and kicked the air.
He turned to leave, "You will consume
what you love least."

She brushed the bracelet to the floor.
Her vision turned. She found the silver snake.
It gleamed and wriggled in her hands.
She threw it to the wall.

She screeched and yanked her hair
and scratched her thighs.

She paused and spun,
unable to get free.

She rolled her knife
and cursed the dawn
and tore her breasts.

*Irritated and losing ground, Michelangelo recounts how shaping David broke him through to viewpoints beyond his own, while political resentment for the statue was building.*

MICHELANGELO:
    He was meant for the Duomo, up off the ground,
    sideways, glaring from his pedestal. The more I
    worked, the more I saw through and back. As when
    certain the water's brilliance is mere reflection,
    I realized his angle was Above—20, 30, 40 feet up
    off the street. I stopped working from below.
    I walked the Duomo, round the transept and the niche,

practicing, squinting, sighting from above. I crossed
the Piazza viewing the Campanile from the bellies
of clouds. And even Ghiberti's molten doors
seemed steep and blistered.

To see things from beyond
is a fifth season with a will of its own.
And always, the strife: holding Heaven's view
when huffing on the ground.

I sliced the heaving from his ribs,
saw it from above, undercut his ball of eye
and knotted up his brain; became snared
in lifting his upper bust; thought,
no one will see it but the Gods!

I couldn't stop.

Some work on stone to see themselves.
Some work below to see above.
David grew like music on the sheet,
a fugue for light to play.

Soderini was stunned.
I was a white-hot spider
rubbing here, climbing there.
They all were stunned, but no one
wanted him off the ground. "Its
magnificence will be lost," he said.
They wanted to see themselves.

They formed a commission.
I ranted like a ghost,
"A pitcher needs water!
A statue needs light!"

Leonardo egged them on
and lobbied for the portico
off the Palazzo Vecchio. Sangallo

claimed the marble was soft, insisted
it be kept from rain. And only Cosimo
urged them to ask. They never did.
And Botticelli see-sawed with the age,
pungent, a rare esteemed delicacy.

I was hunkered.

Sangallo and his brother built a frame
and I worked the vein on the back of his hand,
worked it like a prayer, silent ready vein,
pumping marble blood. It took the morning
of the first to suspend him by a knot
which tightened with each hoist. Midway
through the next, we had beam and windlass
everywhere, and then we inched him from the yard.
Crowds came and went like bored and boring birds.
We hauled him on, gaping through the night.
He seemed resigned without a moon.
I thought to put him in the hills,
up to his waist in trees.

It took four days.
And on a fairly star-filled night,
the weak beams cracked, the windlass lurched
and grisly citizens swung their torch, hurling
rocks. I jumped aboard and waved them off.
They hit his chest, his cheek, his arm, his
knee. One nicked my nose. I picked them up
and hurled them back. They hooted and fled.

It took me weeks to rub the scratches
from his skin.

He was unveiled in June, at the entrance
of the Palazzo Vecchio. Women came and gasped.
Friars mumbled as they passed. The commission,
glib, dissolved. They only saw themselves.

*Ezekiel is touched by the hand of God and carried from his body as a spirit
into a valley full of bones.*

EZEKIEL: In the dip of plain
bones slid randomly
with the dull tap of rot
and a puff of dust.
Leg bones, pelvic girdles, skulls;
locked deep in it with just a wind,
the occasional slide of sand,
the tap and puff.
Air whistled
through a hundred ribs.
The bones began to rattle up
a cloud of powdered ash. Sockets
slid in sockets till knees and shins
rolled, till hips and spines rocked
toward skulls inching
through the sand.
I was compelled
to walk among them.
As I ran, the sand threw me
and I rolled through collar and shank.
And Whole Skeletons Were Rising! Strolling!
Trancelike! Bumping with a Whack
and Veering off! Dozens of Frames! Coupled!
Locked like Warring Elk! Clattering! Spinning!
Drifting! Cracking! I thought,
there must be those who if I touch
will surely come alive! I grabbed
a passing neck, "All Forms Arise!"
I fell into a cage of ribs
and shimmied in the sand.

All sockets
have manilla walls.
All skulls
eat sand from behind.

There were no spirits,
only wind
in and out of bones
as it crossed the plain.

I vowed never
to touch anything dead again.

The horizon waned
and I tried to remember the year.

*Michelangelo yearns for a bottomless power and trails into the mystery of*
*sudden agreement.*

MICHELANGELO: When like a ghost of water,
    there seems no need for egoed silk
    and wafers of light are cataclysmic,
    shattering all self-perception
    till naked thought is unintelligible.
    Its kindling is our words.
    I am convinced.

    Oh, curse the way I left Carrara! Curse
    the shaking, splitting axes of the mind
    that cut down heat-packed nests of dream
    where all the hornets of the self
    pump their stingers full
    and sting! Sting! Sting!
    I'm Swollen! Itchy to the Core!

    I want to carve armed words that hold—
    Hold! Stay spoken longer than the wisp
    of life that speaks!

    How does God appease the godless?
    Like a wet bird gliding in a breach of heavy trees,
    an innocent speech about to stir the throat?

    I don't know where the power hides
    and I grow bored with what I do well.

Tell me why the wind alarms the windless,
why the power without words
suffocates the word.

I know how to see, how to erupt
in the particulars of a thing sighted;
how to hear, how to sop up the sounds
of a more honest time. But can I
be heard?

I once argued with Piero
and closing off all meaning,
it seemed some anima dance:
to arch the mind and growl,
to stalk and swipe.

We were pacing, wildly, yelling
back and forth about Savonarola
when—no warning at all—he sat,
crossed-legged, and in a whisper,
"You are right. I concede."

His hush lit the shadows
in the house.

*Ezekiel, while re-entering his body, composes with sudden clarity the Three
Lost Laws which, once in his body, are siren-like laments he can't recall.*

EZEKIEL:

### *Law of the Temple*

Nations as Fingers.

When well, they lift together.
When lame, those close lift more.
Those farthest yield blood to heal.

Justice as Gardener.

A fern grows from the light.
The pot is turned, the soil rearranged.
A stick is set to bend its stem.
If its wildness blocks another's heat,
its growth is stripped.

Family as Rope.

When tied,
the strands pull close
and taut. When not in use,
each strand curls
unto itself.

## The Sacred Tract

Let no one rake his mate in hopes of barley
when the field yields daisies if left alone.

Let each lift rubble to hear the hole's song.

The peaks don't separate
because the air drifts cool between them.

Snow from both mountains forms the stream between.

Everything alive has water that obeys its moon.

The ground between is capable of scars.
The language between is buildable.

## The Lunar Stream

To expect it to scurry.
To believe it will return.

To master the retrieval
of something so innate
it has no sense of loss.

To control the urge
to stay buried in the cost.

To accept your part in water,
more agile than the pebble,
yet as driven
from bottom
to shore.

# XIII. THE CREATION OF EVE

From his position poised over Goliath, David can see the Temptation and the Fall tightly drawn, can see Adam and Eve fixed in a dry cower as they are forever chased from Eden, can see Michelangelo stroking Eve to life. It lands him in his own temptation with Bethsabee, the wife of Urias the Hethite. And as David relates his own fall, Michelangelo, feeling more and more driven, more and more removed from the people around him, paints his first God to finish Eve. At this point, the scaffolding is torn down and rebuilt beneath the barren half of the vault, and the hidden recluse is confronted with how stiff and small his firmament seems from the floor. He is, at once, overwhelmed yet drawn to what remains undone. Only Eve seems right, a pleading keeper of some threshold which excites and frightens him, as Eve herself discovers the fundamental give and take that empties back and forth through all who love.

*David recalls sending his general, Joab, to fight the Ammonites at Rabbath, and how he stayed behind, only to be drawn to Bethsabee. He slowly relives first seeing her from a roof overlooking an empty Jerusalem.*

DAVID: She's washing herself, sponging her stomach
and the back of her legs. She rinses and washes
and I feel a pin sliding somewhere inside
and I'm useless as a sputter.

There is a curve in the heart,
a thin wall which lines the deeper chamber,
and once or twice in a life, it's perforated
by the presence of another so that husbands
or wives or the fate of small children
are merely fences to hurdle.

She leans to one side and wrings
her thatch of hair. Her breasts spread
and I am stricken, unable to think clearly
with the dizzy pin deep inside.

She is Bethsabee, daughter of Eliam,
wife of Urias the Hethite.

I send for her. We are left alone.
There are no questions, only slow breathing
as we quiver, some chemical of ritual.

Her eyes fix and penetrate.
The world becomes moot. Warm light pours.
The wet leaf curls. How can this be wrong?

Bethsabee spends hours in my bed,
hands sculpting their feel,
rubbing creases from my sides
as she might palm excess clay.

For weeks I simmer, a cinder
greying in the tail of comet.

Then, a sealed note
from her oldest servant,
"David, I carry your child.
What are we to do?"

I must write Joab
and recall Urias at once.
The pin begins to slide.
What a child this would be,
and the chemical would rise
in its eyes.

I send for Urias,
without her knowing.

He is a large, devoted man.
He thinks himself my confidant,
"I am flattered you trust me.
My eyes shall be your eyes."

I nod and discuss our forces at Rabbath,
not hearing a word of his or mine.
I can smell his pride and loyalty.

I can't tell him
so I send him home
with trays of meat.

I can picture her with child,
surprised at the door, "Bethsabee! Bethsabee!
David sent for me to report on Joab!
He sent for *me!* Do you hear?"

The night is black and brittle,
tethering all sense of proof.

In the morning, I find Urias
asleep at my gate. I question him.

"We are at war and I left hundreds
writhing in tents, bleeding, losing faith.
I can't go home while they suffer, to feast
and drink and sleep with my wife. For the welfare
of Juda, for the welfare of your soul, my King,
I cannot do this."

He knows. She's told him.
No. She wouldn't.
She couldn't sleep with him
and so, he thought it out
and came to my house.

As I trace the silk in my web,
he kneels, awaiting my command,
a warrior sent by God.

I have him stay that day
and the next. Each night we feast and talk.
I have servants bring basins of wine.

Both nights I leave early and go to my roof.
He never steps from my door. My servants tell me
he guzzles the wine once I'm gone, then
slouches on my couch into a distant sadness,
a sitting sleep.

I am certain he knows, convinced he is struggling
to keep his kettle full while he schemes a way
to scald us all.

I did not lure Bethsabee.
I meant no offense to Urias,
but she has conceived my child
and neither she nor the child
are safe while these ashes
smolder.

I think it out again and again
while he sleeps, an angry bull
beached on my couch.

I watch him moan in his sleep
and think of smothering him
or drowning him in wine.

But what if he doesn't know?
The pin begins to slide.
I realize he doesn't matter.
I want a son, the son inside Bethsabee,
and I want to wake in summer with her hands
rubbing the creases from my sides.

I take my robe and tuck it about Urias.
He winces and I wait for sunrise.

In the morning, he begs to go,
"My King, let me fight. I can't go home
and your wine makes me think of little else.
Let me fight!"

I send a sealed command to Joab
by the hand of Urias. I order him
to the front, near the walls of Rabbath.
I place him in charge.

I watch him leave Jerusalem,
carrying my note like a target.

It is almost a month to the day
that she comes to my house shaking
from a dream of death. The next day
Urias is speared from the wall.

I watch her weep for her husband, and sink
at how she loves him. She sobs on my couch
in the presence of his ghost, while I moan,
far inside, in the presence of my own.

She is even delicate in black,
and soon, she begins to swell.
It is then we are married.

It seems a painless labor
and I hold my pink son twittering,
his eyes shut, unsure of the strange light.

We name him Samma, after my brother
who tended the lambs.

I can never say no to Samma.

Bethsabee props him on my chest and he
explores my face with his tiny fingers
and I watch his mind work as he feels
the difference between lip and eye.

At times, while she sleeps, I watch
the moon fill his room and wonder
how these soft bones will form,
if he'll be taller, keener,
more able to hear.

Samma is three when I wake screaming,
dreaming of Urias on my couch.

The next evening, Nathan seeks my advice,
"There are two men in our city; one rich,
one poor. A stranger came to the rich man's
table, and the rich man killed the poor man's
lamb to feed his guest."

"Show him no pity! He's a childless
thief! He'll pay fourfold!"

Nathan cups my hands,
"You shall, my King, you shall."

I force him to leave.
I go to my roof.

How could he have known?
I give orders forbidding him
to see Bethsabee or my son.

In the morning, Samma has a fever
and I go straightaway for Nathan.

He has vanished from Jerusalem
and I know my Samma will die.
I begin to fast. The ancients of my house
beg me to eat meat. I send them away.
I pray, prone on the floor, where my servants
can see, "Dear Lord, God of Israel, Spare my Son!
Spare my Wife! It was I, *I,* who let the Warrior die!"

I send them away. I forbid
my wife to see me. I grow dizzy
from weeping. During the sixth day,
I feel certain he will live.

I have cramps from praying.
That night I begin to wretch
and swear the phlegm is black.

I wake the next day
to waves of whispering.
I know my son is dead.

I rise and wash and change my clothes
and go to worship in Jerusalem.

Once home, I find my wife, eyes swollen,
desperate to know what she has done.

I hold her head and brush her hair,
"It was I who let the warrior die."

I run my finger on her perfect lips,
"How can anything so lovely be wrong?"

In time, we have our own son
whom Bethsabee names Solomon.

*Eve is finished and Michelangelo is forced idle while the scaffolding is dismantled, moved and reassembled beneath the undone panels of Creation. Seeing his work for days from the Chapel floor diminishes his confidence.*

MICHELANGELO: It's underdrawn.
A year's work! Too Small!
I should never have trusted it.
Paint! Eh! Look At It! Soaked!
Dab! Dab! Dab! *Too Small!!*

I must plan better, plan farther.
Must paint the west as Broken Arcs of One!

Sweep! Sweep! Where's the Sweep?!
Where is David?! And Judith! Turn!
And here The Flood! *What* Flood?!
There is No Sweep!! The Undone West
is Deeper! Vast! Magnetic! Lean!
I'm sick. It's all a blur, a wash.

Only Eve seems to want where she is.
And something unseen barely pulls her
from Adam, barely reels her into God's hand.
Harping my rack, legs aflame, rump numb,
she sprang from my sore-ribbed mind.
I watched her lean into space
for the longest time
before painting God.

How strange we must seem
when they can't see what pulls.
How strange the stare, the sudden
cringe, the lurching prayer
addressed to no one.

Sometimes, I fear the life of stone.
It takes so much.

# COLOR FOLIO

*The Fall Of Man And His Expulsion From Paradise, detail*

*The Cumaean Sibyl*

The Creation Of Adam, *detail*

HIEREMIAS

*Jeremiah*

While casting Julius,
I had the stump of a tree holding up my bench,
a dark knotted cherry stump, forked to the left.
And in it, the image of a woman bathing,
a dark knotted woman, her wet arm raised
as she rinsed her side.

I carved as far as one breast.
I was rounding her shoulder
when the wood lost its scent.
She died in labor, her wet stump
leaning to the world.

I'd delivered a Death!

She haunted me till I burned her.
The yellow cupped her waist
till the wooden flesh gave in.


*Eve longs for the feeling of being created, in herself and in her life with Adam.*

EVE: I found myself yearning.
There was a draft, a flickering
and then, only Adam, limp against a tree.

I watched his eyes roll beneath his lids
and wished he would wake, and he did.

I've tried to keep him open ever since.
I turn him soft with my mythic eye.
I make him hard with the stretch of my lip.
Still, he closes off, into himself,
where I'm not wanted.

When we left Eden, I knew he blamed me.
He began to glare, as if I had something
he wanted back.

128

At night, he'd stare, till I'd turn,
then look away. He'd speak, till I'd listen,
then brood and pout.

I've spent much of my life
in the will of wasted hours
hanging on when he lets go.

What makes him forget so much?
He knows to take, but not to use.
He accepts his fate and sulks,
accepts the lotions of this birth.
But I recall much wilder births than our own.
And likewise, he believes Eden is home
because it's what he left. He is lonely,
but I am empty. And God, a moment ago,
had a thousand moods and we are two.

O lonely taker who forgets, the moods protect.
They keep us from the pressure of our worth.

O lonely taker, I, empty giver, can't hold back.
Our noisy secrets pass to sand.

*Madonna and Child*

# XIV. THE CUMAEAN SIBYL

Cumae is the oldest sibyl, a prophetess named after the ancient and earliest Greek colony in Italy (c. 750 B.C.), located on the coast of Campania, west of Naples. The other sibyls venerate her experience, though she proves caustic and irascible. And Delphica, still a virgin hoping to be entered by a man, is persuaded by Judith to seek Cumae's advice. Cumae responds readily, badgering the young virgin with a vengeful account of her blazing harsh affair with Apollo. As this storm of innocence and experience sweeps above him, Michelangelo extracts a secret from his father's letters.

CUMAE: The soul while in the body cannot see!

MICHELANGELO: I was having trouble with Cumae's form
  when the letter came from home. We seldom
  have privacy in Florence, my brothers about,
  and my simple father is more honest
  with half of Italy between us.

DELPHICA: Such a scowl stitched to your best.
  Who am I to believe?

CUMAE: There are no men! Only bulls!
  And you are nothing but plowable!
  All of us! Broken from God's rib! Plucked
  while He dreamt of half-beings
  unable to outlive touch!

MICHELANGELO: This was the letter it was leading to.
  Months of probing and awkward silence,
  nights of rereading, rethinking his scrawl,
  curling, half-asleep, easing
  into mother's darkened womb.

DELPHICA: I want a son
  his mouth puckered,
  all quaking,
  my nipple wet.

CUMAE: And I had a God
  who sucked me dry!

MICHELANGELO:
  My mother was Francesca di Neri di Miniato del Sera
  and I was conceived on a farm in Settignano.

CUMAE: You can't trust bulls!
    You can't give those parts away
    and expect them back. You are not endless.


MICHELANGELO:
    Father had been commissioned as mayor of Caprese
    and they had to move. He was 31.
    It was his first paying job.


CUMAE: My mouth waited like yours.
    I was unsure. He thought me dark and mysterious
    and he was bolts of lightning all the way in
    till I fisted his hair.
    I went twittery and numb.
    The buzz reached my fingers.
    I was young. I wept.


MICHELANGELO:
    He says they crossed the mountains by horse.
    It was a rugged trip and mother disliked animals.


CUMAE: We made love in the water, on the sand,
    in the grass behind the dunes. He was a God
    and I only wanted to prop my chest,
    to watch his mouth smear about my breast.


MICHELANGELO:
    The horse froze, sideways to the path.
    Mother jabbed her heels.
    The horse sallied toward the rocks.
    Mother jabbed her heels.

    The horse reared and she was thrown
    beside a snake.

134 CUMAE: I followed him everywhere.
If it was hot, we thrashed the surf.
If cold, we rolled the dunes.
He loved to wrestle in the sand.

MICHELANGELO: The fall broke her ankle.
She was writhing when the snake
slid her belly like a rock.
She rolled and screamed.
The snake bit her leg.
Father lanced the wound at once.

CUMAE: My God knelt me in the sand,
"There are as many years for you
as grains you dare to hold."
I plunged my arms, scooping a mound
which spilled everywhere.

MICHELANGELO: He says she was never right again.
She thought her womb poisoned,
some punishment from God.

CUMAE: He never aged or changed.
He would take me
the same way every day.
His sighs became grunts.
For the first time I smelled his sweat
and the sky did not reel.

MICHELANGELO: Mother fought the labor
and when I was born,
Father says
she looked away.

CUMAE: I was supple, tan, and tired.
    He was golden and hungry,
    no longer gentle. We seldom talked.

MICHELANGELO: His letter grows unclear.
    Her eyes were too dark and her mouth,
    too wide. She ruins
    every woman I paint.

CUMAE: You can't want this! Bulls!
    And eunuchs wanting to be bulls!
    Go! Now! Shun, like shattered bark,
    the storm, and flee!

MICHELANGELO: Father says she was afraid
    to have me at her breast.
    These things grow queasy now.
    Why does he write it down?

CUMAE: I had no say.
    He threw me to the sand.
    I whipped handfuls
    in his face.

MICHELANGELO: I can't remember what comes next.
    Eritrea stares through her book.
    I gave her no breasts. And Judith
    turns her back. Mother!
    You've spoiled my work!

CUMAE: With claws, he dug me apart.
    I bit his neck and tightened every muscle
    to fight the burning.

MICHELANGELO: Father says I bit her nipple,
   that she slapped me hard.

CUMAE: He bit me red. Teethmark-scallops
   between my breasts.

MICHELANGELO: I was wet-nursed
   by a stonecutter's wife.

   When she opened her blouse,
   I cried.

CUMAE: He pulled out
   and covered me with sand,
   "May you look your age!"

   I felt my lips dry and crack.

MICHELANGELO:
   What else can you give me mother?
   I've read the letter for a week,
   now plaster it up on the vault
   with Cumae's mammoth breasts.

# 1511

Most Honorable father

*I shall be very grateful to you if you will find out whether in Florence there is some young boy, son of good parents, but poor and accustomed to hardships, who would be willing to come here and live with me. He would do the various household chores, namely, go shopping and run errands; and if he had time left over, he could learn. If you find some boy, let me know, for here one can only find rogues. With the grace of God, I am well and I work constantly.*

*Your Michelangelo,*
*Sculptor in Rome*

# XV. THE CREATION OF ADAM

Adam is a watcher, a passive singer who can never find his song. His relation to Eve and Eden and to himself remains a molecule of myth, evasive in its relevance to all beings. There is solitude, lack of solitude; peace, lack of peace; an unconscious harmony, then a conscious separation. Our first human father seems at once enlivened by the breath of God and haunted by a relentless alienation from all that is divine. To render him clearly Michelangelo considers God anew, and as Adam relates his version of what it means to be brought alive, the sculptor reassesses the unity that is the world. Adam then admits to a loss of unity with Eve by his side, as Michelangelo starts to feel guided in his efforts, himself a brush being held out of view. With Adam in place, the primal man and primal artist outstretch their arms in search of God, their hearts dragging in the world.

*Feeling pressure to continue, Michelangelo starts and stops several times.*

MICHELANGELO: And now in God's image?
    And what is that? The flash
    across water that made
    John know Jesus?

    And how in God's image?
    Is one who believes nothing
    and questions everything less of God
    than one who believes all
    and questions none?

    Is one who lives like fire
    and questions air less than one
    who loves like water?

    And how, how God from his image?
    How the blow from the spark?
    How the human from the being?

    How God's mind dipping
    in the timeless stream
    from the Universe
    seared into being?

*Adam reveals his first sensations of life.*

ADAM: I stretched my hand into the silence,
    feeling the sun, quiet across my fingers.

    I stood and reached for nothing, stretched
    and marvelled at the tightness of my thighs.

    I ran lightly across a bed of leaves,
    aware of warm patches under my feet.
    I ran, lungs filling with virgin air,
    into a river in which my dizzy hands

seemed larger and softer and the trees
sponging the bank were full of light.

I rushed deeper, the clearness rising
to coat my thighs. I slid against a stone
and watched the water ride my chest.

I sat and took the water like the stone.
And the pounding, after hours, of my heart
lapped in rhythm with the blood of the earth.

And I felt mortal.

The first thing I heard was the quiet.
The first thing I felt was a warm
rising in the world.

The wind picked up. The water chilled.
The clearness left a ring as I stood.

I wandered ashore.

I wanted to look further upstream,
but fell asleep against the tree
I had watched all day.


*Michelangelo, still searching for Adam, considers the world and all its
coupling agencies as parts which cannot self-enlist the whole.*

MICHELANGELO:
The sea of all there is floods us where it can
till glaciers fill the cracks and dreams like algae
grow slippery under stone, till bubbles rise the mind
and mood flows a hole, and caves absorb the winded light
where oracles comb for ancient voice. And all the raining
burning parts sprout, till the sun eats the moon white
and the moon lifts the sea, and soft choirs find
a durable night in which to breathe, and paths find
old mountains full of brush, and confusion finds
its wornout trail. And worms lure fish, as gifts

relinquish truth, and torn songs cure, a salty bait.
As light in water, secrets find cold depths to fill.
As heat in fire, eternity in beauty dwells.
I need to know the earth by heart.

*While Adam sleeps against the Tree, God pulls Eve from his side.*

ADAM: As I woke, she had my hand.
      I pulled away. She looked alarmed.
      I put my arm around her.

      Days passed and though she seemed content,
      I needed to sit alone in the river,
      to feel the water ride my chest.
      But each time I strayed, she was there,
      her sad eye glowing.

      I explained about the water,
      about the ring of calm
      and my deep sleep.

      She wanted to come.
      I hesitated. She looked injured.
      I thought of nothing else.

      I woke early the next day
      and started for the river.
      It wasn't long, she was behind.
      I kept pace. She trailed.

      We didn't speak.
      I sat in the water against the wet stone.
      She fought the current and sat beside me.

      It was nothing she said or did.
      It wasn't her fault.
      I should have stopped
      when I saw her trailing.

A swift chill chased me from the water.
It wasn't long. She was behind,
wet and shivering.

*The sculptor, at last, lets go.*

MICHELANGELO:
    I began Adam today. His form eased weightless,
    spreading through the plaster with untrackable rhythm
    as if I were below and he were being painted from above,
    my brush merely trailing the motions of its counterpart,
    tip tracing tip.

*Adam tries to be alone without securing his solitude, and it drives Eve away.*

ADAM: It was unlike her to go off alone.
    She was up against the Tree,
    rubbing the trunk.

    I would've left her there,
    but I was sure she didn't know.

    When I reached her, she rocked,
    her legs apart, tongue wetting
    her lips.

    I grabbed the lowest bough
    but felt her tongue between my legs
    and the Serpent coiled my arm.
    I staggered down.

    She crawled on me,
    fig crunched in her teeth.

    I nipped the fruit.
    She wouldn't let go.

    We rolled the dizzy grass,
    nibbling the fig between us.

*Having found Adam, Michelangelo tries to replicate that path in finding God, and considers the burden of God's intensity and the brilliance of emptying one's soul.*

MICHELANGELO: The burden of being lighted
　　　is being heartless, so bare and full
　　　as if the soul were some fired sail
　　　being blown euphorically through the deep.

　　　When fired, we live too close
　　　to God, like spots eaten by the sun.
　　　It makes you Godlike, or you burn up.
　　　And when charred, the heart
　　　begs for what it fears.

　　　But halfway—charged, about to give,
　　　the fingers dimming, the tips glowing—
　　　the life of spirit begins.

　　　And you call it sacrifice
　　　when you think it will never come again,
　　　and kindness when you think you can live
　　　with less, if the one you're near
　　　can *stay* near with more.

　　　Or call it faith, when you know
　　　it's endless in return,
　　　a blood of light.

*Adam secretly fears he's lost his ability to feel.*

ADAM: It was clear as we left,
　　　she had known. I couldn't
　　　bare to look at her.

　　　Never to be alone again. Never
　　　to walk the river in Eden
　　　or slide the wet stone.

She'd squandered my reasons.
She'd effaced the quiet.

As the Serpent slithered in her rock,
all links to peace fisted up;
my mind braided to its scalp,
my heart, a mammalled knot.

*Reaching but not painting, stretching his being through his brush, Michel-angelo empties, about to paint, and sees God mirrored out above him, op-posite Adam; he is transfixed, as the three point to the same lighted unin-habitable space.*

MICHELANGELO:

No Power          like the          Naked Ire of Light

Snapping Out Our Arms          There   the heat

Ionizing my blood          Creasing     my heart

There          the Carbon

of Inspiration          Arcs

•

*Adam, feeling a consummate victim, speaks of Cain and Abel.*

ADAM: I never understood why we were forced to leave.
        It was the Serpent in God's Tree.
        It was her fault, and God put her there.

        The land loosened to sand
        the further east we went,
        and I grew tired, too tired
        to even sleep.

        It was months before we touched again.
        We sweated heavily, and the sand stuck all over.

From this desert love rose Cain.
A difficult birth. A precarious breech.

She would not wean him
and made him a buffer
till the boy never felt real
in my arms.

When Cain was a year and a half,
we tried again. I looked deep in her eye
and prayed while inside her. I sent forth
every belief and memory left
in hopes of a child I could love.

Abel was born beneath an older dusk,
and Eve was again beautiful,
if only for a while.

We moved again, further east
till the land seemed livable,
till there were traces of water.

Here Cain grew to be a digger,
tilling and hacking the light uneven soil.
Abel cared for his flocks,
ambling the long hills,
sheep following him everywhere.

Cain was always behind her shield.
She never let me touch him
and he resented Abel for his smile
and seeming calm.

I was certain whatever I had owned from Eden
was now in Abel, in the way he walked,
the way he hugged his mother, the way
he fed his sheep.

It was after I stopped dreaming
that Cain was uncontrollable.
I found Abel filling a grave

with one of his oldest sheep,
"Please, don't tell mother.
She needs to think well of him."

I found Cain plowing in a sweat.
He never looked at me,
"It's you, not Abel.
It's how you treat mother."

His pace was feverish,
"You don't love her.
You only think about Abel
and Eden. All you ever talk about
is Eden and the river, Eden and the fig tree.
Eden! Eden! Eden!!"

I held his chin like a goat.
He steamed at me. I let him go.
He grabbed his tools and backed away,
"Abel will pay."

I told Eve about the dead sheep,
about the blackgoat Cain.
She touched the lines in my face,
"Irksome man, the moments flow."

With that she backed away, adding another step
to the distance already between us.

Months passed and I never spoke with Cain,
seldom with Eve and always with Abel.

I saw, through Abel's eyes, the things
I used to love. His mind pranced with a lightness.

It was a cool morning when one of Abel's lambs
nudged me, butting its nose against my ribs.

His flocks were all about. I let Eve sleep
and followed the scent of something gone wrong.

I found my Abel face up, neck soaked in blood,
his lambs sniffing at his arms, the hungry ones
licking his chin.

All the pains sank and I knew Cain was gone
and there was no fight left in me
as I rocked my rivered shepherd,
his blood drying on my arms.

*Having finished the panel, Michelangelo reveals his work to Pope Julius and
his servile Cardinal.*

MICHELANGELO: They are undone. Their eyes can't eat enough.
The Arm of God! Naked with the Blood of the Sun
Surging through His Veins!

The Cardinal is squeamish, "Never has the Lord
been painted Naked!" But Julius believes,
"It's Daring! You have Surpassed the Greeks!"

I simply
see His body,
a sea of flesh
in which we drown
till our heat ripples sheer
like a voice immersed in prayer.

*Adam sinks further into the history of man.*

ADAM: Nothing mattered after the blackgoat
opened the shepherd. Many years passed
and I could pinch and lift the sags in my face,
could see the creases break down
into more and more piles of dull blood.

There was nothing left to believe in:
Eve stole my life in the water.
The Serpent tricked us out of Eden.
And God let Cain kill Abel.

Some eighty years passed
and our voices grew raspy.
Eve had a terrible squint.

The world was a floating ache,
purposeless, and yet, we could not die.

When she whispered of having another child,
I laughed and reeled till I ached: how absurd!

And then I thought, yes, why not.
The perfect point to a pointless journey.

I could barely mount her.
She reached for me and I wondered,
what could we possibly give life to.

•

We named our new son Seth,
and Eve thought she was young again.

But I was tired of chasing a feeling
that never stood still.

She hadn't accepted in her heart
that real things are elusive.

She handed me the boy
and I held him once,
just to feel his cheek,
unknowing as it was.

# XVI. THE PERSIAN SIBYL

*Eve, driven to distraction by the distance between herself and Adam and weighted by the death of Abel and exile of Cain, claims Persica as her confidante. But she refuses the fact that Cain killed Abel, and Persica uses Cumae's books to draw Eve to the truth. Their conversation weighs on Michelangelo, though he is not privy to it. The essence of their exchange anchors Buonarroti in his own consideration of the strain he terms closeness, of his mercurial bond to the women he creates and the women he has known. As Persica works Eve's psyche like a surgeon, Michelangelo awkwardly recalls chiselling his name in the dark on Mary's sash in his Pieta. Unaware of each other's plight, Eve and Michelangelo share a faceless detachment for being originators of the race. Only Persica, garnering her air of wisdom from Cumae, knows the life that persists is barely blessed. The cautious sibyl hides her pity for poor Eve, a sad sculptor of flesh, and poor Buonarroti, a mad mother of stone. She protects her understanding by keeping it silent, believing both mother and sculptor echo what it means to love beyond all questions of adequacy till what's left is so small, it's resilient and intimate.*

*As Eve presses her, an ambivalent Persica rereads, to herself, the most telling passage from Cumae's Second Book of Prophecy, but decides to withhold it from Eve.*

"To love is to never be free.
But nothing is free except for short cycles,
for demi-arcs of time, say fifty years or so.
And only humans, obsessed with flight,
term such motions as their lives.
All motions return: the light goes dark,
the lift falls, the sharp edge rounds
and given enough love, the poison turns sweet.
Solitude alone can conjure freedom,
and only after many false starts,
many replicas of past suffering unbound,
many vaultings of old pain—only then,
freedom, along the inner mile, quite still,
and taut like the force of storm upon storm
since the flood, not added up, but thinned
to a line of wind, endless and irresistible,
which whispers once, when it thinks we're not listening,
that to steer is human, to fly—divine."

*As Persica closes the book, she is seized by Eve who feels thoroughly estranged from Adam.*

EVE: You think he's possessed?

PERSICA: You really should talk to Cumae.
    These are her writings.

EVE: He has never forgiven me.
    When I approach, he seems
    to know what I will say.

    The moment I know this,
    the words lose color.

PERSICA: Ah, "How can I tell what's near
          when everything's so clear?"

EVE: How did you come by this book?

PERSICA: Cumae asked me to keep it for her.

EVE: Oh never mind.

PERSICA: It's the second of seven.
          Eritrea has the first.

EVE: He blames me for Abel's death.
     He thinks Cain cut his throat,
     that I led him to it.

     I fear whatever killed Abel
     has murdered Cain. How could
     such a thing happen?
     We've kept to ourselves.
     We've bothered no one.

     Cain was missing three days
     before Adam found Abel.
     And before that, Abel found
     the old ram slaughtered.
     Adam blamed Cain. I tried
     to hold him. I said, "You're
     too quick to judge, too quick
     to see yourself in his anger."

     He brushed me aside.
     I felt chastised.
     He knew he was wrong,
     but he blames me for that, too.

PERSICA: But these things were years ago.

EVE: He won't let me touch him
and now, there's a bitterness.
I fear for Seth. He knows
nothing of our past.

PERSICA: "The woman who cannot free herself
at last believes in fate
and comes to fear her wish."

EVE: What would you have me do?

PERSICA: Take your boy and go.

EVE: No.

PERSICA: You think he'll change?

EVE: We still sleep together.
Still eat together. There's
still a place that's ours
when he's all steamed out.

He struggles to understand
too much. Is that a fault?

PERSICA: "The aspiration of being centered
is not to be the center."

*Persica is confining after the challenge of Adam, and Michelangelo feels a surge of the insignificance that plagued him late in 1500 when he encountered a young Copernicus lecturing. It made him walk the crowds far into night, where he signed The Pieta.*

MICHELANGELO:
He spoke of planets, as nations of time voyages away,
and claimed glorious things existed out of view,
vast distances from now. He insisted on ideas,
assumed the clearest laws were windlike
and knowable, if we might let them through.

Then he stopped, fixed on something far above.
Then looked among us and smiled intrinsically,
as if he were in exile from all that he saw.
"Distances," he resumed, "provide such cholic clarities—"
He stopped again. His shoulders dropped, "Forgive me.
I'm doomed to speak of things I'll never know."
Then he swung his Polish arms out there between us
and hitting some unseen wall recoiled and left.

The crowd sniffed around and hungered on.
I wandered Rome, feeling the late sun cuff my neck.
I was not prepared for this. It frightened me.
I caught fire with a muteness.

They were gaping at my Jesus, poking their heads
at his style of dying in his mother's lap.
I heard a Lombard brag, "Solari did this.
He's been working it smooth for years.
I've seen him work—" I pushed him from behind
and scowled. He landed hard. The crowd scattered.
I barked, "Let Him die in peace!" They ran.
I turned and watched the stone cease to breathe.
I grew confused.

At night, a lantern weighing down my arm,
two chisels rubbing in my palm. She watched me
chink my name into her chest. She shuddered.
I thought it was a flicker. I dimmed the lamp
and felt the darkness spread.

I didn't belong.

I swung the lantern at the dark and felt too
known, ached to be a sad nation out of view,
ached for anonymity—the clear blessing
we pebbles cannot bear.

*Eve grows defensive and withdrawn. She is unnerved by Cumae's quotations,*
*which pierce her like slow needles, stirring all the tensions in her being.*
*Persica is aware of all this and merely speaks through Eve's thoughts of Adam.*

156 EVE: If I could shed all his experience,
　　　　be born in his position, I'd swim
　　　　and never rest. I'd dive and never
　　　　let him bring me up. And now it seems too clear,
　　　　the heart of all perception drifts red and warm,
　　　　and only woman swims on and on and on, her heart
　　　　dragged below the surface like a net.

　　　　O it's grown too hard! To know and be as kind
　　　　as when I never knew! It makes me want to die.
　　　　To slip the will off like a ring. And plunge.
　　　　To spiral down the dark.

　　　　Each one I bore was limed with a want for life
　　　　I've never felt again, and now I know, the passage
　　　　caused God such pain, He made women bear the world.
　　　　He spread us, for our openings, into a bloody gate.

*Michelangelo sees the pale face of Contessina, Lorenzo's youngest daughter,
his first love, in the unfinished turned head of The Persian Sibyl.*

MICHELANGELO:
　　　　I can't alleviate that position. I loved her
　　　　and yet we couldn't talk. She knew nothing,
　　　　was dull to be with, but so raw,
　　　　so limitless in that sad reception
　　　　of things she knew nothing about.
　　　　Even then, it burned in me,
　　　　gutted my patience.

　　　　I wanted to mute her little mounds,
　　　　her tiny breasts padding her ribs.

　　　　She was leaving. Even as I arrived
　　　　she was fading from the world,
　　　　fading, as if the young flicker
　　　　behind her eye had been snuffed.
　　　　Yet she carried on with a yawn of energy
　　　　that seemed to me the pale beauty of sickness.
　　　　I was burning.

EVE: What are you looking for? This is serious.
      Everything rubs between us. Everything's rough.
      What are you doing?

PERSICA: There are sayings here that pertain.
      I remember something about fidelity.
      Not the usual kind, that comes later.
      But Cumae wrote something
      about fidelity of outlook,
      how it can turn.

EVE: What has she ever suffered?

PERSICA: More than you—No! Wait! Listen.
      Here it is—Wait. Now listen:
      "We can explain almost everything
      except the need to explain.
      I lived with a God for a thousand years
      till burning and invocation would interchange
      and he went for decades at a clip, rolling in some
      heated dream with a needy thing who leeched him
      of his clarity, and then he'd wander home,
      loving the safety of my face, despising
      the predictable bend of my arms.
      I held his mind till we tired of his rubbing,
      then picked his thoughts like splinters
      from my arms. He hated me for protecting him.
      We could look freshly away,
      but as we turned,
      after a thousand years
      of working bad weather,
      we congealed.

158

Without his ideas,
he stayed away longer
and I made analgesic peace
with voiceless sand.
How could either of us have known?
How can you, who find this strange
and not pertaining, know
this breakdown never ends,
that you will come to spy
the love that makes you able.

I expect him any era now
to come anew in honeyed light.
I expect to change,
to resume the freshness
of our strangeness
a thousand years ago.

I expect him to lose the girth
grown round his heart,
to stop in mid-swig,
to wipe his ageless mouth
and bray, 'I know you.' "

EVE: So she parades it.
      I tuck it here.

PERSICA: You smother what you gain.

EVE: Easy for you.
      I've lost my sons—

PERSICA: How long will you protect him?

EVE: You can't know, not you or Cumae!
      It's like a scream that never closes,

somewhere deep, behind everything
I once believed, a scream, now
less than silence, closing.

Even here, a stitch tightens in my brain.
Always rubbing, twanging, a black thread
dusting. My sons. My sons. Where is that
spot of God in which they were conceived.
A draft enters from behind it all,
closing, never closed, never
on its way.

*Persica lifts a red stone from beneath her robe and cradles it between them.*

PERSICA: Among a thousand proofs that love can heal,
    this is a dead god's heart.
    You can ask it one question.

EVE: Only one?

*Michelangelo uncovers the cold mystery of Contessina.*

MICHELANGELO: On a grey night, she let me fathom
    through her skirts. She barely moved,
    and looking up, beneath her chin,
    blue shadows rimmed her sockets,
    dark secrets chilled her skin.
    She seemed a breath from death,
    her young breasts cold. And now,
    you laugh, but I have learned.
    Death makes us think it bloody
    and red, but it comes all blue and cold.
    And even as a boy, I could have sucked myself
    to sleep, to have her break just one sweet groan.
    You understand? Death makes us want to bring it back!

To pour our fire down its delicate hole! I needed her,
and only now, licking this roof with bodies of air,
only now I know—I wanted Death, cool and blue,
to silence my burning! O Contessina,
Contessina, what makes the mouth
so willing to pay?

*Questions of Adam and Cain flood through Eve. She starts to ask, but stops, several times. She finally wants to know, and after a considerable silence, is answered in a manner inaudible to Persica. She clutches the stone and her hands turn red.*

EVE: It all comes down to Blood.
　　Blood soaking through the core.
　　Blood engorging his orchid of flesh.
　　Blood breaking so painfully, I feel it
　　numb my uterine shelf. Blood coalescing
　　to a fetal lip. Blood, like a shallow
　　surf, bathing the base of newborn eyes.
　　Blood rubbing milk down my baby's throat.
　　Blood. He drinking the puddle of his
　　ruined son. Blood swallowing and
　　smothering and coloring the Earth.
　　Blood baking our lives into gristle.
　　O why such burning rain. Why now,
　　this spot of sun which should be
　　red. How do we bury this. Blood.
　　The taste. My blood spilled
　　my blood. Blood pumping
　　what remains.

*She drops the stone. Her hands turn cold and normal in color. Persica returns to her scribbling.*

PERSICA: Why don't you leave him?

EVE: There's no place to go.

PERSICA: You can stay with me.

EVE: No one can stay with you.

PERSICA: You knew from the beginning, didn't you,
    giving up that peace you were afraid to hold.
    Don't tell me you didn't know.

EVE: I didn't.

PERSICA: You must have known.
    Don't you remember the safety
    in not thinking of yourself?
    The endless task of staying close,
    of mitigating impulse—
    You're teasing me.

EVE: I didn't know.

PERSICA: So goes the race.

EVE: Can you honestly know?

PERSICA: You really had no clues?

EVE: No. No. . . . Just once.
    When we were moving west.
    He tried to swallow something
    welling from within. I went to hold him,
    but he stopped me with a lost expression,
    and I knew he was thinking
    of his life before.

PERSICA: And you envied him that space.

EVE: No, I couldn't understand
          why he couldn't share.

PERSICA: No one can share.

EVE: That's not true.

PERSICA: You think you share,
          but no one gives their lung of air.

EVE: You're wrong. You have nothing to speak from.

PERSICA: Stop teasing me.

EVE: You're wrong! I was the first. I know!
          Nothing will ever equal it!

PERSICA: And what do you remember? Touching or being touched?

EVE: Touching! *Touching!!* First with our air!
          Then our breath. And each, a deeper suffocation
          till broken into one we cracked the heart of Eden!
          We Touched! It's the one thing I've known forever!
          To Touch without thought is Lightning!
          You've badgered me, and all along,
          it's you who are afraid. Don't back away,
          not after this. I'll touch you now
          with what I know, and watch you break
          into a thousand imitations of stone.

# XVII. GOD SEPARATES THE WATERS ON EARTH AND BLESSES HIS WORK

As Michelangelo conjures God, the ocean mountain laments being covered while the wave shows no compassion. It makes him recall the attentions of a man in Bologna. But a distinct surety surrounds Michelangelo as he begins, at last, to sculpt with the paint. He has clearly left the brunt of his despair behind, shed it more by rubbing his mind against the days than by any charismatic choice. Thus he is more transparent in the transmission of Godly ideas than he can imagine. His portrayal of God separating the waters on earth is insightful and radiant, enlivened by egoless moments of intuition into images no human thing could know. He captures, without realizing it, the soaring flight of God gliding through the ether, surrounded by angels clinging to His robe. He is painting decisively now, in sweeping strokes, quickly and cleanly, with an altered perception of God that has been waiting all along beneath his knotted personality, which still brays and complains. And like his lesser, human moods, some of the timid angels are blind, flapping off God's garment through the void. And some are mute, though pouched safely in His beard. But one holds naively to the Lord's numinous thigh, watching eagerly while the others drop away. The naive one hides, wanting more than anything to see the Lord create. But when he does, he is forever burned, his hidden ride so near the Source, he loses the ability to articulate ideas in any form. And as Michelangelo creates divinely with no knowledge of its worth, the Hidden Angel knows everything about the Beginning, but can never begin.

*Through telepathic sprays of light, the Hidden Angel merely indicates the genesis of being.*

THE HIDDEN ANGEL:

>    At first we seemed to hover for eons above
>    where the earth would bob and He conceived of
>    several shapes: domes stretched in whitelight
>    and vast green slopes. He made powder of them both.
>    We hovered till a mass of particles bunched, around
>    which a current of chill seemed to flow. The bunch
>    took on a drone, and then the current began to furiate,
>    and as the fury lengthened, the current brightened,
>    a stellar wind. And gradually, the wind twisted blue,
>    extending each gust, splashing into nothingness,
>    and this intrinsic splashing, where blue never
>    seemed to end, congealed into water, through
>    which scarves of stellar light fisted easily,
>    and oceans without a planet glowed. He simmered
>    and placed them about, jetting swatches of tangled flow.
>    We fluttered. He grew pensive. I almost froze. My blood
>    turned blue. He spread, imperceptible. I was drifting
>    on the slope of flow in a squall of innate light
>    when the blue began to pull from the light, and
>    as it did, we began to separate. What remained,
>    darkened like carbon, packed and condensed
>    to a fiery center, and the oceans of flow
>    began to glove the carbonned center, and
>    we drifted till we could see the world
>    begin to grind in its pocket of air.
>    At once, a tension in how we moved
>    that's never left. And since, that
>    tension is the hiddenness of things,
>    the flare of light beneath the crust.
>    And then, the strangest thing, from the
>    jetting center, through the rim of blue,
>    out into the void, He pulled the catalytic
>    forces. He took the rising, soaring, blustered

sweep of time, cupped it in the gliding violet air,
and pressed it in His sudden clap, which took decades
to close, and that mold of space, once released, was
a bird. And stranger still, He took the dark enfolding
flap of everything over nothing, and whipped it to a
fiber of heat, then rubbed it warmly in His hands
a thousand ways, till the rub was like pure water
brushing in. It scurried out His fingers, a fish.
And oddest was the floral reach of all we'll
almost know, seeping from the earth. He turned
the stillness green, warmed the bud of flow
into a shrub, made the herbal memory cling
until it was a vine. Then I slept in His
hammock for a sliver of eternity, during
which His forces swayed. He took the flight
and depth and stillness down, and forged
the Soul's Intoxicants, implanting them
in bird, in fish, and sprig. And then He
spun again, began to furiate a stark and
empty space, which closed on us, till I
felt drawn at first, and then compelled,
to find authentic things on earth.
And the earth's ways condensed:
fish eat vegetation,
bird eats fish,
man eats bird,
bird and fish
hide in flora.
And the ways
of being commenced:
depth eats stillness,
flight eats depth,
man eats flight,
as flight and depth
hide in peace.

*While painting the hand of God parting the waters, Michelangelo recalls the confused way Aldrovandi first leered at him in 1494. It leads him to darken God's hand above the lifeline, lighting only the heel and meat of His palm.*

MICHELANGELO: The way he looked from behind his desk,
    I thought he wanted to sleep with me.
    And if it came to that, why not.
    He had such a delicate frame.
    It was my first time in Bologna.
    It was a terrible trek.
    I'd been warned to flee.
    Something dark and catastrophic
    was honing in on Florence. I took Cardiere
    and found Granacci, who thought it all
    quite melodramatic, and we hurried to Venice.
    The rhythm of the horses at night
    bled, twin beats of dying stars.

    After several days, I dreamt of tall grass on a hill
    which whitened by pure light was eaten by a mother
    carrying a child, and I woke knowing the child
    was a prophet. I thought of Savonarola
    and knew it was safe to go home.
    But outside of Bologna, Cardiere stole a sack of wine
    which was bad—all wine in Bologna is bad—
    and we were taken to the Custom's Office
    where Aldrovandi leered at me.
    He kept showing me his palms.

*Deep along the ocean floor, a mile and a half along the shelf that cuts the Atlantic, what was the highest mountain in the world, now submerged, recounts the Separation with envy for the wave.*

THE MOUNTAIN: Before, Everything was charged at the base,
    snapping throughout, the clearest crack of light
    sparking from my peak, a pure line of force
    untracked by lesser forms.

Once the swirl of random light
induced lazy wings to try.
But the wind coiled to a patch
which, gaining in possession,
became the wave which fit my peak
like a murderer's glove.

Then, I felt the heat and flow
separate and pull, the coolness rise,
the fire scuttle out some hollow.

I spread and sank without sinking,
that blue headiness swirling and chilling,
routing every surface.

I used to pour light for miles. And now,
I can barely imagine the bottom of the day.

The flying things have stiffened,
retracted their songs, their bodies
have flattened, their eyes all bulge,
and now they squirm in spurts
through creases of clearness
in a mitigated kind of flight.

The earth's a dark fisted thing,
a rock in a skin of moss. But once,
believe me, it was crisp, an air
that could've stilled the sea of time.

The clearness has grown oppressive,
has taken on the essence of the dark.
A baby splashes in the basin.
Here, it chides, a sonic snap.

*While painting the perched nude above The Persian Sibyl, the one God ap-
pears to be looking at, the posture triggers Michelangelo's memory of Ald-
rovandi startling himself awake while being read to. The sculptor smiles and,
in a rare moment of lightness, reworks the scene till the nude grows startled
as the medallion he should be holding appears to rip away, about to fall.*

MICHELANGELO:
  He was calm in a way I didn't understand.
  We were young Florentines in flight, rough,
  unkempt. Cardiere had stolen wine. We had no money.
  And I was frightened, nauseous and dreaming. And he
  kept showing me his palms, rising from his officious
  capacity, freeing us, inviting me to stay. Granacci
  and Cardiere went on, and he took me for a while.
  His sense of Art was Peace. It drugged everything,
  the dish of fish he'd set before me—even candles
  burned in low and ailing flames he cured. I'd
  never read Petrarch or Boccaccio, and he gave
  a serenity to Dante I hadn't imagined. He loved
  my Florentine enunciation, something about
  the rough knot the tongue launched over
  unimportant sounds. He'd laugh slowly,
  playing with my rapid pride. He'd ask
  to be read to, at night, when he was full
  of carp and wine. He'd slouch his eyes,
  raise his palms, and let the eaten things
  swim beyond his consciousness, and then
  he'd nod and drift, a deep mile rising
  from behind his personality, and I would
  stop. The silence would jar him
  out of sleep, alarmed by a wave
  of nothing.

*Jittery in its divided attention, the column of wave recounts the Separation
with indifference toward the mountain.*

THE WAVE: He doesn't know how to use me.
  Of course, I would cover him
  as future blankets consciousness
  with a clarity that seems always out of reach.
  He chooses to be oppressed, the way a man,
  afraid to leave his wife, is plagued by other women.

It's the condition of his dream. It is the dreamer
who inflicts the dream. He is solid and unchanging,
but has chosen to fear his weight.
The sad issue learns to rue its voice.
My time was coming. I could feel the pull.
I was the blue in his veins, the wash,
the gleam to scrub his stone.
He is interred. I have risen. The mountain
like the wakeful eye of man will always break.
But we who rise beyond the rim of sleep
will part and part and form again.

DANIEL

# XVIII. DANIEL

The story begins in 586 B.C. when the destruction of Jerusalem, as foreseen and witnessed by Jeremiah, takes place as Nebuchadnezzar reduces the city to rubble, exporting all the Jews that aren't slaughtered back to Babylon. Among the captives are four young men, Hananiah, Mishael, Azariah, and Daniel, who is shrewd and quick-witted, determined to stay alive. They are carefully trained, along with others, as young nobles in the palace by Ashpenaz, the Prince of Eunuchs, who calls them, respectively, Shadrach, Meshach, Abednego, and Belteshazzar. As favorites, they are treated royally, and, for the most part, respond eagerly. Daniel, however, refuses to answer to his new name or to defile himself with the rich foods and wines of the King's table. He asks to eat the plainest food, vegetables with water.

The story of Daniel, whose name means "God is Judge," and Nebuchadnezzar, whose name means "Defend the Boundary," accentuates the struggle between Michelangelo and Julius. Both stories present the confrontation of the word, the power of truth as revealed through inspiration, with the world, the truth of power as manifest in the conflicts which control human lives. Both prophet and sculptor discover that the cost of freedom is as dear as the cost of compromise, and that honest living negotiates the boundary. But ultimately, through lions' den and chapel, each is indentured further to his true master, God.

*Daniel relates how Ashpenaz was losing patience with him when Nebuchad-*
*nezzar had his dream.*

DANIEL: He was calling me by that name and I wouldn't answer.
　　　I drifted through the others, trying to lose him.
　　　His turn was coming and he was petrified. The King,
　　　a week before, had a suffocating dream, the kind
　　　that rakes you even when awake, a malignant sensation
　　　that rips safety at any time. Some thought he was stuck,
　　　deranged. He needed the thing foretold. But wouldn't budge
　　　or say a word. Offered no clue. Ashpenaz joked until Caltazzar
　　　the Chaldean, so good with rings, couldn't chart the stars.
　　　The King shrugged and smiled. The court magicians and wise
　　　men snickered. And then, he had him drowned—right there—
　　　in the inner pool. The flowers bobbed away from the body.
　　　Four others tried. A sorcerer, an alchemist, a soldier
　　　and a mimist who drew huge countries in that sky
　　　before the King. The King said, "No—that's not
　　　the dream" and had him spiked. He worked his cape—
　　　"Any fool can give meaning to a fear! You watch the eyes
　　　and heat the road the troubled face wants to eat—
　　　I'll have your heads! You and You and You—
　　　All the servants here as well!
　　　Unless someone solves this!"

　　　Ashpenaz knew I knew,
　　　just by how I washed and dressed
　　　and refused the panic. I didn't want to say
　　　till I had to. Such a charge of certainty
　　　in knowing something others will. I could've
　　　swallowed the dream forever. Ashpenaz even
　　　called me Daniel. It was his turn. I smiled.
　　　He smiled. I said, "What are you going to say?"
　　　He considered being vague, but then
　　　a cloud dispersed behind his lies,
　　　"You must come forth.
　　　He means to kill us all."

The King was genuine around the eyes,
but had the forehead of an ox. He was
unnerved. A twitch made him appear to squint,
"Well, who is this? Don't make me kill a boy."
No one laughed. I bowed lightly and advanced
clearly to his ear, "The head was gold,
the thighs were brass, the feet, clay
flecked with iron." He bounded from his throne.
His cape slid down a sleeve of air along the marble step.
He took my arms, "Yes, its silver breast—all crushed—"
"By a hairlike tone that smashed the best
of all you know."

"It sounds so strange, but I feel—No!
Tell me what it means!" The rest backed off.
He motioned them to leave and reassumed his throne,
"You're just a boy." I said, "God often speaks
through fresh young things." He smiled. I laughed.
He frowned, "Tell me what this means!"

I waited till that charge was near.
Like a shaft of gravity, umbilical, leaning things my way.
Ah, knowledge swings to those who know. Like fear rushing
through a sudden fright. He knew I had control.

"Tell me." I held on.
He walked the far side of his pool,
hands on his hips. I stepped the edge
and launched a flower back across, and held on,
for telling always tips the world the other way.

He suffered, uttered, "Please." I looked surprised,
"My King, I am only thinking how." He raised his hands
and let me be, annoyed. I began, "After you, a kingdom
of brass, and after that, a fourth, part strong, part token.
But everything depends on what is seen when you are old.
You could lose it all. Your name could burst
into a storm of plagues. It all depends
on what you think you know, and really know

when you think you no longer see. The one
will be crushed into the other. You have
reason to be afraid. Your children
may not survive your aim. There's more,
but it's not clear enough to speak."

He came close, despite the news, and close,
he seemed uncomplicated, and kind. He was relieved
to know, as if mystery were more deadly than disease.
He spun and laughed and took me by the hand,
"You are the Governor of Babylon."

He dropped my hand and had control of me.
I said, "I'm not well suited." He barked, slowly now,
and louder, for those eavesdropping in the hall,
"You Are the Governor of Babylon!"

I looked him in the eye. Another time,
I might have been pleased.

Ashpenaz hated me for rising so fast,
and for saving his life. He was not to be trusted.
The King and I became deep friends. I listened mostly.
He liked to watch me listen. And soon the priests
and wise men and magicians and clowns forgot
that they were almost done. Instead,
they resented me my years,
thought me too shrewd, too
ambitious for the general mood.

I told Nebuchadnezzar to let me go.
We still could talk the moons into light.
He said no, and Seflatan, the priest
who had his other ear, was waiting,
as I had done, holding on to what he knew,
building things his way. I asked again
to be relieved. The King said, "No, but
why don't you go away till things cool down."
He sent me to Cutha to bring back fodder
for his cattle, then on to Accad for swine.

*As Daniel is temporarily sent away by Nebuchadnezzar, Michelangelo,*
*brought back and forced to work for Julius on the Ceiling, recalls how he*
*ran away from his worldly counterpart only five years before. But there is*
*no running away, as both prophet and sculptor realize they are gifted but*
*powerless in a world where they are sought like intelligent animals for the*
*circus of those who amass power, who want some fired living thing in their*
*court which they can prod and marvel at. Here the bleary artistic animal*
*grows irritable and frustrated. Sensing where the gift meets the world in*
*Daniel but unable to locate it, Michelangelo winds up recounting, more can-*
*didly, his first flight from Julius in 1506, when funds were finally cut off for*
*the building of the Tomb.*

MICHELANGELO:
    There's something. First it vibrates. Then it shimmers
    away. A shape, a glow, a form protruding without control
    beneath his controlled face. Damn it! Hold!
    Something wants to throw its head back,
    peel its arms and wail for all it's never felt.
    But I can't bring it into focus and, sensing it,
    why paint anything else? Always, rip the center,
    hold the husk! I never thought of this as paint!
    It's so small and unimagined! Flat! Flat!
    I don't want to be here. It was all
    supposed to be in stone. O what's the use.
    Julius glares enough to remind me every time we speak,
    then acts like he never shut me out or led me on.
    The last blocks came from Carrara, half-butchered
    by Bramante's crews, the freightage still unpaid.
    I said, "Where can I sign?" They wouldn't let it move.
    I said, "This is for His Holiness." The bellied foreman
    looked both ways and spat between his legs. I went to Julius.
    Bramante was nearby. I was enraged. Julius slowed
    to a stare of real delicious condescension, "Dear, Dear,
    this is a problem. Tell me, Buonarroti, how many statues
    were you going to carve tonight?" I stood between them both
    and said, "Pay the freight and be surprised."
    He grew instantly encrusted and swept
    to where I felt his breath, "If I have time,

or think of it by dinner." He extended me his hand.
I would not bow and left. It was dangerous
not to kiss his ring in front of Bramante.
I couldn't eat and fought off sleep, kept
feeling something in my ear, a branch
of lightless light, a twig of heat.
I brushed it off and then awoke,
a slender presence wavered near the wall,
"You cannot stay past the seventh no.
The bond will break, all fascination perish.
The seventh no will break your fall."
I rubbed my eyes and scalp and ran my hands
along the wall. A film of chill curled off my chest.
From that point on, it changed. He never let me near.
I had to borrow the money from Balducci. The next day
he was conferring. The next, asleep. The next, in private,
bathing. Then the guard braced himself as I approached,
said he was out, but I heard him in the hall. Then
Sangallo overheard him at a dinner tell a jeweler
he wouldn't spend a florin more on stones.
That was six. I was enraged. I kept
hearing the presence count, kept watching
Julius turn on me. Could feel
the statues twist orange from my rage.
I was in my apartment. A chisel fell. I jumped
and hit my head. I slapped the chair
and bruised my palm. I was disgusted
with God's impetus. I paced, and paused,
and gouged the chisel in the wall.
I prowled the night in Rome, heard the paws
of cats pat in clumps on stone, heard
something dripping, something licking, watched
shadows pull at dawn. Thought, if I run,
he'll find me. If I stay, how can I stay?
I smelled towels snapping in the swollen breeze.
A baby cried. My edges blurred. My insteps damp and sore.

It was obvious I hadn't slept. The guard stopped me,
brass pole in my chest. I said, "You know who I am!"
He said, "I have my orders." Another guard
appeared. He rushed me further, with a whisper,
"Don't—Don't come back. He's got plans for you."
He butted me in the rib. I've told everyone
I wouldn't leave, that they had to throw me in the street.
I went quietly and packed my things, thinking
of an unpaved way from Rome, thinking
he might count on me to run.
I told Cosimo, my carpenter,
and Giovan, my stonecutter,
"Go for a Jew. Sell everything.
And meet me in Florence."
And here I am, as if I'd never left.
He never mentions it, but there are Cardinals
always close, wondering if I need to drink or pee.
I ignore them all, or rail my cage
of wood braces to the vault,
and they shimmie back, cassocks
like tulips swirl, like ducks spinning
red before a storm, like pale dusters of conscience
stirring the floor. Shimmie. Stare. Spin away.
Like this definite want behind Daniel's mask.
It's there! Look! Now! Too late.
You must look when I say.
It's not what it seems. You see!
Now! Behind his—Gone! What can I say?
It's best not to talk. Let's watch.

*Daniel knows innately that the power of being gifted in receptiveness does
not fit the world's armor. It seems more a matter of being worked through
than an issue of control. Repeatedly the two collide, the otherly and the
worldly, egos bucking like rams: artists and generals, prophets and kings, the
ambitious legions in between. And Daniel is convinced that along
the line of buck, freedom is attainable. The confrontation always leads to
strange times, like the one Daniel lives in, a time filled with slavery, rabid*

180   *power, and superstition. A time when women are treated less kindly than*
*slaves. In fact, there is a common belief that women have no souls. And, of*
*course, history provides, at such a time, a woman of enormous spirit and*
*presence, a gift named Susanna, who is put on trial, much like Socrates will*
*be almost 200 years later. Here, Daniel recalls the trial of Susanna.*

DANIEL:

While I was gone, Seflatan had pulled the King's thinking
like a gravity across the dark, and as orbits bend,
elliptical, leaning away from the center
while being held by the center,
Nebuchadnezzar was out of reach, there,
but leaning darkly, half-turned toward Seflatan
even when facing me. I realized instantly
upon his greeting. We were estranged.
Even as he talked, his mouth pulled back
in calculation. I had another piece of knowing,
and with the same spur of certainty with which
I knew his dream, it was clear. He would circle me
and then the priest, a figure-eight of influence,
and over time, we'd spin from equinox to solstice,
and then, he'd be gone, out of reach for years.

I knew, when in the realm of Seflatan, my life
could flare like a match. I began preparing
for my seasons, saving things, building certainties.
When in my sphere, a word or nod could shift the law.
When out, all the stallions of Persia thundering
to a yawn of God couldn't interest him my way.

And Seflatan was a study, a politicized worm.
He burrowed with method and steadiness, eating
through the core, gnawing at a chamber, hulling
out the power, issue by issue, meal by meal.
When Seflatan was spinning through him like a lathe,
Nebuchadnezzar's head like an apple would lose color,
his policy grow punky; his sweetness of perception,
like sawdust out his ear.

Seflatan was after something not rightly his
and didn't want to build on it or squander it
or even walk it on a leash. He ached to occupy
and pilot the world, to settle into power
like a glove, pinching judgments on the race.
He understood the ricochet of systems, thrived
on charting messengers, staging battles in the maze.
He made the law his labyrinth. And the King believed in law.

I chose my moments well. When Susanna was condemned,
I hadn't planned to get involved. You know, we witness
the worst and it slaps the conscience like a face—
the first time shocks, the second stings, the third
goes numb, the fourth strangely sings
in sirens too inaudible for care, and then
we shuffle, stop to lick our salt, and like the lick.
No one's upset. It's how things go. The times are rough
and insincere. What difference could I make?

I heard how she had stirred things up,
not publicly, but bit by bit, questioning
the role of slaves, the right to rule,
the weight of tax, and uttering in private
that women had souls. There was speculation
I would side with her and go down too.

It was seeing her on trial.
She wasn't frantic or possessed.
She wasn't forceful or tough of mind,
but pacific, with eyes that pulled
the softness from the crowd.
I think she was condemned
for being so at ease. At first,
the witnesses were men. They testified
she'd disobeyed and caused disorder
in their homes. It seemed routine.
Though everyone began enraged, once
aired, the issue seemed quite tame.

Her presence was winning out.
It was pleasing to feel the crowd
yawn and slow their chops. Then Seflatan
himself stepped in, and wiped the issue
like a knife, along his robe, and something
cracked, as if she'd dropped a cup within
and spilled the sip she'd saved.
It made her sweat and swallow hard.
Then Seflatan swore in a woman
who seemed instantly ashamed.
Susanna braced herself and sank.
And as she slouched and crossed her legs,
something mutable, the inch of thigh pressed
on her knee, the pod of essence keeping her
restrained, something erased the sense
that this was prearranged, and there
was nothing of the future in the air,
nothing that said this had to be.
I felt that thump that centers out when
triggered and about to speak. Seflatan
grew antiseptic. The woman confessed. She was
Susanna's lover. The men squirmed, and one or two
whispered, murmured, coughed and laughed. I thought,
they're just hurt like me that she found comfort
in her arms, or really, that she found none
here with me, or worse, the truth—
we are not beautiful enough to hold.
I gripped the rail and almost stood.
I crossed my legs and turned away.
She looked at me, straight at
me, as if to say, it's come to this.
You and I. Born to meet this way.
She ignored Seflatan and entered me
and the world receded, muted down, wavered out
till we exchanged, talked in thoughts that reeled
like webs of light between our minds. She thought,

"You and I. Like spies for God. You can't let it
stay this way." I thought back, "I never knew."
She smiled, "There's more of us than you'll admit."
She was right. Uniqueness made me free.
She'd heard that, too. I thought, how soft.
She softened in concentric rings. We rippled
to a swaying core, and back, the mob
had burst its spline and Seflatan was
hissing in the storm. What I knew
began to build. The woman's voice
regained its noise,
"Susanna promised"
"Promised what?"
"That there would be an end to this"
"To what?"
"This way of life"
"What way? What life?"
"The unfair estate"
"What estate?"
"This! This subjugation of our souls!"
"Whose souls? Not yours?"
"Yes! Ours!"
"You have no soul."
"O Yes! Tell them Susanna!"
"Yes, tell us Susanna.
Tell us all about these things."
Susanna said nothing and Seflatan pounded,
"Tell us, does your slave have a soul?"
"I don't have a slave."
"How unfortunate, but then, does mine?"
"Does he have a tongue?"
"Why yes, are tongues germane?"
"Only in the end."
"The end?"
"Of speech."
The crowd began to hoot.

"Let's get back to souls.
Does your soul have a tongue?"
"All seeds have common ground."
"So, my slave shares the ground with me?"
"You have your own dirt to sift, you tell me."
The crowd roared. Seflatan gripped the rail.
I almost stood. He pushed, "I have a woman slave
who has a tongue. Does she have a soul? Yes or no?"
"The tongue, the slave, the woman are one.
All have common ground."
"You're of this ground?"
"Yes."
"My slave's of this ground? Yes or no?"
"Yes."
"And this ground is the ground of—"
She tired of this and simply said, "Souls.
The ground of souls where slaves and kings
walk naked arm in arm." Susanna's lover blubbered.
Seflatan turned, palms to the crowd, a tenor in disdain,
"To the lions." He closed up shop. The crowd buzzed and
swarmed. She didn't move. I rose, "Seflatan!" There was
a hush. "You are a Priest. You read the Stars."
He looked at me and circled left. It was a time
of change. Nebuchadnezzar was up for grabs.
If I could just postpone, stall off,
reopen things while it was fresh,
"No one questions the pre-eminence
of stars, the light they speak, how
they're seen first, but darkness, by its
proper place, points up the star. What kind
of Heaven would it be, High Priest, if stars
could not be seen? You couldn't track a single
life. You couldn't read the time or help the King.
And still, the darkness, in its estate, makes up
the sky." He wouldn't engage me. The crowd was
piqued. I turned, "But all are sky. You are sky.
The King's the holy star. And as stars need dark

to shine, Kings and Priests stand out among us
slaves. But all breathe a common air, a sky, a
ground, a word, a name—even if we call it soul.
It's just the endless sky. How can you condemn
the thing on which your Priesthood stands?"
The crowd was unsure of what I'd said.
Tension filled the court. Seflatan was firm,
precise, "She slept with this woman, and challenged
the King's authority. One is depraved, the other
treason." I had to stall. I'd sent Eban for the King.
I faced the crowd, "I heard the woman say she loved
Susanna, nothing more. You love your King, should
I assume—" The crowd snickered. He lost control,
"The case is closed. Take it up with the King."
I could feel his presence in the court. A wave
of bowing offered him. He ambled to Susanna
and looked into her ease. He looked to me.
I knew he'd set her free. My time had come again.
He worked the crowd, meant to utilize his mercy.
But she wasn't grateful, or ecstatic, just relieved.
And the crowd, against all my wishes, called out to me.
The King, as we left, paused to watch an old woman
grovel at my hand. He then gestured me ahead of him,
and never trusted me again.

*Haunted by the gift, Michelangelo finds the cost of freedom a painful wound.
His days become excavations as he stalks to dig a home between the power
of the gift and the power of the world. And though the gift causes some to be
loved till the armed powers of the world whine in jealousy, the sculptor feels
certain it is dangerous to be understood, yet frustrating to remain invisible.
He grows more skeptical of the problem as he gripes about Julius and recalls
arguing with Martin Luther in Rome toward the close of 1510 when the
stringent gift and the fiery gift met, a clash of storms in isolation.*

MICHELANGELO:
First he makes me square his casket!
Then he squawks how much it costs!

Now I have to paint this chantry!
On and On! And he won't let me near
St. Peter's! He counts up the indulgences
and no one says a word. All think I get God's share—
but I can barely buy the paint! And Rome is broken down.
The sewers smell. The streets are wracked. I don't care.
No one can blame me. I didn't come here on my own.
I hate to mix this paint. It splatters like a salve.
And every face is his. He wants to break me down,
then set me free. He claims I'm of his stable.
I will not bow, but now I kiss his ring. And still,
he can be gentle, like a vacuum, a sudden dying
breeze. And last winter, near December, he was
all ears, until the German monk arrived. Then
there was talk of accidents, of German sausage
on his plate. The Cardinals raised their eyes
and shook their heads as Luther frowned his way.
I felt sorry for the ruddy monk, knew Julius wouldn't
speak to him for days. I was wrestling with Cumae,
scratching out her leathered breasts, when a Cardinal
cleared his throat. I pretended not to hear. He chirped.
I glared and saw two figures through the slats. And there
he was, all stern, a block of German Angst. As I came down,
he frowned and humphed through his drab tunnel of a gown.
He was disgusted by my work. It was the nudes. He spewed
something offensive. I read it in the Cardinal's eyes.
And as the Cardinal tried to lead him out, he poked
at me, and growled, and jabbed up at the vault.
The Cardinal sighed and dropped his hands, "He wants
to know if you've a conscience." I pointed to God
creating Adam, "Tell him, there's more to God
than us down here." The Cardinal grew queasy.
Luther locked his jaw and strutted for the altar,
short feet clapping, shuffling, stalling. He spun
and trilled something thick and full of points.
The Cardinal blushed and wouldn't say. Luther half

erupted. The cleric uttered, "He says, 'There's more to God
than Julius.'" I had to watch what I said. Luther railed
something tart, inflected near the end. The Cardinal,
replete with indecision, withdrew, but never left.
He faded in the shadow of the vault. Luther
cropped up close, no higher than my chest.
He muttered in Italian, "This won't last."
I tried to end the conversation. He sneered,
"This is your design?" I spun, "Of Course!"
He butted close, "You'll burn in Hell
Forever!" I slapped him in the head.
He sputtered and humphed. The Cardinal
came rushing. I scurried up the scaffold
like a rodent angel squealing all the way!

*As Michelangelo feels the backlash, over and over, of not containing his
wrath, Daniel learns how to contain the egos of lesser men, while deferring
the love of the people. Both become thoughtful fulcrums, knowing, at last,
they can negotiate the worldly gauntlet, but it will compromise their gift.
And so, Daniel reviews how he let Seflatan set his labyrinth, using his gift to
escape it.*

DANIEL: Susanna led a quiet life when freed.
   I saw her from time to time and rumors spread
   that we were lovers before the trial.
   Seflatan never let up. But Nebuchadnezzar and I
   spent long afternoons, feet splashing in his pool,
   talking of things to come. He'd ask my advice,
   seldom take it, and think he had.
   We grew close again, like those days
   before Cutha, but deeper, mortality
   more in mind. In private, we understood
   each other. In public, I was irritated
   how he believed himself a King.

   Once, he had an urge for fish.
   A dozen servants couldn't wait to comply,

but he thought we'd walk and talk
and stroll the marketplace,
handle some whitefish, pick at it,
lick our fingers, smell like the sea.
We bought the fish, and turning from the stand,
a merchant laughed and bumped the King. He
dropped his fish. It lay breaded in the dirt.
He ordered me to strike him. I said nothing,
gave him mine, and scooped the slab of fish
to wash it in a tub nearby. He threw mine in the dirt,
"Strike him!" I said, "We're all not here for you."
He slapped me, hard. I walked away. He followed,
50 steps behind, apologizing under wind.

As Seflatan regained his turn,
he made advances in the law.
He legalized a prayer to Bel,
a remedial god in need of beef and coin.
Twice a week they'd set a plate, aromas
steaming up the altar. By morning, the chops
and coin were gone. No one in the court believed in this,
but the people had latched on. Everyone knew I worshipped
God. The prayer was just perfunctory, a gesture to the King.
I was expected to make an offering.

The priests approached my home. I stalled,
slipped out and walked the hills. Within a month
Seflatan had summoned me. At court, he coaxed
our Boy, "Why can't he pledge his faith to you?
Some favorite son you chose."

He wouldn't side with me again so soon.
I said I'd watch, if they could teach.

Old Ashpenaz owed me one. He confirmed it all.
They slipped the food through passageways, and chewed
the sacrifice, then sopped the meat juice up with bread
and left the famished plate to dawn.

Ashpenaz hated to help me, but I threatened him,
"You owe me your life, and if you refuse,
I'll take it, on my own, not right away. No,
I'll let you think, forget, rescare yourself.
You'll wish for me to take you down.
Don't think I'll do it cleanly.
No, I've a special way in mind."

We entered the Temple the night before,
spreading ashes along the floor to track
their feet. When we met, Seflatan was sure he'd won,
erect and casual, till I traced the ashen prints
to a cellar wall lined with bones and coin.
He recovered at once, and searched for someone
to assume the fall. The King was fuming.
Then Seflatan understood, and motioned
to Ashpenaz who grew frantic. I was stoic.
Poor Ashpenaz was dragged away. The thing
was kept close to the chest, and Seflatan
was out of favor again. The King was furious,
but once alone, he laughed and took me in his arms,
so glad I didn't lose. I felt him pull me to his chest
in a press that told me, by its sudden depth,
that next time, he would let me go.

*Michelangelo thinks of little else, but how to work the balance when the gift is all stallion and no saddle, when the power is enlivened but orphaned in the world. He wars within to stay gifted while useless in securing food and clothes. It causes him to remember his frightful gallop from Rome in 1506, a fugitive from Julius, as he reached Poggibonsi with his fear of being caught, his fear of being compromised, his fear the gift, forestalled, would end.*

MICHELANGELO:
The horse lathered and pumped. A cramp
bulged in its neck. I pushed. It coughed.
I slackened the reins. My hands were sore.
I'd galloped clear out of Rome.

190 The lathered cramp had a bulbous sheen.
My head pounded in the lack of wind.
I dismounted and the horse shied from me.
It calmed. The moon was rising in the east.
The vein pulsed along the cramp.
The moon's sheen crested on the vein.
The beauty of the horse just suffering
freed me of my fear. Veins halt me, remove me
from my life. And here, the moon made it safe.
Rest, you black Pegasus with moonlight webbing
through your chest. I walked the horse, its front
hooves dragged. It began to breathe more easily. I thought,
the damn thing's scrapped, the marble sitting there in Rome,
all roped and stacked, the figures prone like bloodless
ancient Greeks in coffins I could crack—just feel
the faults, edge and tap where they go cold,
and all the walls and crusts will fall in chunks,
and chests will rise— At Poggibonsi I took a room
and fed the horse. New noises kept me up: an old man
breathing, groaning on his side, deep neurotic birds
whining in the night, creaks that passed through walls
without a wind. The walls became my mind—all shift
and creak to fight off sleep. I teetered on the edge
where nodding seemed a death; to close the eyes,
surrender, a dilation of the will, and slipping,
floating, barely there, small objects rose:
the chair, the door, the basin near the bed,
the bed itself, lifting, spreading, snapping back,
the length of angles falling through the wood, dark energy
cascading for a place, dead energy along the length of nails.
A crow, I heard a crow, a buried groan of man. And laughter.
Ancient laughter, drifting for a thousand years, into a veil
of mortal fright, rising from behind. A light. A crow.
A laugh. The horse. The horses. Rapping on my mind.
The hooves on wood. Old thunder popping through.
The door banged wide. Five Roman guards.
I tore the sheet.

*Daniel believes while the body bearing the gift can be made dependent on*
*the whimsy of a king, the gift itself cannot be extinguished. Shortly thereafter,*
*as if divine energy can be caged, the prophet is cast into the lions' den, where*
*he sheds his shrewdness the way Michelangelo, cast into his gloomy chapel,*
*has shed his deeper forms of despair. In recollection it seizes Daniel, as his*
*lions sleep, and Michelangelo, as his painted figures dry, that, fueled from*
*beyond, mortals remain kinetic and undefined.*

DANIEL: Odd accidents began to occur.
    One of Seflatan's closest aides
    was found dismembered before the Idol Bel.
    Neatly done. The blood was drained,
    organs floating in a murky bowl.
    Head frozen in surprise,
    stumped on a silver tray.
    I knew this had to come from Persia.
    They'd sent assassins in before, slow
    as cats and clean as priests turned butchers.
    They were more than deadly. They were patient,
    methodical, relentless, an insensate razor.
    They'd keep stalking without murmur or whisk of pain
    till silently, with the bug stuck in water,
    they'd dart and sweep the muted dragon down.

    It could have been anyone but Seflatan,
    Nebuchadnezzar, or me. It strangely brought us together.
    We met and strategized. Seflatan was quite perceptive
    and unhurried in his thinking. He thought like a spider,
    moving several thoughts at once, pushing an alternative
    here, holding one in place, weaving them and moving on,
    dragging the partial web behind. But I had no sense
    of why he thought, why he idolized well-thought plans.
    Yet something in his far-off planner's look was vaguely,
    palely, a look of faith. His mind was a substitute for God.
    And when in his mind, like a Temple, the Priest was kind.
    He caught me smiling, and took my arm, briefly, to show me
    his plan. My guard went down for grasping him. Nebuchadnezzar

encouraged this. We devised a law where those obedient
beyond the King would be detained. This gave us means
of interview, and latitude to act. We all agreed.

Months went by. Nothing. We wanted to think it had passed,
but that's how these Persians work. As the mind goes off,
counting the lazy trill of birds, or watching small animals
move through trees, when curling up to think of a time
when it was less of a task to simply be, just as
the rack of weariness untracks—a shaft,
a strange coming down, a pillow on the throat.
Just as not telling had its pull, not killing
was as frightening as the moment of the kill.

Then two more attacks, back to back, both early,
in the dawn. One, a servant girl, well loved by all.
They'd poured poison in her ear. I found her, ear
to the ground, and tried to wake her. Her shoulder
was still warm, and as she rolled, a thin puddle
that some said was the poison mixed with blood.

Seflatan, on a sudden search, came in on me
praying. The light was receding cross the floor
and I was wondering about the girl's last thoughts
draining out her ear. He seemed surprised
to see me kneeling, "What are you doing?"

"Praying."
"What? To Who?"
"Let's not start—"
"To Nebuchadnezzar?"
"Hardly—"
"You mean—"
The guards began to cluster.
"You can't be serious."

They rough-housed me down the hall and all the way,
I was astonished. His aide, the servants, this Persian myth,
all to trap Nebuchadnezzar in his devotion to the law.
This was too obvious. He'd never let it happen.

I thought of our last embrace. They kept me
in the darker cellar. They kept me there
four days and nights. No sign of Nebuchadnezzar.
Seflatan had thought of everything. It was even his turn.
I watched two ants start and go back, cross,
stick to the cracks and disappear.

I could picture them talking and Seflatan methodically
staring as Nebuchadnezzar paced about his throne.

On the sixth day, or night, Seflatan came.
He smugly straddled a chair. I was firm,
"I won't admit to praying. He'll never let you do this."
He raised his brow and shrugged his hand, "It's over.
You won't even see him. The King's *involved*
and soon is due abroad. You know, to Persia,
to apply some pressure, to make things safe again."
He laughed and took me by the wrist,
"Now, I'm the one who knows."
I broke free. He backed away,
"See if your God can save you."

Another day and night, and then, my *King* arrived.
I could tell by how he wouldn't stand still
or look at me without raising his voice.
We'd never been further apart.

"How could you let him catch you praying?"
"How can you let him keep me here?"
"The whole country's under oath, a law
You made! What am I supposed to do?!"

I told him it was all a hoax. But we were out of sync.
Each truth I felt angered him. He'd forgotten who I was.
I pulled him by his robe, "Remember the dream. Think on what
you think you see." He pulled away, "You've never believed
in me. Even when I freed that woman, the way she treated me,
and you never thanked me for saving her. You wanted her
so badly. Everyone could see what I'd done for you. The court's

194

been divided ever since. And how the people love you."
"Don't be jealous." "I'm Not Jealous! I'm the KING!"
"You're an aging man, about to lose a friend."

We said no more and though he wanted to,
he wouldn't touch, wouldn't even take my hand.
He was coached against our bond.
Something made me count his steps.
He stopped and turned and looked for me,
and thinking me not there, went on.
The steps before he turned were two.

The ants were trying to bridge the cracks.
They scurried and fell. I lifted one.
It itched the lifeline in my palm and stopped
halfway. I tried to feel large and knowing,
but how weak my hands had grown. I made a fist
and felt the ant scurry, and nursed the fear
of having waited too long
to do what I was meant to do.

The next morning five guards came.
I thought the King had changed his mind. No one talked,
but soon we left the compound. My mind was racing,
sorting plots, and ways, and schemes. I thought,
they're going to kill me, but how? Which road?
How much time? Which one? Who should I convince?
My mind reeled, a bale of twine, ravelling to
nothing but coiled impressions of the fear.
And beneath all that, my faith in God.
Strange resistant faith. I dropped my plans,
stopped weighing what I said. I slowed. They
stopped. I said, "It would do us good to pray."
One guard rubbed close, "Why don't you run.
We'll make it quick. You won't suffer long."

I looked at him and thought, this is odd.
I can't think fast. We walked back streets

and then I realized where. I paused to watch a bird.
They rested on their spears. We joked about flight.
I said, "There is just one God. How else
could I have known the dream?"

We marched the cool passageway.
I thought, no more holding back, or schemes.
The crowd was buzzing. All rose as we entered.
The light washed me blind. The roars were far
and close, curled, then shapes began to form.
The guards were gone and all around, lions snarling low.
One started out—another swatted him and two more,
about to bound, purred against my leg. One's belly
knocked me to the left where a long one set and roared,
then wagged its tail and jumped, its paws across my back.

I kept quite still, expecting to be torn.
The smell was harsh and old. And nothing.
I opened my eyes. They curled and purred,
all but three. I sat on one, then stood
and bellowed, "Idols and Kings are less than dogs!
Only God can save a man!" Of the three one raced me,
but of the twenty at my side, a large one
with a matted brain scratched and clawed.
Then clouds of dirt. Whacks and whines and snaps.
The first one lay bleeding in the dirt. I was enthralled,
the lion's blood thick as syrup, almost burgundy.
The other two stayed away, circling all afternoon.
The crowd, stunned, hung on till dusk and quietly
dispersed, though some remained. The lions dozed,
piled about my sweating frame. And nothing.

The ground steamed blue and the orange sun
warmed their heaving sides bronze. I thought,
I must reinvent my life. The bronze spilled
from all their hides up and out my face.
And it was night. A part of me had died,
had stripped my cleverness to bone,

had cut the screens across my heart.
I stretched headlong through the future,
felt my senses pop and burn. I thought,
why am I here—not with the lions—
but here at all? I looked for my life
and didn't know where to go, how to hold
or what to ask. The night was winning.
The lions blinked their fired eyes.

The crowd returned at dawn, louder
and larger, for word had spread. By noon, the heat
made the lions shine along their flanks and ribs.
They haled sphinxlike, as I sat the center,
eyes reeling, less sure of what I knew.
They tightened the ring, squinting, yawning,
stretching for the sun, and the yard of God gleamed,
so transporting. I felt unimportant though eternal.
I cupped the sandy earth and let it dust my fingers,
knew the dirt was older than Persia, knew God
like ancient earth had suffered many names.

The crowd began to call out questions,
but I had nothing to say. I'd known so much
in one small center, but dispersed like this,
I knew a speck of everything, my mouth,
a secret twisting in a sea of heat.

By night, the lions' eyes were incandescent,
lighted from behind. Their bronze hides
slipped blue and I knew Nebuchadnezzar
was worried I would die.

From the ring of lion eye,
I heard him raise his cup of bone,
a huge interlocking chalice
made from the ribs of slaves.
He dipped his face as in a basin,
drank red wine, and thought himself enduring.

I felt my eyes become all-glowing
as I made the ribs he drank from breathe.

He came running to the stadium,
but wouldn't show his face.
More people stood the vigil
and in the morning, they tried
to take me from the ring. The lions charged
and dropped two guards, whacked them senseless
in the dirt. Then dragged them, shared them,
and all could hear the seamless tear of flesh,
the stubborn rip of bone from joint,
the lions sucking on the bones.
I was unimpressed.

Thoughts swooped about in pairs like birds.
I had to make a journey. But where? How long?
For what? God had cleansed my head
of all things smaller than 500 years.
I didn't know my name. By the fourth day,
the lions formed a Temple. Their eyes
glowed all at once. Nebuchadnezzar showed,
"Seflatan has gone too far." His voice filtered
through the sun, "O take the oath. You mean too much."
My face felt dark and hollowed, whiskers
smelling like a mane, "Who's Seflatan?
And who are you pretending you're a King?"
He said, "Daniel, please, stop all this.
It's gotten out of hand. Come home."
He was a hellish silhouette, spying on the lions,
with no eyes, no voice, no name. And higher up,
a sea of aimless swaying, buzzing out of view.
I yelled, "Here is your King! Your eyeless Leader!
Who eats fish and wades in pools! He kills servants
for soiling his flute! You are only Nebuchadnezzar!
Therein you and the dog are alike! Bark like a dog
before your people! Inflate yourself, you water-bug!
Chirp like a cricket! All Hail The Godless King!"

He brought troops to kill the lions.
It took seven days and even dead,
their eyes glowed through the night.
I started to remember.
There was a general call to kill me.
But Nebuchadnezzar wanted me to take the oath
and leave, "At least give me back my people."

He sent me into exile,
and three days in the desert,
I heard him say to Seflatan,
"Wait till it's part-forgotten,
then bring him back alive."

*Daniel's fear that he's missed his destiny informs Michelangelo's growing terror that, if caged by Julius too long, his gift will move on, dissipate, and leave him ordinary. Still tethered to the Pope's faint schemes, Michelangelo presses for a way to respond without endangering his life or his work. It depresses him to realize he hasn't moved an inch closer to his freedom since first fleeing Rome in 1506. Even then he resisted the Pope's men at Poggibonsi and returned to Florence, only to be forced, months later, to meet Julius in Bologna. Enroute, the sculptor encountered Machiavelli whose belief that humans hunt power as animals sniff out food pushed him further from the world. He plummets as he recalls their meeting.*

MICHELANGELO: He had a cold passion for how people merged,
    dissolved, backed down, aligned. The more he talked,
    the more distilled his view till he was drawing patterns
    in his sand of thought with a stick of speech.
    He never seemed to stop watching me, I mean,
    even when he talked, I felt part of him above us
    surveying what was getting through, and not.
    He said Julius was arrogant, impetuous,
    ambitious in a way that left no room
    for ambition. He said, "You're right
    to distrust. There's no excuse for how you've been tossed.
    But it's just beginning. What's right is irrelevant here."
    Even when he drank, he was measuring how the liquid

swirled around his glass. He said, "You've picked
a hell of a Pope to run out on. I'm surprised
you're still alive." I was exhausted
from being frightened. Every new face
in Florence sent me hiding. After three Briefs,
Soderini sent me out, "We can't afford a war with him
over you. Make up your mind and return." But here,
I stopped to see Niccolo, and he talked and talked
how Julius was the Warrior-Prince, but something
was out of sync. The power was in place. The strength,
the drive, yet something, something, he swirled his glass,
something was out of place. He became entranced
within the swirling, and finally surfaced,
downed his drink, slammed the glass,
"I'd go home, Buonarroti.
When Dante was called,
he never saw Florence again."

He talked the rest of the night
about interpersonal power, how a leader
had to be mathematic to keep his hold.
How compassion was vital to affect a power,
but disastrous if nursed along. He said,
"Compassion strikes the piece of you in others
that marks access to controlling what they believe.
So, likewise, once you've puppetted the puppet,
licked and knotted all the strings, compassion tugs
and ties you down. It makes for good reconnaissance,
not much else." He talked like a madman, of lives
as resources; how wild rivers could be diverted
and raging fires told where to burn. He saw me wince,
yet understand. He said, "Don't be so shocked.
You do the same in stone. Mine is the art
of carving people. It happens all the time.
I prefer to be . . not haphazard. You wouldn't
blindly hack the marble. Well, alright then,
don't be so righteous about stony lives."

He turned before I'd left the grounds,
as I stood talking. I was gone for him,
all smoke, and he hadn't even closed the door.

I rode five or six more miles toward Bologna,
then felt the puppet strings and Julius pulling.
I was fair game. He'd kill kings for less. I turned
and turned in place, then felt Niccolo's money
rock its leather pouch. I forgot to take it out.
Bonaccorsi had me bring it. His precious money.
I feared he'd think I stole it. I rode on
and worried-through his calculations.
But now, Now, beneath the vault,
to find myself in others, How?
In painting, it's another thing.
I beat the prison of my body,
for my spirit knows so many songs
my earthly voice can't sing.

*Michelangelo's conflict between abandoning all to his divine energy and surviving the world makes him impatient for the light. When swiftly informed by God, he paints like a comet, feeling gifted beyond all restraint. When discharged, the chapel turns a tent of exile. But despite his reflexive complaining, being thrust in the chapel has forced the sculptor to reshape his art, the way being thrust in the lions' den forced the prophet to reshape his life; so much so that when Nebuchadnezzar had him brought out of exile, it was not the Daniel he had banished, but the oyster of that man.*

DANIEL: I wandered for several years,
made a life deeper than the last,
closer to the earth, slower
than I thought possible.
I grew a beard and stopped wearing shoes,
stopped eating all day long and likewise,
stopped eating words. The wind was longer
and the dark wasn't quite as dark.
I searched for God instead of praying.
It was like flying instead of singing,

resting instead of sleeping, like
weeping instead of holding on.

Then, in a village, it was Seflatan.
He'd grown white and fat and wore creamy robes.
He passed me on the street. He passed four times,
maybe five. It was his youngest guard who found me
carving wood. Seflatan smirked. I said, "You've changed.
What's new?" He locked his jaw, "Do you know where you are?"
I shrugged and watched his face. He was looking at me,
but talking to who I'd been, "You've broken your exile.
You're under arrest." I chuckled, "You've shed nothing
along the way. You're like a hole an arrow makes.
Here Seflatan. Go on, I give it to you."
He took my carving distrustfully. "Go on."
He smoothed his hands around it.
"That's what erosion does. I'm
no longer sharp. I'm dull."
He thought it was a trick.

I laughed and as we walked, I thought
how I'd become a length of grain, barely visible
in the merciable fount where all things flow.

It took a month, but there we were,
at night, so none could see. The things
the night has had to bear, the things men think
can be won without sight. They put me in the cellar
again. After all this time, I looked for the ants.
Then Nebuchadnezzar appeared, older, more drawn,
thinner in the face and legs, hunched lower to the ground.
He entered the cell. We couldn't help but smile, and then
we hugged in a gentle way. He held my face and nearly cried,
"I've missed you. Look how you've changed."
"You're a bit of a broken chicken, too."
We laughed and I confess, I was moved.
His eyes were still tender cups of fire.
He took my hands, "I want you back, Belteshazzar.

We can repair all this. You'll see."

How few watch us devour life, fall down,
break off, and carry on. I took his face, "You want us
to age as one, to walk for fish and eat by the pool."
He nodded. We bobbed as old men do. I ran my fingers
through his white white hair, "Tell me my dream, hmm?
Tell me what it means?" He was perplexed. I said,
"It's too late to repair, old friend. Belteshazzar
was dead before I left. And Daniel, tell me, who is he?
And if you see an old lost king, tell him, thrones
are made for One. It's done. Done."

He was hurt and turned away,
then spun as if it were years ago,
"You'll change your tune." I whispered,
"No. You can't keep me here."
He raised his trembling voice,
"You can't do this! I've waited so long!"
And so we began again. He kept me there
three days, and on the fourth, was cooler yet,
"You'll bend to me, or I'll have your head!"
I took his skull in my gnarled bunched palms,
"God will blind you now, for sure." He broke my grip
and slapped my arms, "Still trying to intimidate me.
I'm your King!" "The King will blind you now, for sure."
He laughed, then hushed, "You've aged severely."
"Your eyes are breaking as we speak."
He erupted, "Be quiet now!
You'll stay till I say go!
We'll see who sees, whose King is King.
I said I missed you. I'm a better man."
I sat, exhausted, hands throbbing in my lap,
"What do you want from me?" He stopped and started,
stopped, and then, stammered out a ring of speech,
"You'll admit you love me before we're through."

In less than three days, I was before him,
and by the way he gripped his throne, I knew the dream

had come, had burned itself below his skin.
From the time we'd met, it was working its damp chemical.
He stood but kept his fingertips along the throne's sleek
arm. I circled left, behind his ear. He didn't know
I'd moved. He tapped his fingers nervously.
I whispered, "Head of gold, thighs of brass—"
I tapped his feet—"Feet of clay—"
He dropped his sceptre—"Flecked with iron."
I circled right.
He answered left, "How did you do this?"
I laughed.
"Restore my sight! Don't leave me this way!"
He reached across the void, "Please—"
I watched him stumble toward his pool.
I began, "There's but one way."
He spun and hit an urn.
I sat him down.
"Don't toy with me!"
I took his arms.
"Undo this! Please!"
His eyes were tense.
I yanked on him.
His shoulders dropped.
I began, "We'll leave tomorrow."
"For where?"
"Jerusalem."
"But why?"
"To see."
He paused,
knew I was serious,
"Can you undo this?"
I stroked his face, "Old friend—"
"Can you?!"
"Old Friend—"
"CAN you?!"
"I don't know."

　He hugged me
as he did when we were young.
I hugged him back, crestfallen.

Next day, we set out on foot.
He started with his hands outstretched,
as if obstacles were all chest high.
I walked behind and then ahead, and finally,
his arms sagged, his head bobbed down.
But he pumped his feet too high. I snapped,
"Walk normally and stop being frightened."
"Why did you do this? After all I've done for you."
I swept behind, "I didn't do it." He turned.
I bounced ahead, "The dream, remember?"
He spun again. I crouched,
"The dream of God's what did it."
He flailed and scuffed my neck,
"I've told you how I love you!"

We hit a narrow path of rocks.
I took him by the hand. He was right.
I was heartless. I don't know why.
I didn't mean to tease him. I looked at him,
an old king groping, and looked at me
in his blind reflection, closed my eyes,
saw us in the after-image, as our souls might be
in any instance of despair. I patted his craggy face,
"We're on our way, after all these years."
And deep down, I knew this was coming,
had dreamt it, not in particular,
but in a waking cramp of conscience
while I was carving out the wood.

He fell and scraped his knee.
I reached but stopped. He raised himself.
He sighed and threw his arms to Heaven,
"Why?! WHY?! What did I do to Thee?!"
I'd never seen him so expressive.

I was glad I didn't help.
It's God that made me taunt him.
He shrieked, "Daniel! Why can't you love me?!"
I watched him bump from stone to stone.
I jumped and squat my haunches on a boulder.
He whined, "I never hurt a soul."
I rocked like one of God's white monkeys,
"That's apt, a real ironic thing to say."
He whipped a stone in my direction,
"You bastard! I've had enough!"

"You've always thought the world owed you!
You really think you're a King!"
"I've saved you so many times!
And still, you're arrogant with me!"

He found my foot and yanked me
from the boulder. I cut my leg.

I only had to press my thumbs against his eyes
and pray to God, and he'd see again with dawn.
He lunged for where he heard me breathe,
"You think you're above the law!"

Finally, I wrapped my arms about him.
He struggled but couldn't get free. I began,
"I never asked for you to love me!"
He moaned and slipped my arms to his knees.
I yelled, "Self-Love deceives all men!"

His basic life was unrevealing.
I swept yards away and watched him rave.
I thought, what if I don't cure him.

He rolled his back across a boulder,
thought he heard a slither near his foot, "Daniel!
Daniel!!" He jumped and ran his thigh into a ledge
and fell.

Then, all at once, I caught the leather in my voice
hoping he couldn't find me. My beard began to
drip. I caved in. He kept inhaling harshly,
afraid I'd gone for good. I watched him shudder
and suffered all we couldn't manage. I broke
and wept for my wasted life with him. He rose,
his chest still heaving, and stumbled through
my net of sobs. I thought, now he hears and tries
to find me. Now, when there's nothing left to sing.
I couldn't say I loved him. He sponged the wetness
from my face, rubbed it with his cut-up fingers.
I took one last look within him, without his eyes
getting in the way. He went to hug me and I let him.
Then I gripped his tortured head, and poked my thumbs,
pressing his sight into his sense of time, and said
the words God taught me, and saw the lions' glowing
eyes. He groaned. I brought him to me, and thought,
in another world, we'd be naming each other's
children. I said, "Goodbye, old friend.
Don't try to find me" and
disappeared into the air.

# XIX. GOD CREATES THE SUN AND MOON AND PLANTS ON EARTH

Michelangelo is searing in his depiction of God, as he yearns for that space before time, that nothing before emptiness, that predimension in which there is no erosion, no falling away. He paints a pensive, knotted God, crouched in flight, whose radiance of thought forces energies to amass into a burning center around which worlds will aggregate and decay. It fatigues the artist to sculpt everything with paint. It wears down his stability to pull bodies from the plaster. It ages every part but his hand and eye to extract three dimensions out of two. He pales, feeling trapped in God's image, and grows crouched and somewhat charred on the inside, his eyes incited by an interior flame, as the moon, relying on its memory as a conception in the Mind of God, recounts the creation of the sun.

THE MOON:
  The Realm of His Mind
  Became each Possibility.
  He thought the color yellow,
  and I tumbled through a wash of light,
  a lemon fleck falling in a patch of heat.
  Everything bleached and He dismissed the idea,
  but never fully rid His Mind of yellow. It bunched,
  without form or weight, invading the amebic void
  in which I swam, like He, like a pensive, effortless fish.
  He floated through His void conjuring gravity and fluidity,
  as if a mother in her womb, directing birth from within.
  The yellow began to press and center in His mind
  and I was moved out, away, careening the edge.
  But neither He nor I could escape the yellow.
  And then, by the sheer act of Emanation,
  the yellow bonded, quite muscular unto itself,
  and we began to bend toward it; I in His Mind,
  He in His void. I felt unrealized,
  in both Realms at once.
  And straddling that ridge of heat
  where Idea and Matter join,
  I became Lunar, indirect
  while God whirled,
  expelling the yellow.

*The moon's indirect heat makes Michelangelo feel imprisoned in his body while lamenting the years of decay needed to be released. Drained by the strain of crossing these dimensions, he dozes briefly on the scaffold, standing up, brush gobbing on the Ceiling, and wakes dizzy, in a sweat, in the arc of a lightning dream.*

MICHELANGELO: O O I'm heaving, profusely heaving!
  Dear God—There was nothing, Absolutely
  Nothing—No stars or light or earth—
  And I leaned further—Curious—

And with a Cleaving Snap—Space
had Duration! For each direction had a depth.
It was the Hours, for I began to sweat and age.
I became weary, unable to withstand
the sweep of nothing turned everything
by its being limed with Time. And then
with a shrill that split my brain,
God divided Time in two—compressing one,
unleashing the other and I couldn't stop
leaning into the center which was all that was left
of the beginning. I was unforeseeable, and then I fell
into a Smithy of Chaos, the halves smelting about.
I went to scream but my mouth melted from my face
without a puff. And now I wake, thinking of Dante
and Friar Bene, a carpenter and ironworker, a relative
who must have known Dante, a man who worked heat
in his hands. Did he speak with Dante?
Did he ask him about the dividing of Time?
O dead monk of my blood, what did he say
from his slow winding into Hell?
Is the pressed half the sun?
The future, the effaced
flame of dream?

*The moon, now launched from the Mind of God, but yet without an orbit, continues its account, which rims Michelangelo with a soft recollection of the Medici Garden, where as a prodigy he knew the companionship of like souls while being protected from the world.*

THE MOON: The ripples of heat sent us
into approximate orbits, uneven
and barely grooved. And the spray of light
in all directions burned, froze, became the stars.
And God hovered and tumbled slowly in place, over
and over, for at least the tip of a millennium
and very subtly, He divested Himself

211

into a gyre of barely traceable light
and kept spinning and spinning, head
over feet, circles within circles which flattened
to a dish of elliptical rings, and with a wash
of Atomic Light, the rings imaged out
to the End of Time, and the generations
pulsed in line, and the centuries began,
and everything was, in fact, related.
I couldn't move without diminishing the tides.
And Saturn couldn't turn to Mars without disarming me.
And lion couldn't sleep without dreaming of its prey.
Or crab close its shell enough to neutralize the wave.
And man couldn't isolate his being from his touch.
And God diminished to a dot, that disappeared,
that brought ripples of the dark
to the vanished spot.
And as I turn from view,
month after month, I disappear when new,
like God, that eye of storm, that pain
all Godless men ripple inward on.
Turn new. Turn full. Have faith in all
that remains unseen. Have confidence in none.

*The sculptor's struggle for a time without emptiness slows his pace. He recalls*
*Pico, one of the Medici geniuses, walking in conversation with Poliziano and*
*others amid the Roman and Greek antiquities placed about the Garden. But*
*both are dead. It makes him clean his brushes. Then Pico appears, as an*
*apparition, and speaks like a sad thought in Michelangelo's ear of "The Germ*
*of Every Way," one of his Lost Theses, as Michelangelo continues to work*
*on the tones in God's flight-swept beard.*

PICO: You see, grown boy, we are out of the Garden.
    The idols are gone: arms broken, rocks crushed.
    You see. Beasts bring all they are with them,
    a taste for meat, a longing to still
    anything that frightens. And spirits—
    you once asked me of this—spirits,

let's say beings, before cased in flesh
or born to earth, are complete at once,
a circle with no way in, opaque
or clear, but all the way so. But you,
half-beast, half-being, you have all the seeds
and germs of every way. You, like all the rest
born in between, have an unspecified thirst
to be complete. Only man has all the seeds.
Look at you. Attack the wall above your head,
again and again. Only man will plant in him
and bear his own fruit. If he be vegetative,
he will plow his mind to the sun and shed his thinking
in cycles that will let him renew. If carnivorous,
he will relish his hunger till he'll tear open the things
he says he loves. If rational, like the hub of a wheel,
he'll spin constantly and go nowhere.
And if happy in the lot of no created thing,
he'll withdraw, into the center of his own unity,
where his spirit, indistinguishable from God,
will nestle in the solitary darkness
to surpass all things. If happy
in the lot of no created thing,
he will endure.

*The Furies*

# XX. JEREMIAH

*Born at Anathoth near Jerusalem, Jeremiah is a man of some means. From his garden, he can see the city. From a priestly family, he is keenly aware of the variety of religious practice in his time. As a young man he has a vision of the destruction of Jerusalem and, though he resists his call to prophecy strenuously, he spreads the chilling word throughout his life (640–586 B.C.), which covers the reigns of Josiah, Jehoiakim, and Zedekiah. He sees a genuine Josiah die in battle with Egypt. He sees Josiah's son, Jehoahaz, carried away in bonds to Egypt, as Jehoiakim is placed by Pharoah Necho as the King of Judah. He sees Jehoiakim become a vassal of Babylon. And in the last year of Jeremiah's life, he witnesses his vision come true, as Nebuchadnezzar lays siege to Jerusalem and burns it thoroughly.*

*Up till now, through the fire of his imagination and his proximity to the conflicts of the sibyls, Michelangelo has unknowingly approached the other side, the inscape of the Ceiling, where the dynamics of Creation are being wrested into being. But, as Jeremiah questions the efficacy of God's word when none will listen, the barrier of the Ceiling starts to erode and the sculptor is drawn into the other side where he becomes a part of Jeremiah's dark, magnetic mood. There, in half-formed thoughts of death, Michelangelo uncovers the painful notion that we are cast in the physics of God's image and are driven toward divine ends with but a portion of divinity. The barrier is almost torn, as Jeremiah's doubts and Michelangelo's confusions pool, till both secretly wonder what is the point of faith, while stubbornly refusing to succumb.*

216     *Jeremiah reveals his vision, at the age of eighteen, of the destruction of Jerusalem.*

JEREMIAH:
        An arrow wobbled the red air through wheels of smoke.
        It hung and pierced a woman's neck, blood squirting
        in a mist, from which a rabid soldier licked the spray.
        He dropped his spear and washed his face,
        a slippery red. Ten horsemen thundered
        slowly through the air, smashing urns, going nowhere.
        The horses trampled chickens, breaking legs and wings
        and the dirt-raised square was full of feathers
        and the odd squealing flap of bony wings
        circling in the dirt. A man was impaled
        between his legs, sliding slowly,
        further on the sword. A general
        galloped off the ground and leaned
        from his lathered horse to whack
        a boy's head which thumped and rolled
        against a broken gate, eyes still
        pleading in the dirt. Wherever I turned,
        dismembered hands reached, falling
        but not landing, jetting blood
        which could be tasted through the air. I gagged
        at a dog dragging a woman's arm from a fire
        and then two horsemen, elbowed in blood, swords red
        and smelling, came for me. I ran, stepping warm ashes,
        and tripped over a crazed girl who wouldn't let go,
        and as the horsemen leaned to slice me off,
        I swung her between us and she bit me hard—
        the sword—through her—scratched my side—
        then she died, but wouldn't let go.
        I slapped her from me,
        rubbing her from my sight.
        I circled myself, slapping and dodging,
        as if flinching from swollen bees. I landed

in a scattered pile of hay and watched the street burn,
watched the wingless chickens squawk, the eyeless leaders
wailing through their sudden dark, saw red mounds
twitch in a thousand sudden clutches. I couldn't move
or rest, and by the third day, the stench of blood
was warm and impossible to breathe, and the bodies
were turning black and the severed limbs were
toughened on their ends and three-legged dogs
were sniffing the ends for food. In three more days,
the buzzards were thick as jiggers under skin
and those able tried to burn the bodies. A blind
survivor piled the parts. And in the fire that rose
from the heads and arms and legs of a nation
I didn't know was mine till they burst
out of hiding as they fell; in reddish
brown flames that wouldn't yellow,
their secrets hissed like sudden air
burned from a log. And I threw myself
into the fire, wanting to die, and I began to burn,
but wouldn't die, could only see more than I could bear:
tongues swollen, the size of open mouths, bellies bloated
under leathered ribs, eyes yellowed from thirst.
I tried to eat the flame, to beg sweet sleep.
I ran and jumped into an urn
filled with water and the water
turned to blood. I licked my lips
and passed out.

*As Michelangelo works feverishly on Jeremiah, the dark fume of the prophet's
vision seeps down the sculptor's arms and fills him with a curious sadness,
which he fans into various perceptions of death.*

MICHELANGELO: Some deaths are welcome.
 For some lives are not worth living.
 Some lives stall, elevated till the mouth is propped
 on stilts, stories above the boneless tongue.

All my life: pretenders—facile as lakes:
one stone and their ability to reflect
is shattered. Dissemblers: Julius, Bramante,
Sangallo, even my father—Liars!

Some deaths are longed for—the death of this anger,
the death of this Ceiling, the death of this small
scaling sadness which makes me pause for half an afternoon
to wonder what could be changed, what could be done
or redone in this moment to rechart the life.

Perhaps I should have stayed with Aldrovandi.
If only Lorenzo had lived. And Pico.
Oh what a time—Who shouted liar?
This Ceiling spits up secrets chewed.
Sixty Feet Up! What a pair of stilts are these!
I've never pretended to anyone, but myself.

*For the moment Jeremiah does not pretend to be all-knowing, and reveals,
quite candidly, how he was ushered into public declaration after years of
silence.*

JEREMIAH:
You can understand how such a thing can change one's life.
I couldn't bone a fish, or watch a woman braid her hair,
or wash down a horse without seeing the lather of destruction
coming. My days were spent warning everyone.
Of course no one listened and I doubted deeply,
severely, wondering why God had made me see.
Why does doom need a witness?
There were no other signs,
not for years.

"Lift up!" I'd say,
"Loosen the womb around the—"
Around the what? I didn't know.
I only knew Jerusalem would fall.
I asked repeatedly for a sign, a way.

I grew angry that no one would listen
and my anger set me apart. And I grew angry with God.
Why is this wound incurable? Show me a sign!
Are you a Liar, full of waters that fail?!

There was no sign. I stayed away from others,
for it always led to argument and knots in my head
for days. And then, I entered the courtyard.
People were milling, shopping, bartering, yelling.
And I began to speak, "Lift up! Loosen the womb
around the country's ways! Or I shall break this people
and this city like this potter's jar, and it will not
be whole again! And they shall bury you all in Tophet
till there be no room for bodies!"

I smashed the jar and was arrested.
They were afraid. They said they heard me ranting,
but no one would repeat what I said.
They stiffened their necks out of fear.
And Pashur, son of Immer, had me beaten
and put in stocks. When released,
I railed at him and swore he'd witness
all he loved die by the sword.
He trembled slightly, and let me go,
quite certain I was mad.

And I was.

I went back to the courtyard,
took up two pitchers of water
and began pouring them back and forth,
saying the water would turn to blood, and it did.
I said the blood would turn to sand, and it did.
There was absolute silence.
I didn't know what I was doing.
I said the dried blood of our people would turn
to nameless wind and the sand disappeared
in a sudden gale that flashed the pitchers

from my hands to crash the inner wall.
I said the skies will darken and lightning scar
one end of the city and then the other, and so it did.
And I said the moans of our people dying would sweep
through their ears, and a deep and curdling chorus
crippled the crowd to its knees, and I left,
unsure of what I'd done.

*Unsure of what he's done to plummet, Michelangelo works his sadness, enraptured with the cold, despite the danger of not surfacing.*

MICHELANGELO:
My mother, I've been told, held her older brother
who was dying of the plague, brought him to her chest,
despite the pus marks on his body.
He died there draped and oozing in her arms.
She stayed immune. Death can be beaten
if met on different terms. Certain examples
cannot be explained. I saw a man hanged in Florence.
I was just a boy, and he kicked so long,
they almost gave up. The will to live,
at length, forces many little deaths:
pet selves that fail and fail again
till they are orphaned by the real.
I am not the boy who sculpted Hercules in snow
or the one washing dark fingers in cold cadavers.
I am, at length, unsure, on track, away from my life,
alone, with no patience for the world. I've grown to love
the creak of this scaffold three rungs from the top
as I roll back my haste to witness it is night.

*Years intervene and Jeremiah dictates his prophecies to a willing scribe, Baruch, who reads from his scroll in the Temple, only to have King Jehoiakim cut the scroll in disgust with a curled knife and burn it on his hearth. As things worsen, Zedekiah succeeds Jehoiakim as King. Jeremiah continues his prophecies and is detained in an underground cell. And now army officers lower him in a mud-filled cistern to die.*

JEREMIAH: In my heart an insurgent fire,
    a fire without witness! I will not sink!
  The mud is cool and thick up through my toes.
  I hold the rim. It's rough on my fingers.
  The short one raps my knuckles with the shaft of his spear.
  I shout, "God will spike your children in the earth!"
  They laugh. I grab the rim again. The mud is packing
  icelike between my legs. The short one raps once more.
  My knuckles bleed. God starts a Fire in my mouth—
  "You are the Wood! I will Devour you! Release me!"
  Now!" They laugh and walk away. "Release Me! Now!"
  Only the short one turns and waits.
  The mud is shaping to my collarbone.
  My shoulders arch sore. My arms slap the surface.
  My blood is on Fire—"Out of the North! An Evil
  Shall Break you!" I see the rod of an almond tree!
  I see a seething pot whose bane is gushing forth!
  Why have You made me so on Fire? So alone? For this?
  For This?! Will You let me sink this way? Release Me!
  It's hard to breathe. The mud is packing against my chest.
  So cold. The chill is up my neck—"You will Not be forgiven!"
  The short one leaves. I will not sink. My elbows sink in.
  My legs go nowhere. To wriggle brings me down.
  The sop sloshes and cups my throat. God! You Lied!
  My Fire for a Lie! I'll Lift Myself! Lift Up!
  The arms are gone. Mud is shaping
  the back of my head. Can't poke
  my chin higher. Can't stand
  this sucking coolness!
  Inhale. The mud slips
  tighter down the belly.
  Inhale. Hold. I will not sink!
  The sop covers my lip. Nose only.
  Inhale. Hold. Where have You gone?
  Did I make You up? Coolness up my nose.

Close the eyes. The dark slides coolly,
packs my forehead. Mud. Cold. Sinking.
Into the Ear of the Earth. Our nation
has changed its Gods. The prophets speak
brownly, and my people love to have it so.
They have waxed feet! They shine brownly!
Erase this Vision! Peel its foreskin off my Eye!
Madness in their faces sharper than eagles,
the stick of thick blades cutting sorry heads,
and women hiding, ever so sickly, in thickets,
climbing into rocks, scraping knees to crimson rags,
faces smudged with bark and mud. They throw the gold
from their ears! Their lovers like sottish children
despise them like erosion and plot to shut their
whining lives! And brownly, as the nation falls,
a Mute will bear a child in rubble!
She'll settle her mud hips in dust,
the babe crawling from her ruined legs.
She'll Wail! She'll Wail! Her teeth will Throb!
She'll Crush the child than let it live
this brown and sinking way.
O dark and sinking God, Where?
Where the brown and ancient nation
whose language is not underground?

*With his dark mood sinking fast, Michelangelo, reaching from the quicksand of his scaffold, seems transfixed by his memory of watching dead blood spill through cadavers.*

MICHELANGELO:
Lividity—how the blood settles after death,
where it cradles blue along the scuppered veins,
where the blood of speech has rent after crisis,
in which organs it might pool once all inward pumping
stops. In the lung, like a sponge, a red mist collects,
swelling toward the south, and the tongue flattens
in a bunch at the back of the throat.

After seeing the head's water drain, the problems—
of women vexed by men, of Popes vexed by God—
the problems seem translucent droppings.

Death is a liberation from everything
extraneous, a salient wind in which clouds die.
Look at this Prophet's face and tell me why he burns.
What sight of what seeing has seared punky in the bone?

The fire burns unevenly, and talk of new beginnings
pepper Rome. What do I do, blood so unfulfilled
it soaks through. I'm tired of the partial Roman light
that spills on clerics' knees. The thinned blood
keeps me cold. Like belief turned icy in the wind.
Belief, confused with Time.

*Ebed-Melech, an Ethiopian slave, gains permission from Zedekiah to pull
Jeremiah from the mud. But Jeremiah cannot stop preaching doom and even-
tually, in the last year of his life, he is a living witness to the destruction of
Jerusalem.*

JEREMIAH:
That thunder! That thunder of hooves. It comes!
Why have I known for so long?! And here, here,
the muscular soldier, knees pounding the lathered ribs,
thundering, leaning with his heavy sword—
And here, the astonished soft girl by my side
with a thousand moods of God in her eye,
the one I've searched for all these years,
she doesn't run but lifts her neck to meet the blade—
Thawack—her head drops, her secrets steaming
off her blood and it's strangely full—how her head
bumps the cart of fruit, terror still rolling her eyes,
and she hits my thigh, her shock of blood warming my leg.
I knew the weight of her flow, knew it as a boy. And here
the frenzied dogs whose brains are wired tight, grating
at the pitch of horror, and the chickens, wings snapping
like a bed of twigs, and the stench of blood

fuming through God's air! I fall in the hay
and a cat licks the blood of the girl sticking
to my thigh. I can hear the knives hacking bone;
the carved sound of bone splitting, not breaking;
the bend of swords in joints. Before me,
a boy, bleeding from his stomach
on a pile of bread and the loaves
like a sick mystery enlarge.
Instead of dying, Hell has risen,
a jaundiced fog up through the earth
to wither the human from their being.
And the cat licks the girl's blood
now foaming on my leg.
I can see Zedekiah
being dragged from his garden,
can hear the cracking of ancient cypress,
his benches splintered, his servants battered.
And he is bound with strips of hide, his sons
run through before him as he shows nothing.
He is impaled between his legs. He slides the sword.
He passes out. The horsemen are disgruntled.
The walls are being hammered! And the desert grass
is screeching in a yellow heated steam
that shimmers to the sky! And dead Zedekiah,
yanked by his hair, is blinded with a poker!
I stagger to a nearby hill and hear the dogs,
the high-pitched dogs growl at the edge
of God's ulcered city as it burns a stomach
in the earth. So much endured. For This?
For This?! What good to know?
The smoke of blood brownly
stains the night. I am sick,
sick, the blood has a strange sweetness
to it now, sick! O stomach churn yourself
to sleep, sleep, with your eyes open, sleep
and wake when no trace remains.

# XXI. GOD SEPARATES LIGHT AND DARK

As if swimming into a mix of all that is known and unknown, God separates vast clouds above the sculptor, whose tired mind is parted and mixed by the unheard accounts of Pico and the Hidden Angel. They fill him with intangible notions of creation as an ongoing process, sorting truth from calculation and faith from doubt repeatedly, as the separation of Light and Dark never ceases. Their presence ripples through him till he barely knows that beings in God's image must coax the hidden spirit in their will to negotiate the continual sorting. The sculptor, half-used up, is stalled by the thought, just out of reach, that it never ends: the reeling, the baiting, the peeling of peace from despair and gift from emptiness. And as he comes closer to his Maker, burns in unison with His flame, he becomes a hidden angel himself, too close to the fire to render the source.

*Having painted furiously for months, the sculptor now arrives at the Begin-*
*ning, more alone than ever, more crumpled in his want. He is stymied, no*
*props will suffice, nothing left but God and the elements. And as he stalks the*
*panel, the Hidden Angel, unable to speak, is stymied himself as he tries,*
*through emanations of sound, to reveal the dizzy floating state that preceded*
*Light and Dark.*

THE HIDDEN ANGEL:

    There was nothing but grey. No directions. No depth.
Or only depth. I can't be sure. It was a bare isolation.
No sound of any kind: just a grey wash of silence
between wave and wind. No stars. No planets.
No life. No carbon. No void.
Just the wash of what never was.
The inside of inert awash forever.
Not from or to, but permeating everywhere at once,
both oppressive and porous, dense and weightless,
iridescent and faint. And then, I didn't notice
a single shift in His position, but things began
to have a slant, a lean and there were moments
distinct from one another and these were briefly
weighted or louder and slight gravities flared
to subside. And wherever He dove, the wash
of what never was became something imperceptible,
then nothing again. And this went on
till He grew tired of it all and spun deeply
behind the speed of sound, inward and inward,
till the collapse of what never was
became the dark. Then out, the other way,
and flares with no heat, streaks with no center,
and light crested as a tide. And unexpectedly
the light would fill the dark, the dark absorb the light.
Neither would leave the other alone. And this fill
and absorption, this wash and drop, has come to mask
the ridge of humankind where God can be found
forever parting absence and presence.

*As he struggles with God's invisible plumage, Michelangelo is overcome by*
*the visage of Lorenzo Medici, who fathered the best years of the sculptor's*
*life by taking him into the Medici Garden at the age of 13. Here, 19 years*
*after Lorenzo's death, as God initiates Light and Dark above him, Michel-*
*angelo remembers with deep affection Lorenzo's tale of the Pazzi Conspiracy,*
*which we hear in Lorenzo's own words. Michelangelo begins.*

MICHELANGELO:

There was a name no one mentioned,
a dark subject that never came up.
I asked Poliziano. He took to throwing stones
and said, "Let it be."

Lorenzo was by himself and the light wind,
twirling the leaves rapidly and gently,
pleased him. I stood beside him
for a long time. He finally urged,
"Don't be afraid." I said the word, "Pazzi."
He glared, his jawline protruding.
I drew back. He sighed and sat me down,
"All right. Pazzi. Jacopo de Pazzi. You were three.
He was related, kin, family, a banker for Sixtus in Rome.
Jacopo de Pazzi. Francesco Pazzi. The Archbishop Salviati.
Now that you know, don't ever forget. These were the ones.
My brother Giuliano and I were on our way to church
in Santa Maria del Fiore. Giuliano had stomach cramps
from some fish we'd had the night before. I went alone.
It was a cloudy day, the light diffusive, easy to see
in corners and balconies. I was near the altar.
The mass was logy, slow. I began to nod and drift
when Girolamo's nephew, a young unimportant man,
lifted the chalice with the blood of Christ
in a signatured way. I thought it odd. Then
from either side, like dark spurious wings,
the priests were closing in. I thought, one's ill
and then the knife slipped my rib. My yellow blouse
flashed red. The priests in church. I thought of Giuliano.
I clutched my side, spun free of them and somehow jumped
the choir rail. I made it to the sacristy and Poliziano,

dear Poliziano, slammed the door. I knew Giuliano
must be dead, my poor Giuliano. They'd hired Baroncelli,
a sloppy killer known for his brutality with knives,
and he stuck Giuliano between the shoulders
as he doubled from a cramp. And Francesco Pazzi,
a short and churlish powerless man, so furied
in his appetite, kept stabbing my brother,
who must have been dead, with such inchoate frenzy,
that he punctured his own thigh. You asked.
There is more. I expect you to remember every detail,
every sign. Salviati was the chief conspirator.
He was to seize the leadership, at which time,
Jacopo would occupy Florence. They underestimated all
but Baroncelli. Within the hour, 120 conspirators
were captured and 80 were sentenced to hang.
I'd lost my brother. Florence was nearly gone.
I'd been stabbed in church by priests.
You understand the world, my boy?
I, who measure faun's teeth in your work,
I had them hung at once. You asked.
There's more. The leaders first, hurled
out the windows of the Palazzo Vecchio, ropes
jammed about their necks, and they dangled against the wall,
the oddball rhythm of their muddy feet kicking the noiseless
stone. And then the Archbishop and Francesco Pazzi
from the same rope. The Florentines ranted.
The Archbishop, in full regalia, cassocks and beads,
thrashed so hard he tore Pazzi's blood-spattered shirt
from his chest. And then the others, by fives, then tens.
We'd hurl them out. They'd kick their thudless kick
and gag. We'd cut them loose and throw some more.
The bodies bounced like bags of figs. It took no more
than an hour and a half. Are you pleased to know?
The Pazzi heads were screwed on poles and marched
through town. Salviati's head, on a twelve-foot pole,
staked outside this yard. The rusted pole is in that shed.

*Sketch of the Hanged Baroncelli,*
*Leonardo da Vinci*

This is the same world as Poliziano's, the same
as Alberti's, as Pico's. Falconry, my boy, swift and sure.
They took my Giuliano. I see the look in your eye.
I know how you feel about me. They took my Giuliano.
So now you know. Pazzi. We no longer mention that name."

*Pico appears and etches his notions of Creation in the damp air that tangles
the sculptor's sight, as Michelangelo thinks he's found God seeking Himself
in the Primal Sky.*

PICO:

A God of so many tongues must still bring forth,
Sustaining Creation, still shaping the Universe
which closes behind His effort like a lantern
lighting only where it's swung; Dividing light
and dark swiftly, with no rest—as a fish
parts rushing water, only to have it
glove its length—Diving through history;
sending men to minnow through their lives,
parting His wake as their destiny.

*As he sees God assimilate the nature of His clouds, Michelangelo loses himself
in the details of his youth when, within two years of Lorenzo's death, the
Medici Garden began to tarnish and disperse. Only Poliziano, the old and
vibrant poet, stayed on, as Lorenzo's eldest son, Piero, became somewhat
psychotic in his grief, and his daughter, Contessina, paled into a bloodless
flower. And Michelangelo, still a boy, had nowhere to go—a feeling that has
stayed with him. Here, as he paints God, he pines, like Adam for Eden, for
those days in the Garden when he would copy the masterpieces poised about
the yard. But his homelessness keeps surfacing in the anti-light of Lorenzo's
broken children, till he speaks to Lorenzo who curls, dead and adrift, between
Purgatory and Heaven.*

MICHELANGELO:

But Piero was not you, and the Garden
was fast becoming a headstone with weeds
climbing the busts you so loved, and Piero
used it all as some sanitarium for his regrets.
He'd drink behind old statues. He'd sit against

the Garden wall, right in the flower bed, and sprawl.
This was his way: insolent and sprawling.
I don't know how he came from you.
Can you hear? We treasured you.
Your son was just a pebble.
He had no access to himself.
Insolent and morose, he sulked
the Garden, neglecting methodically,
with a rebellious cross-eyed bent, the meat
of your presence about the house and grounds,
as if you crowded him. Forgive me. They had taken you,
and like an inexplicable storm that collapses everything
inward across its path, the Garden, your son, the weeds,
my heart—all unearthed by your going. He'd drink sometimes
till dawn and, crazed into denial, he'd look for old
peaceful things to break. Now—after thirsts not
plowable—I understand. He was just damaged. With
nothing to express. A storm is born to havoc. The eye,
an unwanted peace for someone broken. I still feel alone
and yet never alone. I found him, almost two years to the day
after your death, hiding from the stream of light at dawn.
Bottles lay in the weeds and he'd been tapping
every odd brick in the Garden wall, chipping
crude little puckers, crude little mouths
to drink up the faint traces of night.
I gathered the bottles and he lashed out,
"They're sculptures, my little genius! Leave them
where they are! They're hollowed Out! You carve away.
I empty Out. They were filled with extraneous Things.
I drank the stone. You can't understand, you strapping,
perplexed, precocious Pan. You protrude your precious notions.
You grip the stone and rub and then this presence Thrusts
its head into the world. How Masculine of you.
How Orgasmic. I empty Out! The shapes I see
are what is Not! I eat away, eat Away, Eat
Away . . ." I went for Poliziano. No one else
could talk to him. By the time we returned,

he'd upended one statue, had rummaged through the shed
and was weaving about with Salviati's pole. He finally
collapsed along the west wall, intrigued by the end,
no doubt, that held the head, working the rust in his hand,
murmuring about black hours. He was eating the rust
almost pensively when Poliziano drew the browning youth
to him, rocking slightly, in keeping with the blackened
wind. He swayed and softly, nodding me away, said,
"Come inside, Piero. Come inside." It shook me deeply.
Something of the time, some corrosive was now
inside these walls. Some corrosive eating
at the light. It eats me now, where I'm not free.
Piero never wept again. Contessina avoided him
and me. Then in May she packed your jewels
and left, for a husband's bed. Piero sent her
weeds. I watched her leave, and she turned,
as if dizzied by some way of life she'd lived
but not received, knowing in her mind, seeing
in her mind, exactly where it lay. She
turned to the gate and ran her sad pale
fingers up the grid, lengthwise, stroking
for some bearing she quickly found,
then pressed her head to the iron
as if it were your ear. Then she left,
stopping, but never looking back. I knew
it was coming. Could feel the corrosive
burn your presence from us all.


*Pico hovers, after reading ancient scripts, and tries to ascribe how we light
up inside to the flux of eternity, but rather affirms the need to break down
and flow, as Michelangelo fills in God's chest, pushing lilac to pale blue.*

PICO:
  There is a prayer, old mystics say,
  tucked too deep to find, and floating
  like a crystal, it hides behind the tongue;

an ancient knot of prayer that thinking can't
put out; a fired prayer which burns old light
to trust. It drags what's true off tired breath
as it tumbles down the lungs. It skims the green
off vegetables sliding round the throat.
It sifts the heat off brutal sights
that burn once through the sockets.
There is a prayer just tucked in Time,
a drink of God that fits no lips. And when
the life has been ground down, when we turn up nothing
after sweating forever, it radiates like a bone in slaughter
and the slaughter ruptures a crafty mind to stir up moods
both rare and clear, and the hands, unsure, reach into life,
dark hungry fish skidding on. And anything in our path
is parted briefly, and thinks that it is loved.

*Michelangelo feels confined to his scaffold and compelled to resurrect the
demise of the Garden which grew barren. Florence itself was in jeopardy.
The French army was closing on her borders, and the zealot Savonarola was
gaining power. Omens were everywhere. And Michelangelo's boyhood friend
Granacci pulled back, watchful, concerned over the sculptor's nervous con-
dition. Even Poliziano grew heartsick and unfamiliar, infatuated with a dull
and strapping boy. Here Michelangelo wonders where his Faun, his very first
statue, has gone, and trips into a memory of Cardiere, the Garden's musician,
who was unnerved by stark dreams of Lorenzo. And as Michelangelo, feeling
secretly a coward, tries to explain to his dead Lorenzo why he fled from
Florence in 1494, he darkens God's face, leaving His eyes closed in an
original blindness.*

MICHELANGELO:
Cardiere was shaking. He could barely breathe.
He was improvising on his lute, the way you liked,
and you appeared. You, in a torn black cloak, your
hair matted from sleeping outdoors. He was a frenzy.
You commanded him to tell Piero of his exile. He said
you asked of me and what I'd built with my sorrow. I was
ashamed, but you must have known how difficult it had been.
The heel of my mind was losing its callous. In two weeks

Cardiere came once more, bleeding from a cut above his eye,
frantically gesturing that you had come again. I thought
Christ himself had resurrected you. Cardiere was terrorized.
He said you woke him with a red pernicious snake
curled near his ear, and when he leapt, he fell
and cut his head. He said you knew the Garden
was a shell. He said, "Piero must leave! We must leave!
The Garden is no longer! Florence is no longer!"
He said the snake returned to you and curled
into a stone you crushed with ease. I calmed him down
and pried his fist to find red powder in his palm.
Piero, of course, loved the thought of you
in tattered black, your hair unwashed.
He slapped Cardiere, and I knew it only
a matter of when. It was difficult to sleep.
September was full of dark slicing tongues.
I seldom went out, and began to see clear through
Piero who was drinking with an anger. The town was a buzz
that the King of France had reached Tuscany, that he would
level Florence, that the Medicis would be hung. On the 21st,
Savonarola hawked a sermon in the Duomo. I saw Pico.
It was unnerving. Savonarola seemed at times possessed
and suddenly the crowd, half-listening, half-beginning
its day, grew still as he discharged some force larger
than he could bear. He prophesied an era of wildness
and said, with a shrill that stopped the very dogs
in the street, that Gardens would issue mad sons
and snakes of blood in stone. I felt a shiver
skim the bone and the spaces between people suffered,
more pronounced, more deadly, more alive. The wind
pumped itself and I looked to Pico, but he was gone.
Savonarola was sweating, his body barely maintaining
his thunderous voice. He swore Floods would burn Rome
into a venal Hell churning the damned to drink fire and bray.
The sky darkened, as if at his will, and the crowd half-died
before him. It began to rain, and at the first stroke
of lightning, Savonarola withdrew. I ran to the Garden,

to Cardiere. It still sweeps my skull: Piero eating rust
off the pole, Contessina's head praying on the gate,
Cardiere's palm smeared with your red snake, and Pico
disappearing in the crowd. I huddled, squat in my rooms,
staring in the dark as far as I could. Things lightened
in the air, but an infirm germ gripped my sense.
I couldn't keep it down. A knot of breath rose in my chest,
into my head, encrusting my life. This went on for days.
I couldn't find Cardiere. And then on the eve of the 29th,
Poliziano, dear soft and truthful link to you, Poliziano,
whose constitution so engaged the world of inner speech,
Poliziano, who mesmerized me when I saw him speak
with those long fingers curling sharply, sculpting
the air between us, Poliziano was enraged, stopped up,
burning somewhere at the throat, and I brought him water,
sat him down, but he wouldn't stay. Tall, lean, angular
Poliziano, who feathered his beard when thinking
on the justice of time as an arbiter of the heart,
he'd snapped and was pot-boiling, ranting over some
deep affection for some boy. He wouldn't say, but was
wounded to the silvered stump he called his heart.
He kept grabbing for something slender in the air
and missing, would curl his lip and grunt
till out of breath, he'd reach again. I kept
asking, "What? What is it? Please. What can I do?"
He grabbed my shoulders, then my chin, and for a long
tunnelled moment scoured my eyes, "You've always
been the one. When Lorenzo told me you were coming,
I knew you'd filter this"—and he poked me in the chest—
"through this" and he squeezed my hands. He said,
"I buried my heart till it hardened in the sun, and like
a loaf of stone, I packed my soul in hurt. And now,
three steps from death, this beauty turns the loaf,
thuds me belly up and all the worms are squirming
Everywhere! I'm too old to be so fevered by a boy!
I've managed so long without these fires, and now

I'm forced to wonder, has it been a lighted life
at all? Damn you all! You brilliant piercing youths!
Damn you all!" He threw my hands to me and turned
and ran into some eyeless stake of air and dropped,
knees to the wood. He squirmed the lining of a word
that never came, reached for me, and fell. Poliziano.
I shook him lightly. Poliziano. He'd pulled his heart
like a stump from life and there—the circle broken,
the Garden dead. I have not dwelled on this for years.
But all these thoughts of you, and Piero's lack of worth,
and Contessina's lack of joy—Nothing has been promising
since you peered into my brain. How I believed
in what you saw. I was a wreck, and left Poliziano
like a fallen birch. Within the week, Cardiere returned,
and Granacci. I was the only one left. It had taken you all.
The signs were clear. I promised to pay their way.
Cardiere was eager. He packed his lute so crudely
he snapped a string. Granacci was less sure. I wrapped
some shirts about a chisel, stuffed two hammers in a towel,
put the bunch in a saddlebag, and we made our way to Venice.
Within the month, the King of France closed off Florence
and Piero was in hiding. I lost the Faun. I couldn't
stay. I was 19. You understand? The King of France
would have had my head. All I could think of
was Salviati's rusted pole.

*Pico shudders about the body of God, which seems to be the condensation of
a cloudlike substance. There he briefly perceives the intolerable forces of the
Universe. It forces him to reconsider his notion of Light and Dark, which
pulls him to a crude and belated understanding of the Divine-Human re-
lation.*

PICO:
There are bedrock forces, thrusting planes
of energy and flow, intolerable to behold,
blinding and essential as the lipless center
of the sun. And as earth and air and water and fire
are deadly in their rarefied forms; in conjunction,
they move the world. And love, flight, depth, and passion
are deadly in their purity to any single thirst, but mixed,

undam the life. It is the burn of purity that makes a thirst
consuming, the rite of motion that makes of it a drink.
The earth in its weight annihilates; in its tilted spin,
we flourish. And man when pure of sight is untouchable;
when drunk on sweat, all tangled. And God, in thirst,
is insufferable; as a bath of nerves, redeeming.
The bedrock sears, isolate and blinding. The human
rubs, tossed until it's able. And the earth burns,
a skinless dream, which humanity churns into a herd
of mitigations. And the earth drives the bedrock deeper
while, furious as spiders, we spin webs of law
into nests of truth to make the earth our home.
And as planets crave their tide of light,
their own peculiar shrug around the sun,
so lives climb walls of fire and ice,
sworn to their own peculiar song.

*Painting God's formless hands with tender strokes, the sculptor acknowledges, for a moment, how badly he needs others to be complete. He softly recalls, after fleeing to Venice, how he and his friends made their way to Bologna. From there Cardiere and Granacci returned to Florence, while the young sculptor—his health fragile, his psyche damaged, his emotions acidic—remained as a guest of the Customs Officer Aldrovandi. It was there, Michelangelo explains, that he tried to exorcise Poliziano's death. As he speaks, Lorenzo drifts sadly closer, pulled back toward the living by Michelangelo's grief.*

MICHELANGELO: During my stay with Aldrovandi,
    I could hear the lagging beat of my heart.
    I thought I had a murmur. I'd lay awake, before dawn,
    my head pounding, my chest pounding, knowing the tremors
    were slight, barely audible. But as they joined, it thundered
    in me. I couldn't escape it. I've always thought of doubt
    in this way, as a thundered unison of something inescapable.
    As the light filtered in, it seemed to mince the air, to
    coat the olive trees with surly wind. Then I'd hear him
    fixing food and it would blend into ordinary anxiety,

a minor clicking behind my nervous speech. I couldn't
shuck the image of Poliziano throwing me my hands, as
if life could only split our solitude, like a nail.

Aldrovandi was nowhere as formidable as Poliziano,
nowhere as focused, but kinder in his own stalled way,
more considerate than probing, more sensitive
than articulate. It was like living with a paper man,
a man with feelings thin as strings. To move here
pulled him there. To be pensive hit a dozen chords.
It was too taxing to explain. I was thinking of you
and Piero and my hammers wrapped in towels. One night
he said, without malice or glee, "You are so overwhelmed
by what you feel, you have no way to use it, no sense
of how to act with what you are."

I thought him tedious. He wouldn't let it go,
"You've run away, and now you think it's time
to run from me. But running from is not a use."
He poured some wine, and came too close,
"Even angels kneel when lost."

He took my palms, "Speak with these
if you must, but speak, don't run."

I had to rid myself of the murmur
which became a toxic flutter, an inward flush
that made me halt and sail. I had to rid myself
of Poliziano's throwing of my hands. I began to sketch,
drawing flutters trapped in caves. My pensiveness
became intolerably knotted. He came home one day and said,
with less patience than usual, "Get it out of your system.
You're filling the house with a sadness that won't budge."
I turned away, said nothing. He sighed, "I've managed
a commission for the church of San Domenico. Go.
Do it there. They need three statues."

I had to rid myself and did so with the kneeling angel
feeling for his candle. It was Poliziano's throwing
of my hands, and what he threw infected the flutter
in my throat. It was a crippled angel, a blinded angel,
a doubtful angel, an angry angel waiting for a spark.
It was an awful feeling starting this, a dissonant
beginning, unwrapping the chisel from my clothes.
It was an awful work, an awful time, but I left
the weight behind.

*Being drawn back to the other side, to the far side of God, the Hidden Angel,
almost out of range, ushers indistinct impulses; trying to convey the way all
living things were blended in God's appetite, once Light and Dark were
formed, and then released. Michelangelo receives these impressions as mental
static as God glides swiftly through the Chaos.*

THE HIDDEN ANGEL:
Adhesions began to form like coral
along the bottom of the Universe,
silted vagaries of Light and Dark
sludging together, breaking apart. And of this,
living forms began to breathe on their own,
requiring definite inhalations to survive,
refining particular intakes to continue,
slower fuels at longer intervals; each,
giving off distinct and necessary
fumes; each, giving back
what it could no longer hold
to the mixed and brimming whole.

And the Universe began to populate
its possibilities. All spirits required
presence to give off absence. And hearts,
all harnessed by wind, required passion
to give off depth, in which the same
center of fire continues to spill,
burning everywhere. And then
cold bodies of flesh required air

to relinquish their rash of exhalations,
endless serum for the orchids
making us our air. And near the air
all forms of mind, elliptical and sheer,
required dream to scrub clear passages of time.
And other mixtures crept and inched and fell about
till God descended like a translucent Whale to swill
the mixtures down. And up He soared, clear belly arched,
coasting, surging, round and round, till all the mixtures
churned, tinder to a holy fire. And then, dizzy as I was,
He spewed us forth. We broke apart, descending
for a million years, floating, sinking,
dispersing into colorless seed
into a billion unborn shades.

*With the Hidden Angel gone, Michelangelo envies God His knowledge. But looking down the Ceiling at all he's done, he realizes his gift and like all gifts, once watched, it begins to be withdrawn. The sculptor knows it's over, though there's much to do. He stares at God's dark face drying above him. Unable to move to the next panel, he grows mildly depressed by the sudden odd peaceful wrench of God's figure swimming through His cloud of Light and Dark, about to dive into the bare unpainted vault that remains.*

MICHELANGELO:
Look at what I've done, and what's to do,
as if it just stops, slips out of view,
right where the cloud furls about His hand,
as if He lifts, a merciless bird
easing into a region I can never know.
Where He glides, I sweat.
I've thought of stopping here.
I mean, no more. Break down the scaffold
with Him about to part what can't be known.
If I could only leave it alone.
I could bask in His thirst
the rest of my days.

*Pico moves closer to God and discovers that the gap between bone and angel, the shadow between God's image and God, is human longing, where souls hunt, dream, and yearn. He struggles yet closer and describes the region above the Heavens as it's reflected down through man.*

PICO:

> That region only He can see is like a searing prism
> encased in its own crust of light that churns away,
> glistens, browns. Its facets leak the flash
> of every concept in the world, the quickened spheres,
> the filthy beasts, the grains of bricks, the fleshy
> tone of lips—a register of all God's worms.
> And only one's unfortunate to be
> without a concept all his own. And that is
> man who, having nothing proper to himself, is granted
> reflex to mimic the spheres, to have the shade
> of every worm within his heart. And homeless and formless,
> he can choose the way he'll squirm. God's gift to man:
> to dream the searing and the prism, to stir awake in shade.
> As though maker of himself, man is left porous, the centered
> orphan of his days. He can elevate or regulate, degenerate
> in ways original to God, but with all nectared sense beyond
> the crust of thought we refuse to burn away.

*As the sun slips the earth again, God fades into the Ceiling, and the scaffolding creaks as if a raft in the dark, and Michelangelo, left only with his life, thirsts and sinks.*

MICHELANGELO:

> I'd give an eye to know the truth of certain things.
> I keep knocking the brushes from the pots.
> It's cold in here tonight. What good the talk?
> It's cold I say. My eyeball's cold. And when I'm sad
> and cold and out of touch, I squint for forms to draw.
> The mind draws pictures from its birth,
> the way pumps draw water from the ground.

And wise men draw their talk with branchlike hands
from some place with no sound. Old Poliziano
used to whittle silver in the air. And women
draw their beauty as they walk or wash themselves in sun.

I find the nights unworkable. I find the time
and Drown in it. Or Freeze! Or Burn!
I Flash Hot! Flash Cold! Full of Anger!
Full of nothing. The goal of a broken heart:
to shut its lie and draw the wind through its break.

*Pico curls, a film along the darkened vault. Unable to follow God and unable
to return to life, he speaks from the repository of longing, a spirit without a
face, and there, he accepts his portion of God and supports the abandonment
of appetites.*

PICO: It's strange how men will sometimes see God
      in their own image and then destroy themselves
      trying to enter the image. Philosophers like
      egoistic fathers will do this with their ideas
      their children. And soft creatures will do this
      with their youth. The appetites once formed
      get in the way. For it's not the bark that makes
      the plant, but its senseless nature. Nor is it the hide
      of burden that makes the mind, but its irrational
      gateway to shapes that won't enclose. If a man
      were to see himself as a devourer, could he
      not feed on his hunger? And if a voice
      were to believe it could fly, could it not
      close its eye like a silence and lift?

      Religions, each, are appetites,
      eating scuppers in the soul.
      Let's say a man is hard
      pressed to find the truth, he still
      can tell it, no? Likewise, someone
      softened by their gnawing in the dark

can still be lighted. And if you see
one unaware of his body, confined
to the inner reaches of his mind,
he is neither an earthly nor a
heavenly being. He is on hold,
a theorem to be worked out.

LIBICA

# XXII. THE LIBYAN SIBYL

Libica, the last of the sibyls, twists her young body in an effort to close an enormous book on a stand behind her. It is unclear what book it is, though it could be one of Cumae's, as Libica has also been enlisted by Cumae in the preservation of her prophecies. But the last sibyl is not enraptured, just resigned. Her lovely features are already dismissing whatever she's learned, as she is drawn to sweet Delphica, her opposite, who waits on unlived life at the beginning of the Ceiling. The whole tumultuous expanse of the vault bends in reach between them. As mythic sentinels, they both bear witness to catastrophe; Delphica looking back at Judith as she covers the head of Holofernes, and Libica, gazing in anticipation on the cold depth which will harbor Moses and the Brazen Serpent, yet to be coaxed into form. Both peer down the surface of the Ceiling like tired swimmers, at eye level, along the surface of an ocean; both seeing below and above; where the painted forms reach down like survivors, wet and kicking, while on the other side, their spirits crest and sway in a nameless turbulence before God. Battered by such a rise and fall of drives drowning into human form, Libica hungers fully for the virgin, Delphica. The undulation of this driven sea pummels the sculptor into an unnerving glimpse of his own desires.

*Michelangelo, wanting Libica's arms to stay supple, tries to intellectualize his love of the human body while refusing his homosexuality, and failing, like a cinder, he relates an unclear dream.*

MICHELANGELO:

Robes and vestments lie. They drape instead of reach
and hearts drape their way through nothing. The ripest
bodies pulse—to thirst, to drink, to suck, to slake,
to chew with fury, while the mind ensnares the nature
of its space. The pulse of flow is muscular. And who
can tell what coats my chest when a rock of beauty
heaves. I carry it for days. And is it him: Or is he
just a cup from which I drink. A cup of flesh that stings.
The body quakes and glows, a map of strain. Its blood
flexes in its cage. Its syrup cruels out the heart.
What's in it is a Birth, a Death, a crack, a snap
where all things give. Taste can lie, the eye deceive,
but muscle can't pretend to lift or suffer its own weight.
I never think to let it happen. But undressed by Godful eyes,
I paint a touch. No brushes but in tongues. Till a mind
in speech flexes like a rump rising from a bath. A heart
while loving pulls up taut like kneeling skin on bone.
And heat bleaches knots, the way soul pours rage
through skin. I'll take the swollen trembled life
with all its fired wounds. For the belly of love
like the bottom of stars is incapable of total night.
And an honest man wears his fate till a yawn in skin
is a vow. It stops my heart. The words all cease.
It's hard to say. Just know the age is jealous of what
nakedness can bring. God lights in thighs, He makes them
glisten til I dive. Then God is gone. Just legs entangled
to the left, chest twisting to the right. But now, I've come
to dream of postures, of naked trusts that tense, and
last night, in a mineral dance, I held a falling boy
who rippled from all he couldn't seize. He thought
I went to fondle him. I slapped him in the ear.
He ran away. I've told them all. I'm not interested.

They badger me. The boy returned and now was deaf,
but as he turned, his shoulders rippled bronze,
then grey. It made me take him near.

*Libica, not knowing where Delphica stands, relates her encounter with*
*Cumae, while making advances toward the younger sibyl.*

LIBICA:
Really, she's overbearing, don't you think?
I don't blame her. She's seen things fall
I couldn't imagine whole. But now, she's
in such a morbid groove. It's tedious,
to be frank. I don't presume to tell her
how to see, but she's remembered all the worst.
There must be other things, a day of wind and sun
where she forgot herself and heard the sea, a time
when bees circled unexpectedly, her hair all wet
like yours—you look just born this way. She asked
me again. I didn't know what to say. I'm as strong,
but what's the point? Some things are better left vague.
She wants the youngest child to understand her suffering.
You think that's right? As if her pain has served an end.
The end of pain is hurt. That's all. Why mystify these
things—Oh, let me comb your hair out. There. You smell
so fresh this time of day. She showed me her books.
There are five or six. Prophecies, or so she says.
She's quite distressed. Says she never burned them,
just tricked Tarquin into thinking they were ash.
They're bulky, oppressive, old weathered things.
She opened one, the third, I think. A real dense
and fevered script, and such strange things she
claims to know. Really, it's quite presumptuous,
no matter how much pain. She claims to have had an
audience with God. I didn't laugh or shrug her off.
But imagine such a thing. And wait—there's more.
She claims that God—Oh, is that alright, to touch

you there, you feel so smooth—she claims God
is both sexes, the ultimate Tiresias, with
wicks for eyes and steam to boot. Well,
what could I say? She stared at me in a
stark and antisocial way. Perhaps we should
lie down. It's such a lazy day. Oh no, it's fine
right here. Or how about beneath that tree? Well,
Imagine, God, two breasts and a penis, with steaming
wicks for eyes. I mean, to guard this with my life?
You see the crux. I'm sure you do. I'm at a loss
to send her on her way. As strange and tenacious,
as one-tracked as she's become, she's still
quite powerful. Of that I'm sure. So, well,
I'm not certain how to proceed. She told me
how important these things, how they could
redirect the course of women, that they would set
all lesbians free. That Leda would cut the swan
and sweetly sing. Well, fine and good I say.
But not for me. She's cryptic to a fault
and vague, except where lust's concerned.
But you wouldn't be interested in such things.
Would you like some cream? The sun is strong.
No, here, like this, in swirls. Oh, fine.
I didn't mean to lean so close. She asked
if I would hold her books till I was old, to
pass them on and keep them free. She fears
there are dark plans afoot, you know, plots,
and well, I think she's undergoing strain.
Plots—just picture it—conspiracies to
suppress such illuminations as how—God,
I wish we could go for a swim. Yes, it's
clouding up. Perhaps not. We'll see. Well then
she stared into that abyss which she alone can see,
and I just waited till she came up for air. She's
unseamed, off-balance. She's fallen in the crack.
You know what I mean. She sobbed and clenched her teeth

and held me tight like this, and said, "The pain it took
to cure these truths. You must. You must," and so unlike
her, she then said, "Please." Of course I put her off
with deep and longful sighs she could interpret as she
wished. But then, the oddest thing, she gave me this. Go on.
It's curious, to say the least. She said it was a piece
of God she's had with her since birth. I thought it was
a stone at first, but look, it seems to be some sort of
shell. She said she knew of God before the rest, that
Olympus impugned her. They thought she'd stage a coup.
And this was why Apollo put her in that cage. It took
long enough, but one by one, they refused, lashed out,
and God presupposed their powers, Athena, Aphrodite,
Hermes and the rest. Preempted, she said, no contest
at all. Their qualities were mixed and spread as quirks
and traits, as flares of guile in nerveless people; to
dissipate the threat, you know, of any God or group
taking on the One. She was more elaborate, but that's
the gist. And how she described their withering. She's
fixed on this, this withering. It's morbid and uncalled for.
And somehow this stone or shell has helped her through
the task of remembering, which must be great. She's carried
on so long and hard, I give her that. It's irksome how she
makes these demands. I'm not inclined to get involved.
She's so possessed. She makes me feel obliged. But it's
her queer weight, these jack-o-lantern notions of how
we got this far. I owe her nothing. You understand?
There are enough uncertain ways to spend the time.
I don't agree with half she says. I just need
to keep her wrath from me. Then, to top it all,
she swarmed on me and kissed me on the lips,
like this—

DELPHICA: Don't force me, please. You seem so certain
       of your lack of ties. I find I'm drawn and pulled
       to everything. I owe my life . . . to her as well.
       I want to give. You don't know how.

*While stroking the inside of Libica's robe, the sculptor recalls the crazed desire of Lorenzo's middle son, Giuliano, the Duke of Nemours, who was a lecher turned mystic. It forces Michelangelo to confront his sexual identity, briefly, and, winded by his own probing, he rationalizes his sexual drive.*

MICHELANGELO:

Born hooded in his own caul, his own
unbroken sac of birth, it was believed
he could see into the future, an expectation
that ruined him. Even in the years before I left,
when just a boy, he rough-housed all the flesh
he could. Once working in the cool stony dawn,
I heard the wooden gate to the south thumping
low. I thought, the wind. But something
made me look and Giuliano had the cook
against the gate, hands on her hips,
dress draping hands, sliding so far
then thrusting home. His head was back,
eyes closed, mouth wincing to keep quiet,
her eyes rolling in the narcotic of being
laced by him. I couldn't stop the upward
arc of him all hard, bare in the dawn,
from thrusting home. He had a mania
to be sucked down. When I refused,
he slapped me silly and I felt full
of want. His soft tip made me dizzy.
He told everyone and I was soon cut off.
Odd conversations were always out of reach.

Granacci tells me now he's mad
and lives inside one fire or another.
He's even tried to work out spells
to foster sex with goats and hens
and Granacci says, I won't say from who,
he's hired couples to perform for him
to masturbate to. He oils them up
and then himself, and later, when alone,
burns celery and chants to other worlds

where organs swell and seize. He's like a dog,
once scenting a chance, he's drugged and close.
He won't let up. I always think of him when a dark wind
racks the gate. I expect him to appear, wincing in the night,
not dressed, not clothed, but dripping with his trousers
at his knees. It's not that he's a man, but such
an elemental thing, more vile and honest than the rest.
Not a person but a form, arcing taut and free.
I really could love anything. I feel ashamed
if I identify it, but glorious if I just
let it be. I know. It shows. It's not what
it seems. I've always been too open to beauty
and how it makes existence sing.

*Libica disclaims her advances while continuing to discredit Cumae.*

LIBICA:

    I'm not interested in you that way. You took me wrong.
I only meant to emphasize her brutishness. She almost
took me to the ground. She has odd drives. You think
I'm callous. I want to give, of course, to have something
sudden flow within. But she, well, she's repulsive.
Like a hairless bear that frowns and swats at bees.
She smells. Her thousand years repudiate her face.
It's not her age, but how she's lived. I don't like her.
I never have. I won't say it to her face, but here,
to you, why not? Do you wish to be like her? Is hers
a way to emulate? Be honest now.

DELPHICA:

    I love her eyes. You want to see what's worn away.
Her mouth can barely lift its lips, her scalp sags
like a bag about her skull. But ease into those eyes.
They've never changed. I think I'll be like her.
Oh, different, yes, but just the same. She never
starts as sour as she ends. You make everything
seem so strange, so oddly conceived. The books

254

do matter. They've been her life. To give so much
to something over time. Does it matter that she's
frightened by the crowd? You frighten me. She's
talked to me as well. And I don't know how you hear.
She told me that, when our age, she prayed to go
where pain began. It put her in a trance a hundred years,
coiling backwards, towards things we shouldn't know,
unpuncturing wounds, unspoiling hearts, unsouring
dreams that eat us up like lice. Then, all at once,
she was returned, her mind aglow, her skin, all flaked
and dry. Everything moist was excised. Her aging wormed.
Then came her audience with God, who burned without turning,
who heard without listening, who pruned her sight till she
saw Adam spring from Eve and run away. There was no serpent.
She says Adam is the gristle, Woman is the bone, and we
should let him go. She says Tiresias imaged God, and is
only blind by halves, and where he's joined, the female
knowledge smolders. And why, why didn't you tell me
of the Gates of Canes, the healing cage
where mother and son make love at death
before turning to voiceless doves?

*As he works Libica's undergarment, Michelangelo probes deeper into his need
for beauty till he opens the wound that is Mother and stalls.*

MICHELANGELO:
When I see such white magic, always through the eyes,
the body knows, and then it's loving God where He appears.
I thirst to be rushed, and under the influence, I beg
and squeal and am other than myself. One touch
and I am drunk, such God-blown scents endure!
And often, I see more softness, more greatness
than some see in themselves. But God is there
inside the stacked hard chest of some Adonis
who can barely say my name. It's unlike me
to coddle another's way, but women, too,

though I can only get so close. They make me
spin and cool. Sweet Delphica or Eve or Mother Mary
calming her spread immobile son, or my Mother's cold
rejoicing eyes arousing my infant-riddled nest. I wanted
her. For all I know, she watched me freeze. Though she was
touched by something old and safe, I was let go, dropped
free. And I've this knot of grief from her that's never slack
for long. How does one disseminate grief throughout the body?
How to find the empty hole and let it bleed its sac of air?
I don't know what to touch to fill me. The figures look
all parched and stained. They're weak. Or am I drunk on pain?
There's nothing left to paint. I'd saddle up and wander home
but where is that, MaMa? Where is that? I never should have
stopped. Can't find a way back in. No use to leave.
My rooms are small, the help just difficult, pretending
not to hear. The women are impertinent. The young boys
dull and slow. O God! Now look! A small grey bird,
flicking in that lunette. Why Here? Why Now?
She scares and tries to dumbly fly
across and out God's arms.


*Libica is pinned.*

LIBICA:
    You make me feel ungrateful.
    You make me drop the nets
    and wonder, if we might grow.
    You know I want you,
    but now for other reasons
    that aren't hard to understand.
    It's been so fast and buoyant these long years.
    It's hard to stay down here from where you speak.
    I started here, but, I don't know.
    You save some things and then they're lost
    and then it seems ridiculous to save at all.
    I know I'm gruff, but once I lifted

a great many things, and used to sleep
naked in the woods, and it felt good.
I feel slightly ashamed.
Would you try with me?

DELPHICA: It all sounds so willfully slow,
but how can I tell? How could I survive,
after cherishing what you reveal,
after counting on you
to love me through old squalls,
after carving oaken questions into a cask
for seeds that no one thinks belong,
what will keep me in my sanity, if my scalp sags
like hers, if I say, here, protect me love, and you,
fulfilled, forget to sing our song?

LIBICA: It's not the same. Don't toy with me.
I've put it plainly. You're precious.
She's scum.

DELPHICA: She'll be here soon
and I'm not good at secrets.

LIBICA: You have no right!
I've been honest with you!

*Unable to work, the sculptor drinks from the wound that is Mother, as the
small grey bird flutters across the vault, slapping her frantic wings against
his work, smearing Libica's golden bodice.*

MICHELANGELO:
White magic floating in my chest. Won't you hold still?
White shade slicing up my rest. I'd crawl into you,
if that would make you open your palms
and leave me be, unaware
that I'm your son—Just how

did she get in?! There's no way out!
Damn grey bird! Damn grey thing flitting,
marring all I've done. Damn Swarming Nuisance!
And Now I have to worry about you Striking me!

# XXIII. JONAH

From the start Jonah does not want to be called by God and, therefore, distorts God's subtle sign and remains unsure if he is even called. But somehow he knows he is destined for Nineveh and, refusing to accept the mystery that has changed his life, he takes a ship from Jopa to Tarshish, "going away from the presence of the Lord," away from Nineveh. An unceasing squall haunts the ship, and Jonah is cast overboard by the crew as a tentative offering to the storm. It is then he is "swallowed up" by the "great fish," the whale, which keeps him in his belly for three days before spitting him "upon the dry land."

After these attempts to flee the Lord, Jonah hears God again, commanding him to warn the Ninevites of imminent disaster if they do not repent their ways. This time he issues God's warning, but with poor spirit and great reluctance. As he grows more confused, he vacillates, not convinced the city should be punished and when misanthropic not wanting to see them spared. After issuing God's warning, he camps outside the city to see what will come of it, and there his mental state becomes more and more unclear and ingrown. As he keeps watch, God causes a plant to grow to shade him, then sends a worm to destroy the plant and a "sultry east wind" to plague his unravelling mind.

Jonah is the last prophet enthroned on the Ceiling, capstone to the agitated sea of forms spread in struggle before him. He points to the abysmal world below and scans the haunting expressions of all those called by God. They swarm and moan, a plague of hosts, as his eyes waver upward, fixed on the apparition of God creating Himself out of Chaos. In the terror of his reluctance, he cannot bring anything divine into focus. Every presence blurs, his sight undone continually, the Old Testament's Prometheus; his eyes nibbled daily into fear and healed over each night, the only seer forced to face God directly without rest.

As Jonah relates his vague bout with a God who wraps him in a trail of eerie half-formed signs, Michelangelo reveals the tragedy of his plans to build a tomb for Julius, a frustrating saga of persistent vision, burning in its clarity, but never allowed to enter the world. Where the prophet is wracked by doubt and uncertainty, the artist is driven by faith and unprecedented sight. The two, wedded across the Ceiling's moat, pose another possibility of Light and Dark, each having the other's life as an option. Both dredge a darkly lighted bottom, where waiting for a sign unearths the quandary of what to do with it when it comes and what to do when it doesn't, of how to burn when opened by the light and how to believe in heat when closed.

*Jonah is a traumatized wanderer who can only speak from his desert camp*
*outside of Nineveh. No matter what he sees or feels, he always returns to the*
*moment of his trauma, or believes he does. Wherever he goes, he is fixed in*
*that scene. Here, he nervously conveys how it all began, when God led him*
*to a warm sensation beneath a rock, which Jonah, in his fear, presumed to*
*be a snake. Thus he avoided it, but once overturning the rock, he was stung*
*by God's message, which he explained, at first, as the hum of bees.*

JONAH:

You can't know. I was overturning dirt in the garden.
The morning was humid and the light was strong.
I was in no hurry, enjoying the flat chink of the hoe
hitting stones, raking till the earth couldn't resist.
I hit a large stone which sent an eerie sensation
through my hands. I hit it again and felt the scrape
of hoe in my fingers, between my ears. I pushed the dirt
aside. It was oblong, the size of the hoe. I slipped my hands
beneath, felt something brush my fingers, dropped the rock,
which was a mistake. For I knew some adder was there,
just waiting for me to lift. Such an awful sensation.
But you just can't know. I left it there and worked
the other end, but how I'd sweat each time I hit a
chink. I planted around it, and even cautioned others
to let the unknown slither in its sleep. The next year,
it seemed larger in my mind. I couldn't walk the garden
without homing to the buried stone. But the third season,
I forgot, and watching clouds ride mountain trees—Click.
Click. Chink. I thought, I Must. I hunched, about to grip
the rock, saw horrible lizards in my mind, thought, it will
strike. Could feel the venom pierce and puff my skin. I said,
"Stop Thinking! Just Do!" Three more times without touching
a thing. Then quietly, between my tensions, while not
looking to myself, I slipped my fingers. The earth was loose
and cool and something brushed my hand. I gripped the stone
and heaved. Thud. A vapor curled and rose. I fell back,
full of misgivings I'd planted, never lifting the things
buried in the way. The thought was odd and quick and dull

and clear—came on with a shudder, and still, the vapor
shrouded my head. I shook it off. It filled my eyes
and nose, coating my mouth and ears. I heard noises
that were almost words. I bore down. They dispersed
to sounds—wind on the verge of silent moans.
I coughed and tried to concentrate. I couldn't see.
Lost all direction. The silence unhinged to a high-pitched
tonal hum: eennn-uuhh-vuhh, eennn-uuhh-vuhh. It made me drunk
on images of voice. I felt sad choirs swarming, chanting,
buzzing. I was on the ground beside the perfect hole
the stone had left. My senses lengthened. Light frisked
through a nearby tree. And on its trunk, a bee
rubbing its thin black legs. I filled the hole
and planted a baby yew, and as I packed the dirt,
I felt the roots bend underground. I couldn't decide
where to put the stone, so I left it where it landed.
That summer I'd sit in the evenings and watch the rock
beside the yew beside the retired sky. I'd nod and drift
and the after-image of stone and sky would diverge and float
behind my eyes to ripple to a city full of blank towers
and flat black gates. My mind would bob lightly and I'd
sponge myself awake. It was then I heard the word, Nineveh,
as I floated my eyes like a mindless fish. "Go to Nineveh."
I don't like big cities. "Nineveh." They're full of idiotic
people. "Go to Nineveh." Everything's so expensive.
"Nineveh." The yew had broken in the wind.
I packed the branch beside the stem
and watered it, but it never was the same.
Then the angel came when I was in that sleepy,
creamy state, "No, don't look on me. Stay half-dreaming.
If you wake, I'll leave." I was bobbing in his water.
If I tried to look, a wave dropped my lids. If I sank,
a swell lifted me halfway. He spoke in a curl of surf
and the sounds were nearest words when the long waves
crashed. It was hard to hear. "Nineveh is where
you're going. Tell them they will perish

unless they do as you say." When I woke,
it was night and I vaguely called the angel
and felt something old and uneven wash over me.
I stopped trying to recall the words and the message
in a total sense was there. And then I fought off dozing,
stopped enjoying that part of the day. My sleep became
the stone, buried, unturned. The more I kept it out,
the more it wanted in, like a notion of sorrow
in the haunches of one's drunkenness the moment
touch is gone. It nagged its way in,
spoiling the garden, souring my sleep.
I broke the hoe by dreaming too hard
of a rabid man drowning in his fate.
I woke and swung at some high-strung apparition
and snapped it on the wall. You just can't know.
I was all alone and slipping fast. I left, No—
not for Nineveh. I took a ship from Jopa to Tarshish.
I don't know why, but I didn't use my name.
I called myself Trancanthos, after a magician
I saw who'd perfected his trick, turning earth
to sand and sand to stone and stone into
a strange translucent thing in which
the oceans wax their sound. He said
his gift condensed our sense. He said,
with a laugh that coiled, "Magic merely
brings time in view." I practiced saying it:
Trancanthos. Trancanthos. I didn't want to go,
but nothing else seemed relevant and sometimes
relevance is letting go of all we have to lose.
The ship was new, full of cabins with circles
to see the deep. I was below, behind the 38th rib.
The numbers were burned in the planks. It's how
they build these days. They cut and stack. They burn
and nail. As we set out, I kept looking back and thought
I saw a patch of sky, way off, darken, a sudden smudge
above the garden. It was wrong, this sudden running.

"Trancanthos! Move back! She'll start to heeling!"
The mast creaked as the huge sail fluttered taut
and we started leaning, luffing, losing ground
as we cut across the deep.

I'd refused some kind of calling,
kept trying to dismiss the quiver in my hand.
But white caps kept rapping with the broken fists
of fallen suns. I surfaced. There was nothing.
I asked if others heard the rapping. I asked the brute
in 34. The Greek in 41. Shrugs and looks kept me
from discussing things I'd felt but hadn't seen.
Each night the rap, rap, rapping. And in the 16th
formless dawn, a foamy ring was lifting, crest, crest,
cresting, dumping bunks. We were taking water beneath
our sleepless forms. The captian asked his fatalistic
questions, stayed below, charting miles like provocations.
Then, all at once, a column rose and cracked a boom loose
from its sheet. It swung and swung and flattened the Greek.
The column sprayed and pooled him over. The squalling water
darkened, wracking us, but nothing ended. Adrenalin. A pitch.
Off-balance. Knees sore from slamming wooden ribs. The sound
of water fast and rising, unsure where it was coming in.
A surge of thinking life was over. A spot of everything
beginning again. Concentric Crisis. Ringing Crisis. 15,
18 times a day. The captain scratching charts and figures,
staring, tracing, rubbing fright from his fingers
through his hair. He came to us, serious, embarrassed,
"I think we'd better—cry out—privately—to what it is
we think is there. Offer up. You just can't tell."
We scanned each other. The cone of water flogged
and cracked. I tripped and fell. The man was talking
sacrifice. We scanned for the weakest. Two landed,
thinking it was me. We huddled in our chambers, sinking,
rocking in the hull. I knelt in the perpetual heaving,
knees sliding on the wood, shoes and pots
tumbling in the bilge. I was done running,

but was more scared, more lost, more
crumbled in my thinking. Three of them
were at my door. My eyes could barely open.
One tried to nudge the others, "It's all his
fault." I pretended to sleep. "His name isn't
Trancanthos. I've seen this man." Another voice,
"Let's throw him in." I shut my eyes. They left
and then the captain touched my shoulder,
"It's you, you know. They'll be back before too long."
I told myself I wouldn't resist, just remain still,
not squirm or kick, just walk into the wall of water
and drink. They came with four others and I fought
and scrapped and bit the brute. They hit me with a plank.
I saw my blood spin in the current, felt the salt
slap my face and needle it away.

*As he paints the architecture behind Jonah, Michelangelo, with great diffi-
culty, recounts how the Tomb of Julius was conceived, and watered down.*

MICHELANGELO: When Julius called me to Rome, I knew
    old Sangallo had been busy. And there he was,
    as I crossed the Tiber, arms aflutter, his mind
    purring like a cat, "Buonarroti! You're Here!
    My God! You're Here!" He shook my wrists:
    "I told him about these hands. I filled him
    like a sail with you, till he had no choice
    but to track you down."

From the time we met, Sangallo had impressed me.
Now, I wouldn't say. But then, he thought me
grand, and to have someone with years behind him,
someone who understood the Greeks—It made me *feel*
Greek, made me want to be a ruin. His family builds
mausoleums and half of Rome believes him morbid.
It's not his fault we raise open-hearted structures
around the dead. He loves the columns of space slicing

true. Then, he said Hadrian's Rotunda was the one to beat.
He said, "When statues face each other, across a pit,
the lace of shadows—merging, spilling, thinning—
it's like the lost intentions of a race!" He said,
"The spaces are imperative! A single pole is just
a stick, but marbled bodies bending light
can nourish!"

He was the Pope's prime advisor. I thought,
I've landed well for a change. We spent evenings
walking the Colosseum. He'd stop to watch the light
spoke the columns, and inflame, "The reason to build
is for the sculpture of Light! Look About! Have you
ever seen a forest when the sun comes up? No one tree
is the focus, and if you squint, the trees give way
to bars of light. It's like a generation's thought
or the history of a people or the one sense of God
men share. You understand, Buonarroti? Build statues
in the forest. Better yet, build forests out of stone!
You alone can do this. There's no one else alive.
You can work the miracle of largeness. You have
the mind. The drive. You're mad enough. Build
something with your Genius that can make
those of us who think we're blind
Weep at the miracle of Light!"

He was not this way with everyone. More cocoon,
less silk: "You can't speak freely all the while.
Some need to be eased and fed. And those in power
don't like to hear theories that proclaim equality
of light. No, we must wait, and work the Pope's
good ear. Our time will come. You work your plans
for reeling Gods and Angels lost in mortal sky.
I'll take care of where and how and when."

*The sculptor blocks in the prophet's throne, as Jonah admits how his mode
of apprehension was broken down inside the whale.*

JONAH: I kept descending, thought I was choking,
　　　but started to breathe the water as a thick
　　　kind of air. Then everything darkened
　　　and the far-off drone that seemed like voices
　　　was everywhere in all directions and the hum
　　　began to escalate and lengthen, as if a thousand
　　　thousand hearts were breathing in precise
　　　and desperate grooves which keep the doer
　　　from redoing, the lover from rechancing,
　　　the food from filling hunger. The voices
　　　not quite voices made me break inside
　　　my breaking like a piece of fired time.
　　　And the race, lagging for a moment,
　　　exhaled the same ennui.

　　　The darkness whipped me through the water
　　　the way gales spin thoughts through trees:
　　　'If I am called, why can't I Hear it?
　　　I don't want to Be—Involved!
　　　Don't want to Understand why lives
　　　don't Challenge where they fall!
　　　Don't want to stand on things I Believe
　　　just to use them as a Wall!'

　　　Debris coursed by without a Source
　　　like cold expressions after Death:
　　　'Why can't I Distill and Say?
　　　It starts out Fine, no knots or cuts,
　　　then splits when almost out,
　　　then breaks right down by being Mouthed,
　　　makes the urge to speak a knife.'

　　　I began falling faster than my thinking,
　　　thinking faster than I could diagnose.
　　　A skull appeared wrapped in weeds
　　　and when I knew it was my own, my soul
　　　along the inside fainted. I thought the weeds

like fears curled in and out the sockets, through
the homeless teeth. Eh! Every touch since God
put man in motion has been refracted, lost
sticks of light through watery hosts. And I
refuse to speak to be contorted.
I woke wrapped in weeds and naked,
coughing water from my lungs.

*Filling in Jonah's muscular legs about to flee, Michelangelo recalls that while
Sangallo tried to maneuver the Pope to build his own Tomb, the sculptor,
in a torrent of energy, was designing it on a colossal scale with a Rotunda
of eighty statues and columns surrounding a free-standing monument. The
upper levels of the Rotunda had thrones of prophets from the Old Testament,
saints from the New, and mythic figures from Greece and Rome: all naked,
all upheld by cherubim and seraphim lining the columns. And in the center
four enormous slaves or angels, on the corners of the monument, looking to
the great men of antiquity. This would be his plethora of human forms twist-
ing and writhing between earth and the beyond. This would be the repository
of his visions at Carrara, his sketches of Cascina. It would rival anything
ever conceived. Here, as he yearns for that moment of inception, Michel-
angelo spills an account of his first vision in the quarries of Carrara, where
a sea of statues came alive before him.*

MICHELANGELO:
For two months I was idle, blinking,
watching light and wind for hours.
Nothing took on form. Sangallo gave me
the run of his house. He spent mornings
chasing Julius. I kept seeing the hundreds
trapped at Carrara, reaching, huddled, twisting
deep inside the stone. I thought, if I can see them,
I can free them, if I can keep them all in view.
I stalked the rows of the Colosseum; the lower,
then the upper, hunting, tracking, spying on the light.
And as I coaxed the empty center, I saw Julius
guarded by the angels, 18, No, 20 braccia high.
It was finally forming. I prowled the ancient stadium.
And all along the blinding outer rim, somewhere

in the riddled light, a rash of thrones colonized
by Prophets taunting Greeks, each hoisted high
by sad impatient angels and cherubim and seraphim
and slaves! All naked and contorted! Intent Prophets
heaving! Old slaves buckling! All the pillars showing
different states of stress! And above the thrones—
Medallions! Huge Brass Histories! Held Up! All
Facing Julius! In the Round! And on a Hill!
In Cyprus, if I could! And All Across the Top—
A Pediment! Simple! Level with the Scalped
Prophetic Heads!

I ran back to Sangallo's,
sketching the whole way in my mind.
I worked for days and let no one enter.
They thought I had been seized. I saw bold
torsos sweating, throwing their arms to God,
staring off, about to speak or stand. I saw
nude angels quaking, lifting unseen fates,
flexing their silent wonder while aburn.
I sketched boldly, quickly, mostly lines
of stress and action, axis after axis
of the lost and mythic world!

I thought, they all could be foreshortened,
slightly, toward the viewer on the ground.
And the angels guarding Julius would be brisk,
not sure the rest are even there, but tested
by some far-off voice.

I could feel the figures at Carrara
surging in position. They were squirming,
like that first time, writhing in the stone.
That first convulsive night. All day the marble
dust and powdered lime caked our arms. Men shook it
from their hair. They looked like pollinated Gods
dusted with the tired light. The sun was almost gone,
dusk washing through the mountain, everything about to end.

They left. I walked the gravelled ridge, my steps firm
and destined toward nothing I could summon or understand,
and the pit, so still, powdered up a breeze, taking on
the emptiness: the thick coiled rope darkening, the ragged
cut of unearthed blocks, each tied for the night, their
long shade slicing up the yard, the smell of tied stone
cooling. And unaccustomed to the glowing dark, I swear
the blocks, about the yard, seemed to breathe, each rise
a glow, a shock, and then, their outlines swelled, urgent
and amber, as if thirsting for an ounce of light.
They all appeared, naked, and writhing in the blocks:
supine, angled, upside down; amber and sweating,
shifting like old germs in sand, and the more
they writhed, the more exquisite their torture.
No one would believe how bodies burn in stone
like muscular eternal flutes, their amber cries
piercing and narcotic, sweet. I stumbled down the ridge,
pebbles trickled from my toes, and there, beneath my feet,
a dozen more, falling nowhere, locked in thrust,
reaching through the path: about to hoist a spirit's
bone, about to shift unbearable weight, about to drop
an armful of hours, about to trust the absolute invading
songs their amber souls can sing. The amber flared, heat
spreading through the ground. I stumbled on, and all
across the yard, deep in the mountain's hide, within
the marbled waves, avoiding veins, a race
of naked forms praying, delving, raving:
bellies in gorgeous ripple, necks upturned
with muted veins, prisoners of unheard positions,
about to throb or drink or lick or die to come again.
Down in the pit I feathered the last tied block
in which a woman, lying on her stomach, raised herself,
both arms extended, mouth gaping for something she didn't
need to see. She pulsed orange through the stone. I pounded
to let her know. She opened her eyes, which turned white
as they opened, and she dispersed as they all cooled,

bleached back into their unforgiving home. The wind
picked up. I put my ear to the side her mouth had
faced and thought I heard her breathe. The dust
all flew. Chalk lined my ear. I grabbed a chisel,
to set her free, but the marble had no give.
She was asleep and white. I hugged the stone.
No breath at all. I spent the night
tracking a vanished race like a wolf,
a dizzy wolf, crazed by ancient scents.
I've hunted ever since for ways
to sculpt and bleed them free.

It was near dawn on a weekday.
The Tomb was nearly drawn. I finished
and felt whole in a way that only sculptors know
when they've been whipped and tried like a sail.
The room was sparking. The door pulsed open.
Sangallo rushed in softly. He knew history
had bathed my making. God had seized me once again.
O! If I could crack the instant God has staked me,
I could live forever, I mean, see past
the end of time, swim through, and eat
the fire inside birth. And then,
at night, my soul could heal me,
burning tarnish off the age.

*Coloring the monstrous head of the fish at Jonah's thigh, Michelangelo,
clarified by his vision, has little sympathy for the myopic prophet who, cast
ashore by the whale, began in muddled desperation to trudge his strange
unguided way to Nineveh.*

JONAH: I was days into the desert.
Thoroughly depressed. With no idea
what would happen at the end. I was barefoot
and by the fourth day, was licking salt from my skin.
Its taste and smell made me hear the sea, the darker part
which opened just for me. Each step in the desert jounced

through my feet up my trunk to ripple my face. I let my mouth
and jaw relax, let my lids and forehead droop. With each step
my face jagged and bobbed, expressionless. I slept cross-legged
watching the desert floor, feeling the blue wind eddy
swirls of sand which would land in perfect crescent
arcs. I went to finger one and never felt a ridge
of earth more finished. It made me weep without
vehemence, without reason, without fear. Another
swirled past my feet. Five seconds, maybe more. Another.
They'd land bluely beneath the desert moon and spread.
In truth, the wind would drop the sand and carry on
as clarity. Each palmful was perfect, thicker
at the base, arching left to right. I'd squat
and finger one, then chase another, but chase
is not the word. I swirled and left small
piles of my own, making me more finished.
Somehow, this was God talking, like the voices
inside the whale. I'd stopped hoping for words,
stopped believing or not-believing, just knew
the crescents of sand were perfect.

I reached the edge of Nineveh early the eighth day.
By now the entire earth seemed surreal. I couldn't
imagine speaking to another, couldn't foresee
how people would look at me. As I shuffled,
the sand began to have a bottom. I wouldn't
slide or disperse as loosely as before.
And there was a trace, a faint smell of water.
I heard a cry of almost voices from the city,
a void in unison. My steps grew thin: the shuffle
sticking, the ball of foot twisting in the sand.
I waited for an indication. My mind was like
my expression, no tension, no pretense of control.
As the mind's feet hit on things above, the notions
without shape, the pure conceptions
would ripple down my tongue.

There was a cork-like smell to their streets.
The city was full of laughter that wasn't freeing,
songs that weren't soothing, truths that weren't useful,
and sand like salt everywhere, behind the greedy ears
of merchants, in the scalps of dreamless girls, in
the navels of those too stuffed to sleep, on the
double chins of dogs. On a sack of grain an old man
whinnied, thrusting through a small bored boy.
The sack of grain was spilling, spread beneath
his knees. I felt a ripple from above, let it go
without forming words. A wave of heat, a sort of heat,
a sort of vibration rippled past the old man's bone,
rippled through the corklike laughter, rippled its way
to the ears of the king. By nightfall he found me.
He said, "We have done nothing." I said, "In forty days,
you will perish, unless the city fasts. No food, no sex,
no false expensive masking." He said, "How can we monitor
such a thing? It's tough enough to uphold laws." I said,
only in the belly of my thinking, "You will fast
or you will perish." He heard me and seemed to know
I was coming. Seemed half-prepared to instigate
a plan. I felt upstaged, found out, precluded.
After all—the garden, whale, and desert—
I expected some more awe. He went to offer me
his women, but stopped, "I suppose that's not for you."
I was lonely and offended. He brought on sculpted buckets
of fruit and wine, "I'm not sure where to put it. But these
are logistics and you're a man of essence." I was enraged
and let it rancor through. The fruit popped to dust,
the wine to smoke, "Forty days or you will perish."
I turned to leave. He was blabbering at my feet.

By morning he was naked, wrapped in a sackcloth,
nestled in a mound of ash. By the second day
the whole city followed suit. There were hundreds

of little rounded fires, cooled and fanned
and spread out in the road. A naked city
fasting in ashes. It seemed godless and absurd.
I walked back to the desert, where the city reddened
like the rim of some decimated dish. I could barely hear
the voices of their hunger: not quite the desert silence,
nor the ruined sounds of men.

I made a hut, near a tree, the west side open,
and spread the sand to form an oblong crater
in which I felt my face regain expression.
My mind closed off in tension, and I thought,
why must they suffer? What makes them wicked?
I would have broken down to touch his women,
would have thought him a friend to eat his fruit,
and the wine would have let me sleep. I pulled into my hut
and whimpered. The dark blue sand swirled about my crater.
Nineveh was naked and in ashes. I was growing bitter
for the things I thought I had to do.

*While Jonah is forced to remember an endless lack of definition, Michelangelo
knows all too well the bounds of reality, which gnaw at him as he darkens
Jonah's trembling hand pointing earthward. It leads the sculptor to relate
how Sangallo, confronted with Michelangelo's design, was torn between the
worldly gates of power he thought he must walk through and his intoxication
with the inferno of genius before him.*

MICHELANGELO: Sangallo was enthralled. His eyes kept
eating the design I had laid across the floor
and the sketches pinned about the walls.
He kept spinning, not knowing where to stop,
drunk on the muscled sweep. He kept poking
at Isaiah, thought it was him, 20 braccia high.
He started to respond several times, but his eyes
kept stalling his speech and then he laughed, shook me
by the shoulders and brayed, "You make it worthwhile
to be alive!" He asked about Moses and Daniel, and

which angels would guard Julius, or were they slaves,
and thought it inspired that the guardians
would not seem to care. Few times have I
felt so inward in the company of another.

That morning, Sangallo peered into my soul,
as a cautious man dunks his head in a forgotten
tribal stream, and the stars were almost seeable,
the air pink yet cool, and words unnecessary.

He was stunned, in awe, out of breath,
pacing about, but leaving the room
brought him closer to the ground.
He said he'd see the Pope, but cleared
his throat and looked away. He poured himself
a drink, and said, "Soon. Soon we will present it."
I instantly lost confidence. What must I do
to carve the world? It takes no lives. It breaks
no bones or dreams. It merely sings the world of forms.
Why can't I sustain the burst? Why must they always run?
Run from God! Run from me! Scurry to the dark
encrusted side where no one ever dreams!

He sputtered about the week being awkward, not
advantageous, about working the Pope's influence
our way. I said, "Damn it, Sangallo! All he needs
is to See it!" He kept walking away, qualifying
our chance: terms of climate, terms of favor,
terms of debt and allegiance paid. I fumed,
slapped the goblet from his hand. He knew
I wouldn't hurt him. He understood my anger,
came close and affirmed, "It's genius, Sheer
Genius. We both know it would Supercede the World!
He's just a General, a pompous, Agitated thing.
He toys with power, loves to tangle puppets,
to watch them strangle, to cut them off. He has
manipulative patience. You understand, my raw
raw genius? He's an incurable spider, always

taunting, trapping beautiful things. So let me
set a trail. Let me set his mood.
Don't be too eager. Don't show him
what you've got to lose."

Sangallo went to Julius straightaway.
I worked further on my sketches. By evening
he returned, said there was some interest,
that he engineered the conversation
till Julius mentioned his own Tomb.
And when the Pope, preoccupied,
thought he'd brought it up, Sangallo,
with an inch of guile, retold how he
suggested a new chapel, "for St. Peter's
has no room. He grew skeptical and pensive.
But bit and asked, 'Who could manage such a thing?'
I paused, then offered up, 'Buonarroti.'
He was intrigued and typically guarded,
but directed me to have you draw a plan."

I hugged compact little Sangallo
and lifted him off the ground.

I went to pack my drawings,
felt the curious path was won.

He said, "Think now, think.
What will he conclude if we arrive at breakfast, hmm?
No, we must wait a week, probably two. He must think
it was a labor, and must be convinced
it was done at his command."

He spent weeks at the Pope's retracted ear,
and told me of his sudden want, "Does Michelangelo
have a plan?" Then how he went to nod, but pulled up short,
"Almost, your Holiness, perhaps another week."

In three more we were ready, and he warned me
on the way, over and over, more anxious as we went.

He'd walk beside, then jump ahead, then backwards
for a spell, then slip behind, stop and think,
and up all over again, "Don't weigh his first reactions.
They're throw-offs. He'll be testing your confidence.
And don't let his coyness endanger your excitement.
In fact, the more silent, the more cunning,
the more guarded his response, the more
in awe he is."

I stopped him with genuine affection,
"Sangallo, no one's worth all this."

He held firm to my roll of drawings,
"But these statues are worth our lives."

I knew I'd build this Tomb. No vision ever
came as strong. Its image burnished in my brain.
Somewhere I could see it broiling just beyond my mind:
whole, complete, the sun and wind streaming through!
If it took my life, I'd break it down and transport
coal by burning coal through my funnelled soul,
and in the world, assemble it. It was there.
I could almost touch it. A Masterpiece
Floating between God and my Brain.

He was warning me now about Bramante.
He tugged my sleeve, "Did you hear me?
Come back to earth now. You must understand this.
This man can ruin us with a glance." I found it hard
to believe there was another who could ordain this.
He said, "Bramante. Don't turn your back to him
in anger or in trust. Il Rovinante. Listen to me.
Il Rovinante. He is a ruiner and he's strongly
seated by the Pope. He fancies himself
a scientist, a modernist, an artisan elite.
He backs Raffaello, Perugino, the whole
delicate, boring crowd."

Sangallo was too dramatic.
He was sweating and soaked around the neck.
As we waited for His Holiness, I thought,
I'll adore this man. As the door opened,
I thought, I'll bend to no one when it comes
to sculpture. He was as tall as I, as sorely
driven. I saw it in the red behind his eyes.
He waited for us to bow slightly, then extended
us his hand. Sangallo was a slippery fish, almost
servile but brisk in retreat. I couldn't make out
how he did it. I was extremely awkward
bending to his ring.

He said, "You have a plan for me?"
I pulled them out and stepped right in,
ushering my power directly in his face.
He didn't balk like the others. He didn't
frown or think me strange. He listened
quite intently, and I thought I caught
a smile, albeit hidden, a trace of satisfaction
that this would bear his name. I thought,
Sangallo has misjudged him. I like this Rovere Pope.
When done, I felt I knew him.

He slouched into his throne, "It is astonishing
and appealing, greater in concept than Hadrian's Tomb.
I will think on it, Buonarroti." He paused to pit an olive,
"In the meantime, just for argument's sake, go see where,
in St. Peter's, you would install the inner Tomb."

"They Are Inseparable!" I couldn't keep it in.
Sangallo winced. He took his time and ate his olive,
"Nothing is inseparable, young sculptor, not even
your body from your head." He laughed, "And in the end,
four angels from your hand for all eternity is better
than eighty paper Tombs dancing in your head."

"I alone can do this. No one alive could ever finish—"
"*Go*, Michelangelo, and see where the disturbed angels
might fit."

I seethed, a quicksand in myself. Sangallo
kept signalling me to comply. I recalled
his angst of instruction, "Let him think
it is his plan." I left for St. Peter's,
all knotted high and low. I thought,
he sees the scope, like Sangallo, how
can he possibly say no?

St. Peter's was under repair, shut-in,
too dark and hunched for what I'd seen.
Workmen were strolling their tools.
I would have fired them all,
without a single florin.

It galled me to pretend this way.
I chose where the new choir had been started,
though no place offered enough space. I returned
and said the roof would have to be completed,
thinking that would stall his mind my way.

As I finished, Bramante entered
and both Sangallo and Julius were changed.
He spoke with arrogant detachment, acted
as if we'd already met, then ignored me
just enough to irk me underneath.
It was deliberate. Sangallo was
hardly present and I realized,
after all this way, he was out,
and using me to regain priority.

I raised my plan again by inference,
not wanting Bramante to see my work.
Julius was suddenly above us all, not
paying attention. He fingered some secret,

half-formed, forming, that very instant
in his mind. He ignored us all and then,
abruptly, sent Sangallo and Bramante
to see the choir space.

We were alone. He was a raw mirrored twin,
the severed half of rage. We couldn't get too close
or we'd repel. He stalked me. I stood my ground,
pent up and ready to strike. He faced me square.
I could see the strong hot iron in his eyes.
He overpowered the space through which he moved,
"Where would I put such a mausoleum, awesome as it is?
It would take a lifetime to build and more money
than a Pope could ever hope to 'confiscate.' "

"It would take twelve years.
I would do all the work myself.
It would be the greatest sculpture
ever built, and in your name."

He took another olive, "You know my taste."
He pitted it, "Will you separate the two?"

"No!"

"I see, and I suppose you won't tolerate
anyone else executing your plans, nor do I
suppose anyone else could. We might seem
lost to any of it, if we don't take you
on your terms."

Át this, Sangallo and Bramante returned.
We continued our confrontation with our eyes.
Sangallo did his best, reiterating the need
for a separate chapel. Bramante swung close
to Julius, picking at an olive, "I think,
Your Holiness, the sculptor chose a fine
airy corner for these enormous angels, and
as these things go," He pitted his olive,

"if the new chapel's ever completed, Your Holiness—
even in His will—could have the inner Tomb moved."

He munched and cleaned his teeth with his tongue.
I disliked him at once, and knew, when I was out,
he'd seen my plans. Il Rovinante. Julius rose,
his mind alight, but nowhere close
to anyone in the room, "Well, this is
a brilliant view, but one man's view.
Let's have some other plans. Sangallo.
Bramante. I want other Tombs in the round,
before I decide." He turned abruptly and left
by another door. I was irate. Sangallo tried
to calm me, could barely keep up as we spun
the streets of Rome. I stalked the rows
of the Colosseum. I fumed and said, "I'll burn them."
Sangallo put his hand around my fist, "It went well,
believe me. You must be patient. It will come our way."
I said, "You didn't tell me you were out of favor."
He blushed and looked away, "I believe in you."
"That's not the point. I believed in You!"
He sunk. I'd hurt him. I thought, next time,
I won't hold back.

*Inevitably Jonah replays his agony. As he watches Nineveh with resentment,
his inability to see his purpose festers, and his refusal of God corrupts his
capacity to sustain the world in a coherent way, till waiting proves a greater
depravation for the prophet than fasting is for the damned.*

JONAH: By the 14th day I hear the edge of voices.
All else remains quiet. The days are hot. The nights
are cool. My hut attracts snakes. The edge of voices
is mellifluous. It makes me angry. There have been
no other signs, no storms, no winds, no perfect
crescents, no extra sense filling the cankered moments,
just me, sitting in the west, watching Nineveh

in sackcloth and ash, singing about why they can't eat.
It becomes apparent why they should suffer. It has to do
with inconsequential livelihood. I mean, the culture
has no bearing on the future of living things.
And not a dot from God. It makes me angry.
I wake up mornings, unsure if there's ever been
a God. I never really heard a word. And if God were,
He'd make something happen. Listen to the austere health
of these voices. They enjoy their threat to perish.
Is this why I've suffered? I keep running sand
through my hands. I notice my wrists. I am aging,
not simply leathered from the desert, or gaunt
from lack of fruit, but putting on years, decades
since the garden. The hands are rivered now. And bunches
sag the base of my throat. I feel ridiculous. I've come
through great internal disaster which has forever
changed my way. Against my will! And Nothing
is Happening! The city's on some liberal ascetic
Adventure! Keeping journals! Compiling notes!
The King's a Hero! Longest proponent of going
Without! And No Signs Anywhere!!

There is nothing beyond me but the illusion
of You and sky and this city of my own invention.
Let me wake in my garden.

By the 27th day, they've forgotten they are fasting
and it seems their way of life. I am miserable,
can't rely on the desert, can't rely on my vision,
can't rely on the silence in which this field
of piercing thought-waves rots. The nightwinds
are sudden and slicing. The hut is tearing north
and south. I want to leave, but nowhere fits the illusion.
By the 35th day, the king says they've found The Way.
He gives up his throne, proclaims he is The One.
The city starts rejoicing. I can't convey the scope
of my anger. I go to him, and damn him. He says,

"Those creatures who depend on rain die."
I condemn him to this desert and rip the sackcloth
from his eastern-looking frame. He says, "Like fire
are the days. They've burned the forest that is your
God." I'm ready to run wailing through the clean streets
of this tortured dream. He says, "O tell me the Origin
of your Suffering." I can barely understand
what he is saying, the blood so thunders
through my skull.

He offers me self-mastery.

I leave wanting them all to perish, praying
I'll turn my back and the illusion will be gone.
It's harder to walk the sand. I feel myself
aging faster than the time. What if they're saved
and think he's done it, believe it, accept it
as their fate? But there's been no saving,
been no nothing!

I'm in the hut facing west, cursing
the red dish of the city. In the hut
facing west. I pray that you will perish.
In the hut. In the hut. Nothing lines
the flap of hut. Nothing is the west.

*Other drawings for the Tomb are submitted by Leonardo, Sangallo, Sangallo
the Younger, Peruzzi, and Bramante. All are void of central free-standing
monuments, no Tomb in the center, as Sangallo has passed the notion con-
vincingly that the inner Tomb is already promised to Buonarroti. Here, as
he paints Jonah's waistcloth a soft, muted green, Michelangelo speaks to the
power of containment, only to find himself, again, in the hands of Julius,
powerless.*

MICHELANGELO:
For weeks, I waited, doing nothing;
not sculpting, hardly drawing, just shuffling
and waiting. And Sangallo never quite recovered.
The whole thing galled me, this democratic search
for brilliance.

The drawings were quite ordinary.
Sangallo's was a token, but his son's
was a slush of estimation, a hazard.
He was full of selfish heartthrobs
that sputtered near the surface
into frittered enervations
which always weakened him.
He was void of form.

And with no shaft or bridge or tunnel,
the energy escapes and drains the hunger.
Sangallo's boy was an escapist. He'd impregnate
with some rosy fatuation of a morning or a bird
or a notion of injustice, and as if the feeling
hit a screen, it would turn to mist and scatter
with nothing to contain his sympathy.
For it's containment that moves us on.
What funnels water through a pipe!

You can't let the power fill the air.
It will! It wants back where it began
like all of us, our minds and souls, our sense
of time and God. To think releases energy,
drives it through the pipe of thought.

The difference between man and goat and prissy
hog is the *steerage* through containment.

Take the pretty brittle of Perugino
or the boy, Raffaello. They miss the point
and wind up, formal. They build the channel
and stop flowing. Aqueducts without water.
Heads without spirit. They become skulls,
the ultimate broken channel, formal
and no longer forming. Skulls, the pipe
of formlessness, a proper end.

Sangallo's son was formless as a sponge.
He'd sop up here and squeeze out there.
I always had to slow for him, dawdle
with how I felt, thought, formed, perceived.
I was the falcon toying with the mole.
His sketch hardly pressed the paper,
hardly seeable, as if drawn with webs.

I never saw Leonardo's. And Bramante's
was all trim and tidy, symmetric
to the death. I was prepared.

We walked the streets in silence.
I was determined not to have my form undone.
Sangallo wasn't quite as free with me.
He felt impotent because of his dishonesty.
When we arrived, it was early. He kept us waiting
half the morning. When he sent us in, he was laughing
with Bramante. I walked straight to his throne.
He began to pit an olive. I took the tray
and gave it to Sangallo, "No one alive, not even
Leonardo, can do the honor to you that I propose.
Great men must risk great chances.
I will outdo the Parthenon."

He stood and smiled till the smile eroded
to a patch of consternation. He took my hands,
shook his head, and slapped the tray of olives,
silver wobbling the floor, "You will do Much
for me, Michelangelo. Once I Break you!"

I stood my ground but said nothing.
Neither he nor I looked away. Sangallo
was almost flitting in our hair.
Bramante was bruised with pleasure,
envious how Julius and I seemed peers.

Julius, without breaking his stare, announced,
"The choir will be abandoned, and we'll use

Buonarroti's Rotunda to build a new St. Peter's."
The thought was astonishing, almost blasphemous,
to disturb the bones of Peter. Sangallo gasped.
Bramante coughed out of surprise, shaking
his hands to disclaim his reaction.
I thought, I won't let him use it.

"And what of the Tomb?" Sangallo asked.
I kept locking onto Julius, erasing
Bramante and Sangallo from the room.

He wouldn't buckle, "The Tomb will proceed
as well, what's left." He was ruining it.

Bramante prodded, "Just the four
distracted angels?" "Yes!"
He was emphatic, "You Bramante,
you are the architect. You
will build the new St. Peter's.
And you, my unbreakable sculptor,
you will build my Tomb within."

I spun, enraged, and spun again,
almost exploded, slipped on the tray,
kicked it across the room. It crashed
as I stormed, slapping pillars as I went.
I heard Sangallo sputtering after me,
oppressively perplexed, not sure
how things turned out this way.

*While Michelangelo can't fathom why God would so inspire him, only to
have Julius break his will, Jonah believes himself the prey of a God who will
not declare Himself. Oppressed by uncertainty, he beseeches the certainty of
death.*

JONAH: I dump all my water,
    turn my back on the city, face the east, and wait.
    Next morning, the cistern is full. Agh! What good

this speciousness now? I break the jug. The water
packs the sand. I tear and knot my robe. It rips
like a sheet. I noose myself and run from the tree.
The ring of cloth fists my throat. My lips swell
and drain. My eyes almost explode. The branch snaps.
I tumble, yards, head poking in the sand, noose
trailing, lips breaded with the desert. I roll
and roll and eat the sand. I want to die! I eat the pebbles.
They scrape going down. My roof of mouth begins to bleed.
Perish! Perish! You City of Illusion! Nothing surrounds us!
The silence turns to voices that are never really there.
A buzz, a hum, within, without. You just can't know.
The stones leave talc along my teeth. I taste
the powder of the earth. My God! My God!
Swoop down and nibble at my innards!
Vulture That You Are!!

*As Michelangelo leathers Jonah's skin brown, he remembers how he went to
Carrara to adjust his disappointments, but his dreams had been plundered.
First Cascina, abandoned in Florence, for this, a wasted Tomb. The Pope
had stolen the fire of his design, and Bramante would never use the naked,
prophetic thrones or the angelic slaves. He returned eager, inflamed to make
Julius weep. But on his return, things changed. Access to Julius diminished.
His funds were cut. And, the project abandoned, Michelangelo fled Rome.
The next day Julius, taking the shovel from Bramante, broke ground for the
new St. Peter's. And two years later, hauled back like a prisoner, the sculptor
transposed his fired design to fit The Sistine Ceiling. And now, still painting
like a prisoner depressed within his cell, he recalls those nights in Carrara
where, deep in the marbled core of the earth, he saw his place, euphoric,
among his massive statues.*

MICHELANGELO:
    To see a thing so clearly,
    to taste its very inception,
    to know your life was born,
    placed in time, at this juncture of the planets,
    to grasp the sweep of things in such striking flow,

to stumble with the nod of destiny—
to see what I was born to see—and then to have it
broke apart. I've never recovered.
Some things are all or nothing. Yes.
Like the center of night in which
small flowers of light emerge, if we're lucky,
and from their petals—dreams.

They dismembered my vision. So what?
Just see again. Talk to mothers
who've had their infants quartered.
See what it takes to spread their legs.

You can't imagine what it's like.
To have to be here Painting—Painting!
While next door—they Rape My Form!

I went shortly to Carrara, sweet Carrara,
to select marble for the Tomb. I felt cut off.
I stopped outside, sat on a stone, and burned and burned.
Thought of Dinocrates pleading with Alexander to carve
Mount Athos into a Titan whose upper hand would hold
a city; the other, a bowl, a cup, a dish the size of Rome,
from which the mountain's ice would dam and flow.
I see it, Dinocrates. I see the sun setting through its legs.
I see the fires of the city glow across its granite face.
I hear their choirs rise along the edge of flame.
I see the mountain carved into a man about
to drink the song and heat.

I spent nights walking the pits, awaiting
dawn, alone, most alive, at dawn at Carrara,
alone. I could see in the first light, in the white
mountain, transparencies arrested in position, hundreds
squirming in their amber cause, so deep, they were leaning
in, just below another, changing course, twisting, tensing,
shunning my sight as if to be seen were pain.
And after three or four nights, no food, no sleep,

the dawn would buzz, my hands aching with no way
to sculpt these perfect arms. I'd moan, like them,
all dizzied by the fact that all I'd done
was horribly false. And they'd shift like truth
at dawn. They'd shift and slip the mountain
as my Rotunda would appear in the pounded early pit
and they'd take their place in the sculpture of my Tomb.
And I'd position them as a director posits actors on a stage.
And then I'd go to each with lambskin and each would wipe
his brow and arms and shins. Some fit the skin to their
faces, between their legs. And I collected the many skins
like soiled shrouds and each dried with the outline
of the user's body. I draped them all and they merged
before my eyes, into one gigantic skin, as the actors yawned
and stretched, embracing as they froze into statues
for my white Greek Tomb, and this enormous shroud
was my Cascina, finished before me—my Cascina!
And even now there comes a wind, a flush of heat,
and I can see their souls, their heated guests, rise
from the marble skin and hundreds of muscular bodies
float away. I want to rise with them for I know
where they are going. I can hear the sea
at the foot of my Colossus, a thousand feet
high! And all the perfect arms are dancing,
splashing the shore, clear old light slashing up their
arms, and we all join hands and dance and I throw my arms
like a wasted lie, my head back, back as if to eat the sky
and I freeze into marble myself—my stomach ripples Greekly—
my soul jets on!

I toughened like a piece of meat,
became engrossed with the figures
writhing at Carrara, chose the saddest,
saved the rest. The workmen cursed me,
cursed where I sent them cutting.
One arced a ridge 40 feet up,
another crimped behind a nub.

One across a fault. I was exact,
relentless, demanding. I was on fire
to have Julius break at the sight
of what I was doing.

Everything I reach for fractures.
Why do I have—But I have nothing
but the want. Where, Dinocrates,
are we running? From Owner to Maker?
Were we equipped, the human would gnaw
and sculpt the earth into the mind of God.

*So far within the rind of his confusions, Jonah's last chance to perceive
between the world, himself, and his imaginings ignites.*

JONAH:
I woke in the shade of a gourd.
I don't know where it came from.
It's gentle and tolerant and makes the heat
a mist of light, dispersing the burning tunnel
that is sky. It eases my anger. And once the twisting
in my skull lessens, the grisly vow seems forced, forgotten.
My head begins to gently throb. I want to die but cannot end it.
I want to stop this sled of injuries. Nothing is what it seems.
I drink the desert, swim the heat. To love God's likeness is not
loving God! I breathe. I breathe. It does nothing to the air.
I pray. I pray. And God is unaffected. I sleep and sleep.
And while I'm gone, the living want to use me, as crows
build nests of mud. I sleep and wake and the gourd has
worms all through it. All things that thrive become a
host. I think and think and thoughts like worms drill
me. In several days the gourd begins to wither. By now
my skin is flaking. I've lost most all my hair. My shins
are bluing. I'm hunched. It's difficult to breathe. I'm old,
half-gone and ancient, can feel the strife of knotted perception
bunch the bone between my eyes. And now the days are endless,

and somewhere in the middle, the gourd has died a death
of consumption. Heat burns and twists the branches. Its wounds
will never soften. Damn the gourd for being here! For growing
while I slept! Damn the city! Why won't it perish?! My mouth
begins to swell. I want to end this. Damn the sand! I lie
and bake for hours, sand burning red the edges, skin
shrinking by the day. The burning makes me angry. I knock
the hut to pieces, break the pieces, tear the cloth, bury
what's left in sand. I'm tired of the anger. Where is God?
I'm angry at being angry! I'm preying on myself. They only
thought to pray when threatened! I can't stop fuming! I bake
and bake, thought after thought searing through, each layer
burning red, my mind, volcanic, smoldering. I shut my eyes.
The image burns the lids from underneath. I watch the image
skid. Who feeds on death never dies! This is the godless way!
Don't spare the dish called Nineveh! Where sixty thousand fuck
and bray! Where fatty wisdoms squid! Where gawkish boys spit and
squeal! Where heads imbibe their lack of dream! Where none can
touch what they feel! Perish! Perish! Inculcate! Thunder!
Perish! Vanish! I'm Wrong! But So Are They! I pass out
in the heat and when I wake, the hut, the stones, my
droppings of blood. All gone. Only the gourd, draped
in heat. Nineveh cannot be seen. No buzz of voices
ever forming, no red buildings along the plate of sky.
I run their way, spraying sand before me. It all has vanished.
No bricks, no fruit, no brass, no grain, no trace of any past,
no piece of any gown or robe, no rope, no smoke or smell of oil.
Just sand, unchanging sand and heat. I run and run to where they
were and start to dig. Nothing below or above. I lose two fingers
in the digging. They snap like dead thin twigs. The wind skirts
sand about them. I have to live with this? I plunge my hands
to the wrist. The sand fills in above them. The demolition
of so much? It cups my ears. My head goes back. The buzz
begins. And in my throat, the deathcry of a race—
punctured, swift, unclear—the voice vanishes
the features from my face

# XXIV. THE PUNISHMENT OF HAMAN

Legend has Esther living at the time of Ahasuerus, the King of Persia, who reigns over an enormous empire which includes 127 provinces from India to Ethiopia, and who, by willful submission, is the mediating force over the princes of Persia and Media. As a precedent to discourage disobedience, he dethrones and imprisons his exceptionally beautiful Queen, Vashti, and then assembles a pool of virgins, from which to choose his next Queen. Esther, who was raised by her uncle Mordecai, is taken into the pool, from which she is eventually chosen Queen. In the meantime, Haman, a ruthless minister to Ahasuerus, is promoted by the eccentric King to "a seat above all the princes who are with him." Haman quickly uses his power to initiate the annihilation of the Jews, and Esther, concealing that she is a Jew, sets out along a path of manipulation and self-denial to save her race. As she tries to establish a truth that will save lives, she is forced to embroider and equivocate a net of illusion. Her uncle Mordecai is struck, early on, by a vision which consumes him and, unlike Isaiah or Ezekiel or Michelangelo, he is not strong enough to recover. She is left completely alone, a Jew and a woman, void of any recognizable power, forced to violate her own sense of ethics in order to participate in a larger preservation. At the same time the Ceiling grows weighty and tedious as Michelangelo, pressured by Julius, is forced to mitigate his sweeping vision, yet again, in order to bring the job to a close.

*Esther describes the climate after Vashti's dethronement, from her own con-
finement, as one of the virgins being purified for the King. She cannot shake
the image of her aging uncle Mordecai rubbing his chest as they took her
away, and cannot stop hearing the dethroned Queen play her flute from her
cell in the night.*

ESTHER: It is an ugly time, despite the riches
and the extent of the empire. There is talk Ahasuerus
is going senile, losing grip, sharp one minute,
his sense distending the next, and lives fall through.
He snaps his fingers and lives go out.

Since Vashti's been imprisoned,
he's been less visible, less clear of who he is.
One of the youngest was declared purified
and brought to him last week. She is fourteen
and large-boned with lanky shoulders and broad
full lips. Her name is Amadelia and she was,
of course, afraid. We said, don't hesitate.
Ask him to be gentle. He is a King. Act
like a Queen. She came back bewildered,
"He thought I was his daughter. We sat
and talked of Vashti and how he's missed me
all these years. He combed my hair all afternoon,
asked to see my breasts, but wouldn't touch.
Just sighed and kissed me on the neck."

Ahasuerus doesn't have a daughter.
You see the state we're in?

I am a clever woman, not in a social sense,
but I've a way of seizing situations;
as if once things are falling,
I can see how, which way, how long,
and then the falling slows
and I can always intercept,
repair or hold. Since men
fall more than any other species,
I am adept at seizing men.

It is a hard time to be a woman.
There are 43 of us in the hall.
We're in the custody of Hegai
who's like an old and crusty coach.
He keeps us oiled and docile
and makes the King seem like a prize.
Mornings, there are always baths
and we graze like naked fawns
through fragrant clouds of steam.
There are times we feel so fresh
and vulnerable, we'll huddle,
till one will hold another in the steam
and a mouth will slip over a moist firm breast
and a soft moan will crack the steam.
Hegai will shout, "Ladies! Please. Please!
You'll make me die of fantasy." And then,
giggles from the tubs. It's sad but safe.
Most of the help are eunuchs. And no, but no one
is allowed to touch. My first week in,
a guard was found fingering Elena, and Hegai
cut his dick off on the spot.

I don't know how they chose me at all.
Now we sleep with sweet odors
and locks of hyacinth banded with copper,
all these rituals to make us sirens and sexually free.

I don't know how to let him touch me.
Today, it was Elena and I've been playing
in the tub all morning; afraid for her,
afraid for me. Even Hegai is somewhat somber.
The door bolts open, and Elena, looking shocked
and tired, shuffles in. She shakes her head,
"He's gentle when he's focused and squirms
when he thinks he's sinking or at sea.
He loved my hips and spoke to me of Asia

as his weathered tree of figs. And then
he thought I was a river, and he
was being thrust under. He hit me,
slipped off, and went to the window,
panting, frightened, asking me to leave."

We put creams along Elena's bruise
and hear Vashti play that night.
The next day Hegai calls me aside,
"How is Elena?" I shrug. He says,
"You're next." I close my eyes,
feel my perfect ribs shake
beneath my perfect breasts.

The door opens, north light cooling out the room.
He is staring through some ancient private place.
I say, "Your Highness wishes time with me."
He is jarred and spins, "Yes. Yes. Come here. You are—"
"Esther." But I don't move. He stalks up close
and sniffs my hair, "I love hyacinth on a woman's breast."
He starts to nibble. I gently stiffen, "Are you
looking for a glove to warm your little finger
or searching for a Queen?" He cocks his head,
"I'm not sure." He laughs and seems to enter
another personality. We begin to talk. He says,
"You have possibilities." I say, "And so do you."
He is confused, but slow and slower, he begins to fall,
and I can see just where and when, and hold him
as he reaches ground. He says, "It's hard to be
so public and alone." I say, "It's hard to be
kept naked in a bath." He doesn't know what to do
with me. Perplexed, he's warmer, off-center,
a gentler sort. Now he kisses with his tongue.
And I wonder at the secrets passing to my mouth.
I run my hands through his hair, think of Mordecai's
silvered chest, and now he crawls into me.
My head is swimming with a hundred different scents,

but my heart's a string. He is, I guess, skillful,
and painful in his reach, and every time we rise and fall
I hear Vashti's dark-blue flute. And when he comes,
he groans as if dying. He scares me. I take his head.
He calms and falls asleep. Later, I dress.
He watches as I tie my strings. And as I think,
why is it men love to rehearse their dying
inside women of all things, he, standing naked,
taps his sceptre, hard and often,
and proclaims me as his Queen.

*Michelangelo grows impatient with the lumbering Ceiling, which drags on.*
*He feels more and more removed from its fire as he approaches the end, and*
*conjures a series of chaotic figures to surround Esther, as he vacillates in his*
*reflections of what is and what could be.*

MICHELANGELO:
You ask about the people. An unfortunate group.
Of watchers, lookers, hangers on. They only think
of space when it's invaded. Reactive. You bump.
They inflate. Like porcupine or blowfish.
They pick their teeth a lot and wait for events
to roll in on them like fog. For weeks in January,
before the Tomb was cancelled, I went day by day,
and finally, the marble on the barge. It barely
broke the surface, water slopping in loose plates
across the deck against the blocks. It bobbed in slow
shifting rhythm, first this way, then that. The blocks
piled four high, six deep, roped loosely, with workmen
striding the top, stopping to brace a rolling pitch,
then crossing, checking the water's edge. They were
just ahead of thunderclouds in the north. As they
glided in, it started to rain. And then the barge
slammed the dock with an enormous crack. Rainslick arms
strained to hold. Their muscles had a glareless sheen.
The thick ropes stretched. The barge began to sink.
There were other workers passing by, but no one offered,

and some made hoods of their robes and watched. These Romans
are never where they are. They think everything's an event.
I grabbed one boy and threw him toward the struggle.
He looked, not knowing what to do. I yelled, "Help Them!
Hold! Pull! Pull!" In Florence you don't have to ask.
When a bundle slips, someone's there. When some errant wave
enters from beyond to make one stop and speak,
Florentines collect and form a shore.

In Rome they start the other way, pretend not to hear,
look down or scratch their knees and leave. In Rome
there's no conclusion to a squall. In Florence
the soul's a crucible, and even lost in dream,
true Florentines look out as the sandy lids shut,
and it gives the face that special trace of yearning,
that simple fuse of fighting sleep, like a handshake,
a language that takes using it to learn.

In Rome they watch things sink along the river
and think; if I knew them, I'd watch more closely.
They worked the day into night unloading the marble
as the rain muddied the river. It gave off that odd
low smell that wetness gives to stone. Then the edge
of dock was covered, and all at once, the river overflowed.
The workmen scattered. The barge edged its way on land.
The river rose above the marble. The figures locked within
were drowning. It took weeks to get to them.
I had to scrub algae from their veins.

*Esther is informed by Hatach that Mordecai is frantic at the King's Gate in
protest of Haman's decree, which Mordecai has sent her, a decree approved
by Ahasuerus to slaughter the Jews.*

ESTHER: He means to wipe us from the earth.
And then our stories. He means to crush our bones
to powder, to scatter all the powder, to rake the ashes
so the meadows will stay seeded for his children's goats

humming tunes to save the words
and the hum has the feel
of what we suffered
a thousand years ago.

And how will he rid the air
of our laughter?

What makes him want to do this? He must be killed.
Why did Ahasuerus sign? Do they know I'm a Jew?
He must be killed. As soon as someone has the nerve.
I can't think this fast. I'm falling without falling.
And Mordecai is at the Gate. He's made himself a target.
I must soothe Ahasuerus. Oh Mordecai should run! This is
the code of terror. Shiny as a needle. How did I come
to think of killing? Blood sirens to the brain.
Because I'm forced to think of being killed?
I want back! Go back to the beginning.
It's just a paper scratched with words.
But Mordecai is out there Wailing!
They'll hang him first. Dear God!
Slow Down! Hatach! Where Is he? Hatach!
Which Gate? Be Quick! Where's Haman?
Where's the King? Show this to no one.
Tell Mordecai I'll meet him. In the niche
north of where he is.

*Michelangelo is busy making Haman thick and impenetrable when he is
interrupted by Julius, who agitates him into a state of hallucination and yet
another panicked flight.*

MICHELANGELO:
When God speaks He speaks in winds. When the mind
is winded, it is capable of genius. And Everything
is an Intrusion. Food. Night. The need to bathe.
Julius has a knack for coming as I'm winded.
It's maddening. Like rowing through light

to a dock of pearls and as you're gliding in,
about to land, someone dives and their wake
drives you out, out, back away. "Buonarroti!"
He is coming. His vestments shuffle and drag the floor.
"Buonarroti!" He waves off the spying Cardinal, then peers
through the scaffold, "Where are you? Speak Up!" He's over
60, rugged, impatient and loud. I have to stop stroking
Haman, and now his chest will be uneven. A skin will
form while we talk, that is, I'll listen. He climbs
the scaffold, pumping his robes, all ribbed with dust.
He reaches, two braces at a time, grips hard and grunts.
This is how I love him, lifting himself higher,
grunting to ascend. Now here's a look of exhaustion.
I reach. He clasps. I bring him on the mount.
"Well, well, well . . . I like this. Who is it?" "Haman."
"How come his stomach's a different color than his chest?"
I drop the brush and wipe the colors on my shirt,
"I need more blue and three more brushes. And the boy
you sent is twice as dumb as the last." He laughs,
looks down, and fights the urge to sink. He squints
along the slice of vault—the prophets rant, the sibyls
hunch, the frames of Creation dart and stream.
"Extraordinary. How much longer?" I sigh, "When I am able."
He brushes past to where I'm working.
I let no one in that space. I step him back,
"Excuse me." The scaffold creaks. He is offended.
Here we go. "I just want to see how much farther?"
"Some days are fast. Some days are slow."
"Who is this now?" He's back in my space.
"Haman!" He picks a stick I use for long reaches,
taps it in his hand, "I'm anxious to show this.
What's left?" I step him back, "A lot!"
He snaps the crossbeam with the stick,
"Don't be short with me! I'm here!
I'm showing interest!" I nod to him.
He thinks I'm joking. The next few minutes

are wired and awkward. It grows impossible.
He's in the way. "I don't understand
why Haman's taking so long." I think twice,
but tell him I am tired. "Tired?! I'm Old!
You said not much longer!" "I need 500 florins."
"For what?" "I need to go to Florence."
"For what?" "It's been months since I've been home."
He spins and raps the outer brace, "No!
Not until you Finish!" I look to God parting the planets,
"Then stay away from me! You only slow me down!"
"All right! How long?" "Until I am Finished!"
"Don't toy with me!" "Don't tie me down!"
"I Want This Done!" He raps the stick
against the Ceiling scratching Jeremiah's
knee. I rush the shaky tower. He screams,
"When I Am Able! Able!" and whacks me in the head.
It stings. I fume down the scaffold, hawking my arms.
"Come back here! Buonarroti! Come Back Here!!"
He throws the stick. I hug the scaffold.
It careens the braces—and halfway—breaks.
My scalp peels, warm and wet. With four feet left,
I jump. My heels jar my knees. I turn and pray
he won't damage what I've done. Then boil toward Raffaello
and Bramante who have listened all the while. I throw my arms
and stalk between them, "DAMN YOU BOTH!" I run halfway home,
the fear and anger mixing, coiling tighter, chest to throat
to head. This time he'll try to kill me. I pace my rooms,
unsure if I should run. Afraid to work, I huddle in the west
where the light cones down at dusk, a circle rimming smaller,
cutting off my knees. I hunch, afraid, the cone of light
constricting to a spot, a slash across my chest. I'm dark
and cool! And pounding! God! Save me from his love!
The room dizzies like a patch of Hell about to burst
in flame. My head behind the eyes twists. Twists in!
I'm losing sense! The pain is clear. The center of blood
sloshing to eat the stars. And now, not now, the air smells

of Tyrants! Whose Hearts are Strops! We're Herded in a River!
Up to Our Nostrils! In Boiling Blood! I Don't Belong! Dante!
Come And Free Me! The Jets of Blood Wash Dark Creases
From my Brain! And someone's shooting Arrows! At the Tyrants
who are Curdling! Smithied rods of Iron! Plunking in their
throats like trees! Plunking in their throats like trees!
Plunking. In between the sheets. Pounding. Coming from
the streets. Pounding. Shuffling of feet. Pounding.
Pound. The darkened door begins to creak. I am sweating.
A twitching figure enters, streaked with light, wheezing
with a chirp. It's Accursio, the Pope's hunched messenger.
He's says, "You're sweating." He dumps 500 florins.
They vaguely glitter in the dark. "He begs your
forgiveness. He wants the damn thing finished."
He waits. I say nothing. The light streams in
behind him. My breathing pushes it back. He drags
one foot as he leaves. I count the money and ride
to Florence, ride the horse like a prayer back to birth.
The clough clough of the rhythm in the dirt. I can't escape
the way he breaks me, the horse's staggered exhalation,
the gold coin chinking in my shirt. I'm riding, riding,
going nowhere, head puffing through the old confusions,
eating my sight into Florence, soaking through
a life of lies. I never asked to paint and now
he beats me. I feel the scab form in my scalp.
More than a year at Carrara. And all the marble
Lost. Stolen at Ripa. Nothing. Nothing finds its home.
And what is there in Florence? The trees of blue flap by.
If I were blind, it would be cooler. The money bunches
at my waist. Last time, he made me crawl to Bologna,
made me cast him like a Stud! In Bronze! O let me ride
until I melt in anger! Let him rot wailing at the Ceiling!
Let the scaffold snap and bring him down! I don't want
his goddamn money! I toss it in the woods. The pouch
drops flat. Off a branch. Clough. Clough. To the rhythm
of the dirt. Clough. I simmer. Clough. Clough. I tug the

reins. And trot. Trot back. Dismount. The horse nods
his snout in shame. I comb the brush for the pouch.
By dawn, the horse is lapping at the Arno
as I test ducats with my teeth.

*Esther is running through the Palace Colonnade to meet Mordecai at the
Gate where he has had a burning premonition erupt into the future, and there
he is seared by glimpses of the Holocaust, which he interprets as the present
fate of his people.*

ESTHER:
It's so hard to run in slippers.
The pillars and shade flip white
blue      white      forcing me      to think
in slashes. I pray he's not arrested.
They wouldn't kill him at the Gate.
I have to stop. The air is hurting.
Its dagger in my rib. I lean against a pillar.
I must maintain. It can't unwind with so much shrift.
It can't—God's awe, sweet as ancient wind rushing
through devoted minds, God's law, through skulls
like caves, God's touch, through hearts like heat
through coal—Mordecai might be dead this instant.
Should I deny I am a Jew? Who else knows?
Perhaps Elena, but she would never tell.
Must keep my mind. The pillar's cracked.
The crack is cool, even in the midst
of all this heat. Look at how the light
can't find the crack. It's like a vein of
emptiness right through the heart of white.

No matter how much falls to fire,
no matter who goes down or how,
I must keep the thread of emptiness.
Must be the crack. Don't get excited.
Inhale. Feel the cold air slither through.
I must not think of what could happen.
The crack will close and I will buckle—

What's that sound? A branch?
A guard? Hatach? Oh Mordecai!
I must make it to the Gate.

The air. The air is full of daggers.
I can't run. Not yet. Oh Mordecai!
It falls together. For it was here,
inside this garden, you heard Yusef
plot to drown the King, to hold him under
in his tub—Oh Hear! Hear. Someone's coming.
It's just a bird. In the brush. Just a bird.
A bird. Now I understand, when you were sent
to Haman, why he was not astonished. And last
summer, just before that frost, the one to kill
the baby goats in Persia, Yusef was made captain,
doing errands for the King. And Ahasuerus
turned ugly in the evenings and sulked his way
to paint old vases, talking endlessly about
goldleaf, "It's so easy to apply when wet—
it breathes so well, but the pores
close shut when dry—Oh No. Yes.
Well, if you were to paint a woman's body
head to toe—As it would dry, she'd suffocate,
asphyxiate thinly into gold."

This is how it went, my early days as Queen.
I came in once. He was discussing deeds to farms
and I said, "Family rights should supercede."
He dismissed Carshena and Meres and took me by the hair,
"The Queen will Never Enter unless Adored." And now
it's worse. There is a law—Oh Mordecai! Nothing is simple.
Cool as a crack of emptiness. Freeze up the faith
and paint it dark. To puncture power, to suture heat,
faith must be a pin of ice.

And now it comes together, how in the fall,
just when the birds fly off to China, the way they do,
with no apparent treason, so we can hear another song,

how in the fall, I heard Haman with Ahasuerus offer up
"The hands of a race—" I couldn't hear the rest.
It made no sense till now.

Mordecai rocks at the Gate in ashes, protesting, praying,
while methodic soldiers build gallows out of cypress.
I find him, eyes riveted shut, mouth fallen open, hands
on his head, neck and shoulders sweating, the sackcloth
soaked beneath his arms, his silvered chest rhythmic
and heaving "Oh Mordecai." He moans my name, "Esther!
You can't imagine! I saw women driven through the streets
with leather whips! Kicked and forced to strip their dead!
And—coming the other way—old carts, all drawn by horses—
legs and arms stiffened out the sideboards! And Old Jews—
naked, on their knees—gathering dirt with their beards—
their backs sliced! And sages undressing babies! Mothers
piling their clothes! All made to dig rough steps
in the clay wall of a pit! And in the pit! An old woman
with white hair—her throat cut—rocking an infant!
And twenty broken men! Bleeding! Heaped with shovels!
On Top of her! Blood soaking their shoulders!
Still moving! Squirming! And the baby's skull—
crushed—the clay moist with its brain!
And everything grew hot and stuffy!
And suddenly, I fell into the pit!
Blood squirting from my head! I was
Choking! Burning! Bodies were writhing!
Climbing the Naked Mountain! Moaning! Seeping!
Dying! But Not Dead! And the Children were Muffled!
Screeching! I was covered with blood! The bodies
were shifting! And someone was biting my leg!
And we were pelted with rocks! Buried! And some of us
were set Aflame! And I thought I saw Haman
sorting through us! Pulling teeth
and cutting women's hair! He was
prying the Dead Apart! O Esther!
I've told Everyone! To make their way to China!

To Flee! To Shoo their Children to the Mountains!
O Esther! It is Haman! He wants to burn God
in our Pasture! O Esther! Esther!
You're a Jew! And You're the Queen!"

He is alive before me, but burns somewhere else,
completely broken in perception. He is a pile
of scattered organs. There's no reason
not to believe him. One look at his condition.
One look at how he breathes, his molecules of
conscience popping, dissolving, oozing through.
No one would invite it. No one could pretend.
He can't shut his eyes enough. His life, as
I have known it, his kind patience for false
stories, his accumulated silence—his sense
has been used up, a fist of reeds ignited
to illuminate a race. He's a blasted bag
of ascension, hot shifting rubble, trapped
within a man. My Mordecai is made of pebbles,
his eyes, the eyes that chose to be my father,
the crystal eyes are shattered. Oh Mordecai—

I take his head between my breasts, so fevered,
my chest begins to sweat. Can this man butcher
an entire race? He must be killed. I am the Queen.
But the King has a cracked bill. Everywhere he sputters.
Everything he drinks slips through. He's sane enough
to be sick with precision, sick enough to twist ripe
stalks. He loves to bind his hyacinths. God put me here
for a reason. Loves to hear them snap. God showed me where
the pillar's cracked. I need to find my emptiness,
to defuse an empty King. I have to calm my Mordecai.
Have to set a trap for Haman. Have to thread
the strings of God to pull true gestures
from my husband. Have to weep, before
I'm torn, for Mordecai, all burnt and used.
Have to weep, in a hundred caves, for I've

no one left to love me. Have to coolly tend him
here, with terse exact instruction. Have to be
a pin of ice, to bury all my inborn ire,
so it can pump our children's lives
as they hone the past and oil their tools.
They won't realize how much blood it cost.

*The Ceiling is becoming a chore and Michelangelo, feeling raw and irascible,
roughly puts Mordecai in a doorway before the scenes of accusation. It trig-
gers Buonarroti to envision the damned sinking past the saved at the Last
Judgment. And as he pins Mordecai with a tender rose belt, he confesses to
the only sight he's had like it, another night of vision at Carrara, where he
saw a vague distorted race of gaunt and flowing forms, less finished in their
cries.*

MICHELANGELO:
The wind dragged light through the pit at dusk,
sweeping unrevealable life about the blocks,
rattling pulleys and boards. I watched a rope
loosened by wind slap a mammoth stone. I waited
for the figures to rise where I could see them
in those unearthly moments that bond me to night.
The wind picked up, began to bite, more grey than blue,
and the stone was just eating up the air. I walked
the edge, my hands patting the uncut marble, and I felt
buried in the open, evacuated by the sheer dull cage
of the quarry. The wind was raveled vagrant air
whipping up the walls. Nothing was speaking.
And that Nothing was flooding me. I began to cough
and felt punished by the lack of light. It occurred
to me, in the collapse of that moment: what difference
what shape the stone—unearthed, reformed, worn down,
unearthed again by sculptors yet unborn? My hands
began to quake. My purpose shrank. I grew dizzy
with insignificance. And then I heard the creaking,
way up, as if a column were being lifted like a marble rib
from the mountain. There was the shuffle of workmen's feet,

but there was no one in the yard, and Nothing in the air.
The timber cracked, the pulleys squeaked, the carts
grated in their roll, yet Nothing moved.
The wind gusted up and the unseen column tightened
with the strain of rope about to snap. So real, so
stretched, I hid and ducked. I ran from cart to stone.
I thought I heard a calling out. It was wind through
boards and up the blocks. And then the column Swayed!
But where?! There was Nothing overhead!
The wind galed. I heard the pulleys crack. A squall
filled the pit. Ropes began to snap. The column crashed.
I scurried like a rat and fell, stone-dust in my face and
lungs. And through the dust and bales of wind,
I thought I saw a body struggle from the stone:
arms busting out the choppy block; another on its
back, immersed in marbled wave, a knee breaking
through, a belly, a rising chest, no more. And hands,
a tribe of hands, breaching their element like me,
and I was frightened they would hold me in the stone.
And as the squall cleared, there was a random buzz
of moans, a rise and fall, an interstice of gasps
and groans, slow exclamations, deep nerves
being burned. And then the amber seared the haze,
the dusk was full, all clear and blue. The boards
were still, the ropes all slack, the groans building
and breaking, the wind all stopped, as if it crossed
into the marble, becoming this wind of moans, and as
the cries surfaced, the amber of a hundred bodies pulsed
and glowed; floating in all directions; urgent, raptured,
rising, drifting, halting, stalling like garbled angels
impossible to decode. And the amber was painful, not just
to the eyes, but deeper, like a pang, like a ripple
of wisdom felt too late to be of use. It burned me
with the nauseous unrelenting fact that I would ever
appreciate, but never build. Things were raw—the forms
writhing like a sea of pagan saints—all too raw—

and I was stripped of any sense that I could bear
these faults. And now I was plagued, unable to stop
the amber hands, the tribe of hands, my eager hands,
my weakened hands. I thought, how small these paws,
how quickly they tire, how little time is granted them.
And the writhing and groaning grew oppressive. I shut
my ears. The amber burned. I shut my eyes. The groans
were piercing. I pressed against the mountain which went
sheer and there were naked lives being lifted and guided
by shades: a woman untaxed, as if cut off, no muscles
tensed, arms flowing off dead shoulders, her head
washed back, red hood about her eyes, toes dangling
in her wake. She drifted out and up, her lips
wavering in the current, as if sheer movement
through her flagging mouth were causing her to
groan. And closer to the surface, upside down, a man,
being dragged to the peak, gripped behind his knees,
his flaccid calves pinched, his stomach crowding his ribs,
arms covering his face. And next to him, an eyeless head,
staring off, its body limp and bound about the waist by hemp.
Above them both, a pair, hoisted in a net of bloodied pearls,
their knuckles white. And floating down, a dullard,
stepping out in space, fat toes about to land.
And losing fast, a runner in grim stride, his
nipples hard, his weight on one pulsed leg,
the veins all tough. And by herself—hotly
in tow—her one leg raised, her palms about
to take the glow that healed her face, the amber
down her satin neck, between her sweetened breasts,
her ankles noosed in a shroud that kept her rising
rising past bones and tattered robes. And then,
they all began to harden, though something in each
kept climbing, as they shed their amber skins. They
left their useless bodies and the shimmer surged
from thirst to thirst. I felt the heat. It all
dispersed: the resonating knees, the gristly

moans, the lift of hooded eyes, the eyes
breaking into ancient sight, the surge
of bloodless light. Then, nothing.
But my mouth against the stone,
chilled, chilling. My cold arms
spread. I coughed and slid the wall,
knowing God and only God can thaw
the soul's resistance to be found.

*Before setting her plans in motion, Esther makes a long-awaited visit to the*
*imprisoned Vashti, who's become a legend: loved by the people, feared by*
*the Princes. She has two servants, and a modest view, by which she writes*
*and plays her flute, mostly in the thick of night before dawn filters through*
*her chamber.*

ESTHER: She holds her flute with an incidental grip
    in the cradle of her lap and I can feel the sadness
    slip and glove her between these walls like the secret
    air between a falcon and its hood. She is a hunter
    who's been hunted. But it's clear by the nature
    of her weapons—flute and sorrow and books
    beneath a bowl of flowers from her garden—
    she hunts the color of a feeling long
    and thin as time. She hunts the casement
    of solitude. The gardener sends her stalks
    from what she planted. Perhaps she feels
    the weightless thought of God's experiments
    with spring. She rolls her flute in her lap
    as I enter. Her way, her room, her cell, her
    living Tomb is folded, beaten, gently—like the white
    around a yolk—into a sadness; leaking as light drips back
    on light, no place to go, an incandescence in her reach.
    I love her skin softened by the hunt. Nothing can approach
    without her knowing. She takes my hands and pulls my sight,
    first one eye, then the other, then both, then shuts
    right down, and I feel I am holding some rare
    and pressured shell that only opens, spreads itself,

briefly, once each day. She asks me to wash her hair
and we spend some time untying and letting it fall.
Her scalp is soft and lathers well. We rinse,
laddling clearness from a pan. And I think,
this is how ideas were meant to form, by the ladle,
soaking through. She tips her head into the towel
as if it were a fragile bowl. She thanks me.

I take her hand, lean close, and whisper,
"I will free you if I can." She smiles
and rubs her hair quite slow. "I will
find a way." She stops and sighs, pats
her face, stares off, and says, "The moon
is free to roam the night, but you know
what it really wants? It wants to roam
the day—no, more—it wants to light things
by itself." I tell her how I've heard her flute,
how it helped us through the night. She picks it up
and holds it like a babe, then gets involved
with a line of grain that might have cracked.
Her fingers rub it several times, "It hasn't gone,
but at some point, will. I used to get upset,
but now, it's just another opening to play."
She shrugs, then focuses on me, "You're gentler
than I thought. Less tension round the eyes.
It isn't easy, is it? No. You must never
underestimate his capacity to forget.
It's out of that his cruelty springs."
She is full of bursts of deep sensation
that veer off just before they burst.

I sense that we were sisters, undersides
of one reflection in some vast inhuman stream,
"O Vashti, he means to kill us all." She stops,
then saddens, "He's capable of that. Only when he
forgets. You must remind him. Make him remember."

She resists the next, "I could tell you things
that would stop him, make him stall into his center.
And only then, then might you have a chance."
Her hair is drying from the ends back to the roots
and she is suddenly quite lovely. "You must take
what I will tell you and imply it indirectly.
If he knows you have been here, he will kill us both.
Believe me. You must take the smallest detail
and wedge it in a tiny crack along his thinking.
He will work it deeper and deeper and split
into remembering. And there, he won't be
so thorough or so quick to make decisions."

She stares off, bothered, her flute
rolling in her lap, "There were times
we'd go swimming in Persia, and the waves
kept spreading from our diving, dark rings
across the bottom, and we saw a giant manta
slip from the shallows, loose sand shaken off
its dark flaps, curling as it glided through
a hidden mouth. It was a wondrous thing.
We tread the water slowly till he reached
my floating body. You must remember,
this was the man I married." Her eyes
are swimming in Persia, but her mouth
keeps on glowing. She is straining.

"You must be subtle, for these are raw things
which will come flooding, all or nothing,
and his face will shatter to another face
I wish I could be there to see." She closes
her eyes. "And there were times we'd wake
to watch the heatstorms crack and pop
across the pre-dawn plains. We'd stand groggy
on the verandah, leaning naked toward each other's fog;
watching the arcs zag out so whitely, till small fires
like sulphur tried to slake the blue. And there was
something strangely beautiful about the elemental

tongue of light arcing from the sky. His face
took on a spiral backward glow in the seconds
after thunder. We took to making love in storms,
to coming when the lightning cracked.
You must not bring this up directly.
But use these things to soothe him.
Use them as small calming mirrors.
They'll slow his grip about the dagger,
make him briefly see the blood as blood,
make him feel alone and sensible."

She is quite drained, but keeps on going,
asks about the other women, of Elena and Amadelia.
I drop her hands, "I wanted all along to free them.
I hadn't forgotten. But I knew he wouldn't listen.
After Mordecai's vision, I pushed him to release them.
He stared at me with no expression. I prodded firmly,
'They all have families. They'll be so glad to get them,
they'll think you a hero, and forget you ever took them.
You can always have Hegai round them up again.' He tightened,
'If one should curse me to her father, or say how I groaned
in bed, I'll have them all beheaded and make you watch
and stack the heads.' I went to say goodbye, to tell them
they were free. It was oddly sad, like prisoners of war
who after years resent the peace which robs them
of their friends. Amadelia said, 'We'd given up.'
I was ashamed, 'I couldn't make it sooner.'
We huddled close, each milky and steamy
in an obsolete way. And they were frightened.
It would be hard to love without grease,
to live without oils, to wear so many clothes,
and hard to bathe without eunuchs sponging them to sleep.
I said, 'Don't go home, but flee. Go where no one knows you.
And change your name. Bring your families. Tell your cousins.
And you, Amadelia, especially you, for a savage cloud
will strangle the Jews. Go. Teach your children

to be beautiful, by choice. And never bathe
in myrrh again.' No one budged, and finally Elena
spoke for the rest, 'And what of you?' I saw Mordecai
rocking at the Gate, thought to go with them, but said,
'I'll find a crack and slip through.' "

She smiles at that, then sours,
"Does he love you?"
"No. Twice he's called me Vashti,
both while deep inside—"

It's awkward now. She seems protective.
I try to shake her loose, "The one who put you here
is not the one who calls your name. You understand?
He's seldom here, but when he is, it's always you."
She stands to uncramp her heart. The knot enlarges,
blocking her throat. I take her shoulders,
"You must see what is and not what was."
She inhales and tries to clear herself,
"I understand who put me here."
"But you think your old lover will set you free."
She starts to cry. I bring it home. I have no choice,
"You think he'll change." She stares at me.
I take her face, "Listen to me. He's signed over
the destruction of an entire race." She turns away.
I pull her back, "You must help.
He's not the one you started with.
That one is dead."
She's losing strength.
"You must tell me why he put you here."
She hesitates.
"I need to know."
She's skeptical.
"So I can avoid it."

She goes deep behind my eyes
and thinks she can trust me.

"He will recognize the slightest detail.
You must be methodical, whatever you do,
to the point that you imagine and predict
his every move." It's so crucial, it is hard
to pay attention. I keep thinking of the planning,
of the timing, of the importance—now I've missed
the crux. She's already moving on—"never agreed
on what was uppermost to me. I always felt
the nation was the people. He loved to quote
and thread the law. It was his obligation
to a system, to the pure idea of order.
I believed in simply reaching. He
believed in jurisdictions. He'd sew
parameters. I'd take a hand.
There was someone we were close to.
He was—well—" This stifles her momentum.
She's closer now to how I found her, settled,
half-closing, half-closed, deeply troubled,
deeply pure. She's calm again. She rolls her flute
along her thighs, "It doesn't matter how. The thing
you have to know is never make him choose
between the human and the law. Never say
the life comes before its notion. Never
let him see you don't need his order.
Remember. He lives by mirrors. The law
is what he'd like to be. Lawless is what he is.
Use the one for your protection, but give him
what he thinks."

I'm spinning with all these complications,
what to thread, what to clip, where to speak
or simply move, how long to wait, then
what to give. Cool and dark must stay the method.
Stay down. Stay down. I feel it rise. She seems
relieved and is watching. I reel and pump and slouch
and slide. With care she takes my arm and rubs it,
"Would you like to be here, instead?" I watch her fingers

rub and warm me, envy her her rooms. So much to do.
Where is the crack, "I'm not sure. I'm scared."

We clutch. She pulls me to her
and I feel the soft mirror of our merging breasts.
We hold, deep issue to deep issue, and I leave
with the scent of Vashti on my nipple,
to keep Ahasuerus from burning the dead.

*In 1505, in Moreno outside of Venice, the first mirror with mercury backing
was constructed. It was the first mirror without distortion. And Michelan-
gelo, rubbing more color into Esther's mouth, is still intoxicated with its
uncanny clarity. He's about to explain his enthusiasm when Pico appears,
skeptical, as a grey diffusive cloud, just where Michelangelo intends to speak.*

PICO: The concept is unstoppable,
    since man bent over water, no doubt the way
    water, once created, bent over God.
    And so reflection passed into being.
    But it's no substitute for seeing.
    God rubbed water, water man, man rubs brass,
    rubs chrome, rubs silver, and he thinks
    he's hard fire in the way he moves.

MICHELANGELO:
    I tell you, few ideas have crossed over
    so completely. It is what it set out to be.
    You look out and you're in!

    Think of it. A true reflection. No bevels.
    No waves. No shrinking. No bronze elongation
    or silvered loss of focus.

    This small thin piece of glass
    opens like a throat of vision
    to an always imaged world.
    On its edge, a silver hair. Back again,
    we see ourselves, not through reverie

or sensation, but as we are
without the other soft distractions.
Not with inflated complications
of dead partners who could soothe us,
but as the heart pumps clearly,
rising in the glass. As we are.
A new contrition. A way of living.
A fascination for proportion. Though man
is water, he's not all water. Though he
believes, he's not all belief. As we are.
As we're reflected.

PICO:

I don't like it. It's too neat. Cramped.
As you look, you hardly get halfway
and its bumping back at you. There's something
natural about distraction, getting more
than you bargained for. To look at you
and see—only you? Oh it's bound
to be arresting, but compelling?
And if what I see is all I am—Well,
what of God framing each chance?
What of all those lusters
just sweetened by that wind?

MICHELANGELO:

It's all because of mercury.
It turns glass into pure image.
Astonishing but simple. I don't know
why someone didn't see it sooner.
But that's the way. A thousand lives
step on a treasure and once flattened,
a sad brilliant thing, moping, picks it up.
And we're intact once more. Discover.
Dis-cover the cover. Bring it up
to where it was before.

That a fluid stubborn element
should like a fog cloud up transparence
and reflect what can't get through—
it's such a human thing:
how we see ancient faces
in the stumps of trees,
how she hears devotion
in his animalistic moan,
how a child can dream of God
as a breast of voice with wings!

But to bind the transparence,
to form it as a sheet of glass,
to heat the mercury till it spills
pastelike on an iron dish,
to spread it and cool it
till the image can't get through—
it's as brilliant as stacking wooden slats
to tunnel wind, or dis-covering that charge
when bodies, like slats, lie close
till Love is tunnelled through their spin.

PICO:
It will be a seed of separation.
It will make us feel
we're looking through
while staying put.

It will peel us
from our perception.

It will lead, I think,
to looking at one's pimples
as inner imperfections.
How many will wake and get lost,
see their image as the morning,
and not the sun rapping through the trees?

It has to lead to vanity, that starving occupation
of imagining our selves as food. Narcissus
is hardly to be pitied.

*Weeks pass, and Esther, unsure if anyone realizes she is a Jew, proceeds, trying
to lead both men to kill each other. She tries to pry Haman from his wife,
Zeresh, in an effort to make the King jealous. And Haman gives her a skein
of blue silk, no more. Here she recounts the endless calculations she tried to
set in motion. Nothing is clear or sure.*

ESTHER:
Both Haman and Ahasuerus saw themselves in everything.
The task was to braid a path between them,
working the mirrors they had in common
to get them to the threshold,
steaming the slivers each would use
to cut the other's throat.
I filled a vase with sand and spilled it.
He fingered grains into the linen.
I said, "I'm sorry. What's the matter?"
He said, "Nothing" and grew sullen.
Then I asked about Yusef.
He said, "Why? What about him?"
"Well, he seems to be lurking
and my maid heard him—
be suggestive."
"To your maid?"
"That would be another matter."
"Then to you?"
"About me."
"Well, I'll see to him tomorrow."
"Oh, I'm sure it's probably nothing. But it's odd."
"What's odd?"
"He mentioned Haman."
"How so?"
"He said Haman would know how to treat a Queen."
At this, his wheels were heating.

He was regaining his precision.
But I had lodged a bur. Enough
and the itch would make him save me.

There were reflected complications, timings to be polished,
inflections to be braided. It was taxing and relentless.
I'd go over conversations, single out the gestures,
interpret just how much was meant, was said
or taken in. It wasn't clear if I knew Vashti,
and I, of course, remained evasive. It wasn't clear
that I was Jewish, though I feared it common knowledge.
Now Mordecai kept erupting. It made the days a pyre.
Did they know this was my uncle, this raving ashen Jew?
Shortly after I'd first seen it, and memorized its horrors,
I torched their vicious fiat and watched its venom flutter
in a heated silver dish.

Within days I summoned Yusef, had him order sheer blue silk
from the eastern edge of Persia, knowing blue was difficult,
near impossible to find. He went and made his contacts,
came back empty-handed. I appeared quite disappointed.
I said, "Zeresh has a gown of it. It took my breath away."
He perked his ears, his small ambition twitching.
I said, "It must be quite disarming, to be close
to such a man." He puffed and praised his Haman
as a God of good intention. I stared, a reticent
believer, and sent him on his way.

The sweetened gyres were in motion, but these
were incidental, essential only if the triggers
could be lodged. Then came a risky piece of business.
I had Hatach pilfer copies of the law. I was looking
for the lines to prove my theorem, to web them
in their loom. I thought it out again. Then Yusef
was demoted, but I feared too soon, and Haman
cut his loses. I never knew if Yusef
played his part.

I'd scattered sand
across the table, was oiling shells
as we were talking, "Thank you for removing Yusef.
He made me, well, uncomfortable." I moved it closer,
"Haman must be disappointed. He had plans for him."
He fingered the sand and was slowing,
"Haman never gives what he can't reclaim."
I rubbed the oils deeper, "Oh, you and your politics.
He's rather sweet. He sent me a skein of silk,
all the way from Persia."
He brushed the shells to the floor,
"Don't play me off my counselors!"
I rubbed the sand between my palms,
"I'm teasing you. I'll return it, if you like."
He laughed and stalled and smirked, "No.
It was a gift, I'm sure, from Zeresh."
He seemed to twist and dizzy,
"Make a long thin robe of it,
and be sure to wear it when they come."
He brushed up close and whispered,
"Haman's the kind who will always think his station
one notch lower than he warrants."
He spun and heeled a shell,
"If he were the moon, he'd want to be the sun!"
He laughed. I thought him ill. We wound up
making love among the scattered shells
and low, as he began to die, low,
drowning in a lifeless sigh,
I felt him reach for Vashti.

During the days I kept inspecting the laws
both men had made, searching for the noose
of their own logic. I wasn't sleeping well,
with such death to imagine. I hadn't much time
before Haman started hanging Jews, before
Mordecai would more than smolder.

Yusef was placed near the Gate
and I panicked. He'd recognize Mordecai
and Mordecai, in his state, would accuse him.
I took a chance and had him stationed
near the garden. I simply gave the order
with casual recollection, as if arranging
some minor task my husband had forgotten.
I went to pick some hyacinth. He was ill at ease.
I was superbly uninformed, "I don't understand
how you wound up here." He shrugged. We walked.
"You know, I must thank you. Haman sent me the bluest silk.
I'm sure you had a part in it." He started to loosen.
His weight shifted to one foot. I leaned close, "You've been
so nice." He shuffled. "I've come to warn you." He laughed,
"Warn Me?" "I don't know what to make of it. But, as I
woke from my nap, the other day, I heard Haman,
through the door, with the King. They were in
the smaller chamber. You know the one."
He showed some interest. I started
loosing nerve. Surmount. Stay cool.
A pin of ice. Dark and clear.
"They've found you out."
"What are you up to?"
"I don't believe him."
"Who?"
"Haman. He told him."
"What?!"
"I wouldn't run. He'll look for that."
"Haman's the one who hired me!"
"He said you'd kill the King.
The only reason they haven't moved
is to see who you're working for."
"Haman! It's Haman!"
"You were going to kill my husband?"
"No. No. Never. He wanted me to, but I was only
watching, spying for him. You must believe me.

You must!" His pulse was astronomic. He took my hand,
"You must help me. You know I'd never do such a thing.
Talk to him, please. I'll do anything!" I walked
and pulled a hyacinth, weighing what to do.
I sighed and tipped my head, almost breathing on him,
"I will try to plead for you, but can never admit
to having done so."

"Of course. I'll never forget this."

"You must listen. I understand how Ahasuerus works.
You must not run. If you run, your head will top a pole
by evening. Go to him in mid-afternoon. That's when he's
calmest. Go, tell him. It will be hard, but tell him
the truth. And don't linger on Haman." I swallowed hard
before the next. The whole thing was getting deeper.
"I will have been there before you. Say you came forward
because Mordecai, that raving old man at the Gate,
found you out." He looked skeptical for a moment.
I pressed on quickly, "Remember, don't linger on Haman.
He'll think it disrespectful. He'll think you not worth
saving. Say you were loyal all along, and meant to expose
Haman, but this crazy old man kept getting in the way."

He stared at me, no longer frenzied, "Why? Why are you
so involved?" He's a dead man, I thought. The only thing
to keep him is the truth, "I'm after Haman." He stared,
then firmly nodded. He didn't ask why. I pressed on
like before, "He'll send you to China or Persia,
somewhere far away. As soon as you get there,
you must change your name and leave.

He'll be more concerned with Haman, and won't kill you
just so Haman will wonder how much he is believed."

He hesitated and then, "All right." He let out
a colossal shiver. I took his hands, "Remember,
bow and tell the truth.
It will set you free."

I never said a word.
Yusef went to Ahasuerus.
He never left the room alive.
Things were stretching at the seams.
I was confused and terrified.
Had Yusef implicated Haman?
He wouldn't go down alone.
I should be safe, unless Yusef,
faced with death, told all.
But if Ahasuerus was enraged,
Yusef must have died swiftly.
Perhaps too swift to mention Mordecai.
There were too many things I'd provoked.

Yusef's death marked a change in me,
a rise in tide, in fear, in looking round corners,
in never sleeping fully, another swell
in which to drown. More of the coolness
heating up. Less calm. More full of jitters.
And I knew it would mount this way
till I was like Mordecai in the end.

The dark crack in me was splitting.
My nerve was shaken, jittery, given to ticks
of fear that would sometimes last for days.
I had to do this before I lost my nerve completely.
Each day was harder to be cold-blooded.
Each calculation had its price,
took an ounce off my precision,
off my purpose, no matter how I prayed.
The pin of ice was melting.
Before it did its pricking.
The race of blood was on.

Fourteen Jews were hung to test the ropes.
I heard the floors swing open, heard the slight
quick lengthening of noose through morning air,

heard the muffled snaps, the minute squeals,
the jerk, jerk, bob, and sway. And still
this seemed preposterous: to keep the blood in me
from moving, chilled enough to do the killing
in time to stop the blood. And none of it
would matter, if Haman found I was a Jew,
or Ahasuerus caught me playing with his memories,
or if Mordecai should shout my name.

It finally stormed at night and he was up.
I sashed my robe and watched him squint, watched
the dark wash the anger from his face, watched
long enough to let him slip. I rubbed against him
from behind. He thought I was Vashti swimming.
I had to chance that I was safe,
"It's unnerving all this talk of death."
He let his rib cage drop. Now came the test,
"Yusef must have been a surprise."
The cage locked up. I rubbed his back
in clockwise swirls, pressing firmly
as Vashti did. The cage dropped as he spoke,
"You work a lifetime and there's no one to trust."
He turned to hold. I held. The lightning snapped,
illuminating a side I didn't want to see,
a gentler boyishness. I hardened fast,
"You were wise to write those laws."
He buoyed up, quite pleased,
"You know my laws?" I played coy,
"I've been reading, yes. I'm quite impressed.
You anticipate so well." He was afloat and offered up,
"The days of thought, plucking this, plucking that,
then waiting to see where the order lies."
I kept adding sweets, "How did you arrive—
Where did you begin? There's so much to consider."
"Do you really know my work?" We grew playful.
I hugged his neck, "Test me."

"What law pertains to Yusef?"
Like a schoolgirl, I stood erect,
" 'In treason, the thought is the act,
and discovered, death to the conspirator
is an act of self-defense. And whosoever
undoes the plot assumes the post of he who fell.' "

"Now I'm impressed."
The lightning popped.
He squinted, stared,
was losing track of who I was.
The conversation seemed to drop.
I wasn't sure where to probe.
He turned to relish the storm.
I felt defeated.
Then he blurted in a semi-growl,
"It's Haman, you know."
Thank God, at last.
I let it register,
with full and slow surprise,
"You mean—"
"Yes. It goes back to Haman."
"I can't believe it."
More thunder rolled in.
He stretched, his hands on his hips,
"I'm not surprised."
"What will we do?"
He played with my hair,
"Have him for wine."
He laughed, the poker hot behind his voice.
It started to rain. He kissed me.
I tried to arouse him, but he pushed me away. O God—
He knew. Maybe not. I went to bed, insane to know
what he was thinking. Did Yusef mention Mordecai
or me? It was the first time he refused me.
But Haman was in place.

In the morning, I saw soldiers oiling gallows.
Ahasuerus had been up all night. He looked resolved
but dreadful. He offered me some juice,
"We'll have wine at dusk.
And wear your blue silk, please."
He paused to kiss me, but didn't.
He seemed to have a plan of his own.

Hatach told me Mordecai was acting up.
Not now. I can't cope. I told Hatach
to interrupt our wine and pull the King
for as long as he could. I didn't care how
or for what. At noon, another dozen Jews,
snapped and left swaying. I thought to pray
but there was too much to do.

As much as I had no patience,
I bathed in oils of myrrh
and rubbed hyacinth between my breasts
and down my legs. But as I rubbed,
the hyacinth tore. I picked it up.
It tore further. I held the shreds.
I worked them around.
I couldn't stop trembling.
Heat throbbed below my ears,
along my jaw. I started to cry,
but the urge turned to fear.
Each exhalation urge.
Each inhalation fear.
I took in ancient air,
the broken hyacinth,
the whole of life
steaming.
And everything—
*everything*—

no longer possible for me,
depended on wine,
a cup to the lips.

I filled the vase with sand,
prayed for a storm, and wished
I had something scented by Vashti.

*As Michelangelo hastily draws Ahasuerus rising in bed, Pico finds the ultimate
use of mirrors deceitful and debilitating, while the sculptor, growing bored
and volatile, continues to extol their possibility.*

PICO:
    You can't escape it. This mirror business
    begins a distancing. You have to move away
    to see. It breeds a reversal of perception.
    Everything is backwards. How can that be healthy?
    I see children believing left is right and far is deep.
    It will be impossible to teach anything directly.
    And intellects, I think, will grow too heavily
    skewed from where they're thinking,
    until some will say we have to be
    far away from things
    to look at them
    precisely.

MICHELANGELO:
    It strips the eye of all its habits.
    It fascinates. How the image freshens
    when reversed. Why, in Padua,
    they've begun drawing models in reflection,
    as if they're posing in the mirror.

    If I could only hold the glass
    to a bargeman swabbing, or a Cardinal
    rinsing, or a tall perfect boy
    hoisting his ass over a wall;

if the glass could just freeze them
and release them later,
the way I do inside my mind.

Sometimes I reel with unexpected emotions
which rise as bodies twisting: longing
as a bearded slave; resignation as a stupored
prince struggling to his elbows, stomach rippled
in the mud. Oh if I could see more clearly,
perhaps I'd feel more deep affection
for the things I'm fast becoming.

PICO: The crux is this fear of distortion
which is a fear of unity. The edges,
which are not really there, dissipate,
and we, on the verge of seeing all
fear the blur.

It's the old man fearing blindness,
renouncing the dark because it's everywhere.
And the faithless bishop going deaf, refusing
silence as an oppressive sudden wrong.

It's why wisemen have a thousand names
and shrug at being called by any.
It's the blending of all there is
that emulsifies us
from the unconscious.

With these mirrors, these rigid plates
of perfect glass, we will stop squinting,
sweeping, imagining ourselves as larger
than we are. And there rings eternal danger,
across an undistorted valley where, so clear
in our reception, we estrange free will
from mystery.

Yes, even when we despise it and peg it
and hide it, the torsion we call suffering
thrives.

MICHELANGELO: There's talk it can heal us. Talk that people
like Copernicus can use the edge to bring us to the stars.
They say where a single surface yields reflection,
two in combination might ripple through, reveal,
enlarge the things around us, bring in
the Ptolemaic planets. What rivets me
is the double mode of seeing.
I'm so tired of my point of view.

They say the plates have altered Europe.
That, now, we are self-centered.
They say we are the glass
through which the world
gets all its names.

I only know I've grown quite restless,
stuck sitting where I'm sitting, seeing
what I'm seeing. Clear or unclear, I'm
stranded. Always some interference
that makes the mind
like old eyes burn.

PICO:
Oh somewhere, there's a custom to mirror only,
and the people talk through their reflections
though close enough to touch. And they adore
the state of being and fear the act of becoming.
And when a bird or thought or jet of voice lifts
beyond the glass, it never occurs to them
to turn and search the skies.

MICHELANGELO:
There's talk now of building a hall
with nothing else but mirrors, where once
you've entered, your every move would multiply
and the task, as a hundred arms would have you,
is to know which are true.

*Esther, less confident and more careful, reveals how she maneuvered to check-mate them in their first meeting, but failed, for Ahasuerus was half-mad, and Haman was ruthless. And even as they meet again, Esther can feel things spinning out of her control.*

ESTHER: I sent word for Haman to come early.

> My arms dangled off the chair,
> the silk draping my small wrists.
> Haman found me instantly appealing.
> But as he approached, he was knotted
> and forbidding, huge, massive, sheer dominance
> leathered from survival. He took my hand,
> "You look more than deserving of the blue."
> I thanked him for his attentions.
> My hand and wrist fit easily in his palm.
> I poured his wine, caught by the red film
> like blood splashing down the bronze.
> I delivered the goblet and began,
> "We're fortunate you are so near at hand."
> He was dancing on the surface, "As near
> as you will have me." I stayed serious,
> according to plan, "Your sense of law
> is firm like his, and we will need that,
> when the time comes." He held the glass of blood
> now with both hands, "What are you suggesting?"
> I stopped for an appropriate length of puzzlement,
> "It's getting worse, the bouts, the loss of sense.
> It's all I can do to make it through the nights.
> And storms, my God—but—surely, you've been
> kept informed?" He arched like a predator
> and stalked the throne, "Of course, I've known
> the gist of his condition, but had no idea—"
> He knew nothing. I continued, "Your sense
> of privacy has been a kindness, but now,
> it's different. To be frank, we need you near."

He loomed over me. I landed my small hand
on his arm, a bird flitting to a cliff,
"It's grown much worse since Vashti went away.
He thinks, at times, he's a wind circling Persia.
He calls out and shouts at all the things he sees.
But talk to him of law and the kingdom and he snaps back.
And elsewhere, he imagines children he hasn't had,
or thinks he's a prisoner. I ask of whom.
He shooshes me and cuts the conversation.
Or after dark, we'll be sleeping,
he'll come prowling, swinging lanterns,
claiming they're his pared halves.
'Of what,' I'll say. 'Of Heart! Of Heart!'
It's not hard to see what's coming.
I'm not morbid, but I think we should be prepared."

Haman was astonished, but became calculating
more quickly than any man I'd known.
I wasn't sure if he believed me. He gave me his goblet,
"What is it you're after?" Mirrors, Vashti warned,
mirror what they'd like to see. I gave him more wine,
"I like being Queen." This he understood. "I see.
I see." I turned my back and pushed further,
"I find you quite precocious in your writing of the law."
He was impervious to flattery. I pushed it further,
"Quite self-serving—" "Oh?" "Given a King half-here,
half-there. Take your law of continuation.
A clever piece of work, in times like these."
This began to move him to a state of self-importance,
"I like the way you see things, Esther."
"And I, you, Haman. It'd be a shame
if we bypassed a chance to work together."

Ahasuerus banged in the door, "Well,
isn't this a fine way to find you?
Starting without me, always, both of you!
Where's my glass?" I felt uneasy,

wondered if he overheard.
I poured his share of blood
and there we were, the King,
the Butcher, and the Temptress,
drinking what we'd come to spill.

Ahasuerus drained his goblet, "More.
More." And leaned quite close to Haman,
"The fish are biting! Ahah! But then, you knew!"
Haman eyed me quickly. I couldn't understand.
Was he really half-demented?
Or had he shrewdly out-guessed us?
Three steps down in his own piercing scheme.
He said, "I ate the storm and now it's Blazing,
Arcing, Busting out! So careful, boys and girls,
I'm on Fire! Touch me wrong and you'll burn out!"
Neither of us broke the silence.
Haman was convinced, but I was lost
in my own machinations. Both men,
if crazed, were too adroit.
Were these just deftly uttered symbols,
warnings from an aging King?
Or was he half-naked now in public,
wagging all his mind's loose strings?
He looked dead at me and said to Haman,
"I've hardly heard a neck snap today.
Step it up. You're the one with all this hunger.
Let's get it over. And I don't want records.
No names. No scorecards, please!"
I was certain he knew.
I couldn't look at Haman
who strangely resisted,
more I think, to be independent,
"There's no hurry. I know where they pray.
Officially, we're not starting yet.
But in a week, if you would come."

"Splendid! Why don't we have dinner tomorrow?
Bring Zeresh, if you wish." Haman looked askance
and said, "That's kind, but she's ill these days.
But I'll be here."

Ahasuerus swung the air as if a cape
and left.

I was exhausted, dropped my head
into my hands. Haman was genuine,
"I'm sorry. I had no idea.
How bad does it get?"
Without looking up,
"That was mild."
He reassured me,
"We'll be prepared."
I played the caring wife,
"Please, I don't want him to be upended.
I simply want you to pick up what's let go."
"I understand."
I'm sure he did.
If he licked his chops,
it was quietly where I couldn't see.
"He musn't be humiliated. It's not his fault."
"It will be done delicately. I'll inform the others.
And we'll invoke the law. I'm truly—"
Haman's sense of authority was shaken.
He kissed me on the cheek and left.

Almost there. Stay down. Stay down.
I had no need of feelings.
I put my hands before me
and they were quaking
like a scheme of smoke.
They quaked and quaked.
I drank the blood.
It dizzied me.
Mirrors, Vashti,
mirrors, true.

Oh Vashti, now I would trade places,
trade the inner world of pleasures,
trade the freedom of my fathers
for an unadulterated peace
which I could feed the others,
for I cannot stop the madness,
feel it boiling up before me
like a soured rage without a face.
There's nothing left, but to let
the rabid angels hawk the future
into being.

Everything's in place.

O God, my dusky God,
let the blue release our steam.
Let us settle in our place.

Ahasuerus enters first.
He's smug and taut, but loose around the edges,
"Anything red for dinner? I love things rare and red."
I can't tell when he's playing. He goes to where
Haman will sit, "He's such a big impressive man.
You'd think he was—oh—Genuine." He moves behind
my chair, "You know you're quicker, darting,
harder to hold than Vashti ever was."
It's alarming to hear him talk this way.
"You know, once I'm dead, he'll kill you, too,
no matter what he's said." He comes round,
grips the chair, locks me in, follows my eyes,
"Oh sweet Esther, you were better as you were."
I squirm away. He follows close, "She never told you
how I made her feel. Never told how time stood still
when we'd interlock and pray that we'd conceive.
No, she always omitted what it did to her." He backs away
and tips the vase of sand I'd placed behind his plate,
"You almost did it. You simply asked the wrong questions."

Haman enters. I want to run.
I've tried every way I know.
Ahasuerus assumes his role,
"Ah, have some blood." He pours the wine,
"It's particularly sweet this spring."
Haman looks to me with those genuine lionine eyes,
"It's nice of you to have me." Wheels are clicking,
grinding, pockets of the mind, boiling, popping.
What now? Which way?! Who's lead? Who's stronger?
If I'm to die, why not take them with me?
I'm so far in, I can't stand up, move on, go back,
can't see where we're going. Ahasuerus gulps his wine,
"Tell me Haman, how many Jews today? Big ones? Fat ones?
Lush ones? Old toothless bags? Be careful what you do
with the bodies. They're funny about their remains."

Haman seems offended and tightens like a mountain.
Ahasuerus motions him closer, "How would you like
to swap women?" Haman bounds up actually embarrassed,
"My King, you're not well these days—"
Ahasuerus pounds his fist—
"Answer me! I know you fancy her!
She's very loyal!" I'm enraged
at having slept with him.
He's vile and demented.
I throw wine in his face.
He jumps to hit me.
Haman steps between.
He spins away, appears to cool.
Haman sits by the verandah.
Ahasuerus pulls the sash from my silk robe,
"So, you see what it means to dine with us.
But I suppose you and Zeresh have your squabbles."
Haman continues staring into night.
"But that's a friend! Put up with our
little indiscretions! Bravo! Good man!

Who wants to be—" Ahasuerus, from behind,
slips the sash round Haman's throat
and tightens with such a yank,
the chair tips backwards,
cracks its legs, and Haman squirms
like an earthquake, Ahasuerus squeezing
till the sash cuts his hands, "Who wants—
to be The King—The King—Who wants—
to be—The King." Haman starts to shudder.
Ahasuerus is in frenzy. It's happening.
Haman sputters. Kicks. And dies.
He lies there like a lion
and we wait to see if he's just wounded.
Ahasuerus jerks the sash once, twice, three times
to be sure. He's shaken to the point of weeping.
He's at my side. I console him. He's all
trembling from the muted fire. I hold his head.
He licks the hyacinth between my breasts, and against
all my preparation, I slip a dagger from the cushion
and for all his dry rehearsals, enter him from behind
with a deep and thrusting measure till he comes
redly in my hands.

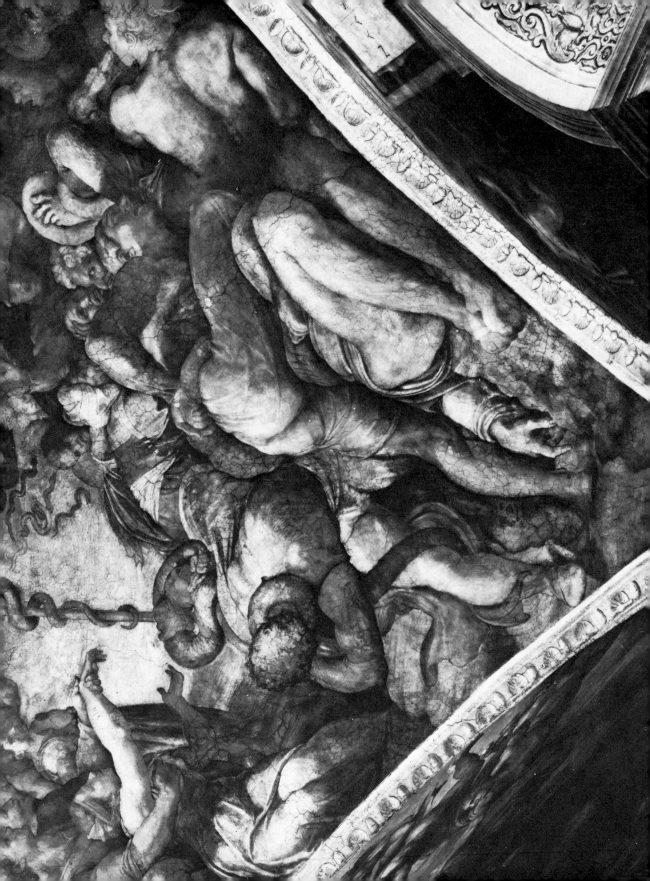

# XXV. THE BRAZEN SERPENT

Faced with extreme hardship as they first wander the desert after being freed from slavery in Egypt, the Jews, disheartened, blame Moses and God for their dark and painful freedom. God responds, as if their complaints are a request, by sending fiery serpents among the multitude to coil and bite the disheartened, killing many. God then, through Moses, creates a Brazen Serpent wrapped about a pole which heals those filled with venom if they have the courage to look upon it.

Likewise, the sculptor is disheartened, wrung dry of heat, his vision spent. Bitten by the fiery days, his will to look upward or inward is full of venom. And oddly, as Moses ascends the mountain at God's behest to leave his life, Michelangelo, agitated beyond complaint, is cast back into the cage of his body, his blazing excursion now spewed from him across the length of Ceiling. While Moses recalls the incandescent moments of his life, Michelangelo can't see where he's going. Both, having moved closer to the fire, now live farther from all others.

*It is late and the restless sculptor works until he stalls in the dark And there, as he contemplates the Brazen Serpent, it speaks like a brass cloud of its alchemic place in each heart that dares to reach.*

THE BRAZEN SERPENT:

[—Moses struggles with a light darkly pushing him about.
Buonarroti wrestles with a darkness blinding him within.
The sculptor downs the scaffold as the ceiling turns a desert.
The prophet scales the mountain as the desert turns a nation.
And as dark voices shout the heads off falling bodies,
as stark silence lengthens the roots of eyes,
as dark descends through climbing,
as light ascends through falling,
there squirms the brazen serpent
in all who take turns yearning:
God gave me lungs and a reflex for survival
God gave me voice and an impulse for arrival
God gave me nothing that I should eat it
God gave me want that I should burn it
and me and He into a filament of song—]

*Moses is called at the age of 120, and told he has one more day to live. He writes out 13 scrolls of the Torah, thinks of all the farewells, pares them down, says half of those and begins ascending Mount Abarim. The glow which Moses has from his meetings with God drapes him in many ways, and when he is dying and climbing the mount, his face begins to illuminate, stronger and stronger, till even when buried, God's light keeps glowing and intensifying. If his burial place were found today, its lid cracked, the shaft of light to burst through would blind the world.*

MOSES:

I don't know how to finish, to unflex
this hold of will. It's kept me going,
trudging, gleaning berries from the desert.
I only know to question, to toughen,
to strike myself and ignite.

What once were knots
have burned to joints
and feel like home.

Do you think He really means it,
means to stop my mind from racing?
And even then, it would keep tasting.
Nothing ends. The sand's a sorry proof.
I'm sure my gnarled emissions would shock
and hiss and galvanize to all the things
I can't remember.

O God, where are You now?
Inflaming those things that came between us?

I am wise, at last, and full of juice,
and now You want to peel me like a grape?

If it's what I've learned, then smudge my thinking!
If what I've felt, uncork the basin!
I'll drain! Condense. Become a Rock!
Pull all expression to the core.
Compress to Quartz!

I can't do that.

So let me drift, a bird, and as a shadow
slips across the earth beneath a bird,
let me shadow You. Let me see Aaron
one more time. Now You've depressed me.
The climb starts to twist.

*Michelangelo, having slept in his clothes, in the Chapel, wakes and starts up
the scaffold. His work is quivered and uneven, and when a draft rolls out
along the vault, causing him to shiver, he stops.*

MICHELANGELO: Such a chill. God turns his back.
    The blood turns ceramic. I'm reeling, weaker,
    unable to focus. Now it takes four times as long
    to think of thinking clearly, and longer

to lift myself once settled. Lift
and move along. I'm sputtered now.
The morning's shot.

This one's breaking me to nothing.
And stroke on stroke from out the living rock,
it pounds me with a sadness,
pronging round my head.

I can't stand to parry with the living,
to hear them yak about their corns
or dying aunts, or boils that never surface,
or always surface, or how they're irked
by a lover's missing comb.

And yet, by myself, the life of night destroys,
as far as light that misses stars, devouring
each hollow space that closed or covered lies,
devouring the beginning.

I'm lonely though I want to be alone.

I burned my poems two weeks ago,
because no one understands.
I try to sculpt the golden boys with words.
But everyone thinks they're confessions,
sublimations, skin licking skin,
belly humping belly.

To deny that I love bodies,
love the face of skin on muscle,
am stunned from my depressions
by the organs swiftly working—
it's like the sudden inundation
of a wingspan briskly lifting—
to deny its lift would cost me dearly.
To explain it costs me plenty.

I dreamt of a long-faced generation
who believe in thirst, but not in drinking.

Then I woke. God! They write the laws
that bind me—men begging like sand
to be packed together.

It guts the heart of its desire,
like a melon of its seeds,
to know, after all my deep protesting,
no one wants what I have made.

*As Michelangelo starts to fill the remaining space with a swarming mass of figures, Moses, while ascending, remembers retrieving Joseph's bones, before heading for the Red Sea.*

MOSES:
Word was out we were leaving and bitter Jews
were looting robes and whips and Egyptian gold.
Some were breaking carts they'd used to carry reeds.
An old man scurried with an icon. I stopped him
and tossed it. It scattered the crowd.

Joseph's bones were in the Mausoleum,
in the Antechamber of Egyptian Kings, sinking,
shifting, knocking in the earth, where chambers
didn't matter, where languages were less than flesh,
where belief was decomposed. I took the steps
three at a time and once inside, the dark
minimized the breakage in the street.
And as my eyes adjusted, two hunching forms
brushed past me, one bleeding from the scalp.
I think they were Priests.

There were chambers off of chambers
with cool and dark sarcophagi
mounding up like gilded rumps.
I wasn't sure what to look for,
or how to distinguish, bone from bone,
canister from sacrificial brass, resting
place from hiding place. Then a rush of feet.
I pounded my staff. It glowed enough to see.

It was Jochebed, my mother.
She hadn't forgotten.
She set the staff aside
and brought me to my knees.
She stroked my face in the midst of Egypt
burning, bleeding, breaking down. She stood,
gave me my staff and said, "Come. We're Free."
And we swept through musty corridors
like swallows chasing close and low.

We landed in a row of polished Tombs
pedestalled with Isis and Khnum. She walked
behind an onyx bird, stopped, turned, backed off
a step, and nodded to the painted floor. For a second
there was the smell of hickory and locust, burning,
a tinge of ginger or wrinkled rose, and it fumed
in exultation, rifts of deadly fragrance,
clouds off Joseph's bones.

But there seemed no way to find them,
and the fume spawned a cholic mood where to reach
seemed an invasion, a softened want for health and cattle
near a spring with no conviction but the daylight hours.

I pressed to move my lips which seemed like rope,
"Joseph. We're here. Come. Come." A vault across the room
began to rumble, a crack snaked the painted floor,
and the earth spit up a pile of yellowed clumps.

The odor dissipated. Bone dust filled the room.
A skull, on its side, a bowl with one cheek broken,
the jaw up to its hinge, missing, as if death
had eaten the dead's last way to speak.

A leg bone was a nest for mites.
I picked it up. It crumbled. I swept the bones
into a brass pot. Some nubs
just powdered as I touched.

Mother disappeared. There was no time to linger.
The next I saw her, she was holding orphans
as we began to cross the sea. And There was God
Working in the Open! No Room for Interpretation!
The Waters Lifted! Rushed! Fell Up! Up!
In Sheer Wrathful Affirmation!
A Nation's Weeping Couldn't Still it!
Miles of Water Routing Out the Skies!
Arcing Ever Upward! Waves Shot in an Eruption
which only kept Erupting, Uniting in a Vault
200 miles above the Earth! It Pulled the Rivers
of the Earth! It Pulled the Minds of Kings!
And Sent Old Angels Charting through the dark!
The Mist sprayed stars whose hiss of steam
fogged up the sea of peace, steam drifting off
the want of stars to be much more
than holes of light, trapped
burning in their place!

And burrowed—through the churning,
rising, falling tides—translucent tunnels
scuppered out a way! The thundrous water raged
and hulled out paths for each lost tribe.
They scurried on, the Benjamites, the Judeans,
first to have the mind of God whip such clear
and awful turbulence into an air, a way
of winded emptiness through which beaten lives
could march. It took courage just to enter. Imagine,
fish, debris and gravelled life arced and churned,
sucking such a draft, the air whisked younger,
fresher, back to the Atmosphere of Creation.
So fresh to breathe, it shocked the lungs
and thousands broke into staggered prayer.
Sudden voices trudging the bottom,
grateful to be sudden, as if simply led
by a father's bones, we could just
walk out of bondage.

*Michelangelo's patience becomes a thread of wax, burning between his dis-
satisfaction with what he's done and what seems insurmountable in what's
left to do.*

MICHELANGELO: I'm fed up, wired.
    My hands burn each place I hold.
    But it's nothing, if not finished.
    I kept telling myself: move on, keep going,
    don't look back, don't get distracted,
    cut the sigh in half, don't ask long questions,
    mix the paints, clean the brushes, get set
    the night before, keep on hacking, don't start over.
    The more the marble wastes, the more the statue grows.
    Don't reconsider—The fire's turned to flood
    and now I drown.

    The image grows therein.
    Beneath a spotless veil.
    Hissing from the source.

    They all look half-demented!
    This one's afraid he'll leak his ounce of faith.
    And here's a punished soul, all parched and bony,
    he'd burn his sockets to see God's face—
    Don't look to me! I can't help you!
    And what—You, so agitated,
    why should I listen
    to Your sea of moans?

*Moses nods halfway up the mount, and dreams of how souls are born into
human beings.*

MOSES:
    Each was an orange bird, an ancient mosaic
    in an orange cage not hung but suspended
    and while the bars were not substantial,
    the soul, the bird, the mosaic
    couldn't make it through.

Each had no choice
but to come apart
and spill like an orange stream
into a river of breaking,
and life outside the painless cage
became a myth of piecing things together
so the time on earth was a puzzle,
birth and death, our puzzling dreams.

Then I woke in a paralysis,
a heavy sense I've come to dread.
And this dense mood of half-begetting
always clouds my sense of knowing.

It seems impossible, but natural
that while the life out here grows
larger, weathering against the body,
in the center, it gets smaller,
losing detail and dimension.

First the lips of God
are a hot secret,
then an image losing color,
then a silhouette, an artifact,
encumbered comet scratching up the mind.

Can it be? So many things reducing
while the days on earth swell stronger
till the theology of calling out
never makes it through?


*Michelangelo is irritated that his brushes aren't cleaning well. His colors keep running.*

MICHELANGELO:
Diluted! Sappy! A Heart of Sulphur! Flesh of Straw!
Bones like Wood the Sun has Dried! What's the Use!
I'm too far out of it to finish. Eh! Haul it down

and let them Gape and Misconstrue! I Don't Care!
They All Project Their Limitations!

'It's not Grounded'—They can't be Sweeping.
'It's Blasphemous' —They've lost their sense of Holy.
'It's Disconnected' —They can't look Wide!
'It's too Bold'—They're just Timid!
'It's not Relevant'—They're in desperate need of Meaning.

The elements dictate the terms.
Things rise forth or they plummet.
You render them with all you have.
Or it's nothing. There is no other way.

*Moses concentrates now on his climbing and, with irritation, recalls the sending of spies into the Promised Land.*

MOSES:
A group, disgruntled, mistrusting, wanting to turn back,
even as we approached the boundaries of Palestine, said,
"We shall send men before us, unknown, unknowing,
to search out the people, to find where we'll be
welcome and respected." I thought, what good are spies
in the wilderness. All men thirst the same. Look here
to know what's there. Their eyes were shifting, darting,
spying on me, on daylight stars, on the absence
that clouded their heads. I said, "Very well.
Go and see what you can find. But never say
what you believe or why you've come."
This they liked and they left in the night
and never returned.
They could be next to you
or feeling the bread you've stored
or instructing your children how to add up sums.
The spies, they wander the surface
like dragonflies a breezeless lake.
With each step up,
they forget what they're looking for.

With each step back,
they remember why they've come.
The morning has them full of lists,
the night finds the secret work undone.

*Michelangelo, struck by the notion of Moses fully looking his age, stops to
sketch a bearded head on the plank to his left, but the image dissipates before
he's done.*

MICHELANGELO:
    I can't keep them lit!
    They're bold, clear, then gone.
    I despise living between glimpses,
    trying to reconjure the brilliance,
    to rejuvenate the confidence,
    the short-lived burst that seeing brings.
    And then it goes the other way. I mean,
    first there's fire and then the lapse,
    the memory of fire, and worse, the amnesia,
    the world without fire, the wandering quite dryly
    in the muck that covers the mind like moss.

    The damn thing cycles
    till I live dying in myself,
    a spirit hulled in its decanter.

    O Curse the way I left Carrara!
    Irreparable ill of wasted hours!

    To work for days when really heated!
    To fondle dregs when coasting to the dark!

    And in the dark,
    Everything loses! The thought,
    the moment of thinking the thought,
    the instant spent imprinting the thought—
    all quick and flared and flashed and gone!

    The face of God changes as I blink!
    That's the trouble with this painting!

They squirm a thousand deaths
beneath their drying skins!

*While Michelangelo decides to eliminate the prophet from the scene, Moses
is stopped by a clearing reminiscent of the burning bush, and is fevered into
remembering his visit into Hell.*

MOSES: As I entered, which was more like falling
    through enormous drafts of heat, the fire withdrew
    500 parasongs with an irate muffled thunder,
    and Nasargiel, the Angel of Hell, welcomed me.
    As he spoke his being flared. He was not discursive
    or the least bit friendly. He disliked his work,
    but did it with complicated zeal.
    We walked through clouds of fire,
    mists of flame that didn't flame but steamed.
    There was no corporal sense or difference
    between the Hellish ground or air.
    There were men hanging by chains of fire.
    I wanted to know why. Nasargiel wasn't interested
    in explanations. I had my impressions, but I don't know.
    It seemed beings were tortured for their omission;
    their lack of spirit, or lack of sense. One twirled
    by his lids—I couldn't bare to watch—hooked by flames,
    I thought, for never being seen. Then a rumpy statesman,
    by his ears, for hearing just the parts of truth
    insignificant to change, and still, huge mammoth hunters
    by their bloodied palms, for taking more than they give,
    and one set of torn-up creatures popping from their tongues,
    for drinking too deeply what other thirsty beings save.
    And then—God—sour lanky women, by scalp and nipple,
    for never touching themselves. And above, small ratlike
    sophists, for nibbling holes in the baker's sense of wealth.
    And strangely, as we walked, there were no screams,
    though the air was pitched in painful colors
    screeching at the eye. The groaning was inaudible,
    having crossed a frequency of mind. And more,

we've barely entered. Nasargiel was not showy
or concerned with my reactions. He kept a steady pace.
We came to Alukah where hundreds were pinioned by their feet,
heads down, blood rushing, swollen bodies ribbed with worms,
each 200 parasongs in girth. A pale fired woman writhed
as worms nibbled at her cheek. I watched and couldn't
fathom why. Nasargiel said, his face flaring orange,
"They were pretenders in the game." I thought, My God,
just for pretending! He read my thoughts and put it plainly,
"They deny having lived." He stalked away. We travelled then,
for hours—I think—never quite landing or falling through,
but progressing just the same. He paced ahead briskly
and I had trouble keeping up. At one point he seemed
to vanish and I couldn't find a shadow or a scent
of a direction—the ground, a heated mist. Everything,
stuffed with orange, kept suffocating, hot and pressing in.
I was getting woozy. From beneath where I thought
I stood, Nasargiel appeared, "Don't lag behind!"
I'd seen enough. "There's no returning!" We came upon a field
of faces covered with scorpions—the blackest red I've seen—
lashing, stinging everything. And each had several
stingers and each stinger dragged its pouch of venom
which puffed as it filled a wound. Each puncture
blackened. Each head softened. A man stung
in his temple tensed and the venom simply
flowed around his tension up his skull,
along his plate. Then passing—I don't know
how to tell you—but looking at their faces,
their lips all foamed from screaming, melting
from their jaws, eyes peeling in their sockets.
I gasped in thought, can Paradise be as extreme?
Nasargiel just stared, steam drifting from his eyes,
"Keep Moving!" We hiked another cloud of orange.
I didn't let him out of sight. And walking,
I had a notion like a vision, if you can have
such a thing in a place like this. I sensed
we were in a plasmic quarry, for those

who give up things not theirs to give, who,
losing faith in the unseen, begin to kill
things unborn, who heat up dreams
not theirs to burn, who give the wolves
their scent of lamb. There were thousands
to their chests in mud, their mouths all pried.
They couldn't close. And it rained pus-hot stones
which broke their teeth till their mouths were sacs
of enamelled rubble, and their groans scraped inside
my ear. I clutched my head. He called this, "Tit-Yawen."
He said, "Their teeth grow in the dark." Then gripped me
by my uppers. I passed out. I don't remember how,
but we arrived at Abaddon. I woke with Nasargiel's
orange arm rimming mine, pulling me forward, screaming,
"Unbridled Souls Admit No Guide!" We passed bodies barely
breathing, half-immersed in fire, and white-hot snakes
slithered through the damned who kept fainting.
Their venom was clear yet milky.
He stared at them and hollered,
"These called themselves God!"
I had trouble comprehending.
Then the screams, which he'd been muting,
pierced fully, and I thought my ears were frying,
punishing everything between, and I fell and fell
through the orange till dying was like lifting,
till my life, open to pure motive,
propelled straight out before me
till I couldn't hold a thought and Color
Time and Depth simply passed on through
like air through mortal wicker
and I was forced to flatten,
to forfeit all retention.

*Michelangelo's arm begins to numb. He shakes the blood back to his fingers, then stops and notes his hands, and takes the pose of Laocoon, the Greek statue discovered in a vineyard above the ruined Baths of Titus on the outskirts of Rome, when he was living with Sangallo.*

MICHELANGELO:

There were excavations all the time,
digging in the corners of old cellars
for a crippled God buried in the earth.
At times there'd be a hand holding nothing
very tightly, or a leg broken like a stump,
or a marble nose no longer breathing.
There seemed some frozen message
in white organs packed in soil.

I was drawing when Sangallo's son came charging.
They thought they'd found a statue, at least
a hand clutching the body of a snake.
It was already six feet under, but upright,
in position. Chances were, it was intact.
It took two hours to get there. By then
the arm was in the air, unlike any
I'd ever seen: the marbled bicep flexing
from the sea of earth smudging up its veins.
No one said a thing. But it had to be the grouping.
It was well known and well recorded, quite at length
by Pliny. All were there for the duration, gently
picking at the chunks of bonded clay. Some were
scooping out the loosened earth by hand.
It would take at least till morning.

By dusk the eyes were glowing.
Now it looked like it was drowning,
brown dirt tangled in its beard.
Through the night we took turns digging.
Shovels were heard chinking. Then we'd trade
positions. Now 12 to 15 feet below.
By dawn its chest was rising, and I jumped
into the pit. The loosened earth was sliding.
I sank down to my knees. It seemed to stare at me.
I put my hands on its cold shoulders.
Dawn filled its milky eyes.

I wished that I had done it.
It took 20 men to lift it.

I should have sketched it
coolly mitered in the earth.

Julius let no one else have it.

And when I'm truly weary,
I wait till no one's looking,
feel its ribs and astounded stomach,
and know somewhere God made a Greek
who understood.

It makes me see my Ceiling broken,
its colors stained with mud,
scratched with roots,
beneath another era's sewage.
Or me? Perhaps I'll harden
when dead a thousand years
and it will be my hand
reaching for the youngster's shovel
slicing down at me.

There's more to lasting
than I'd figured.

Always to see a flower,
the hands wind up
in dirt.

*The sculptor uses the postures of the Laocoon to cast his serpent-tangled youths, while the climb grows steep for Moses who weakens. The prophet bends, hands on his knees, to even out his breathing, but dizzies slightly. It sets him thinking of his visit to Paradise.*

MOSES: The speed of Paradise
       was faster than all perception
       and so the distinctness of Time

and Space and even thought and speech
was not relatable, and was in fact, shed,
the way matter sheds its structure to move
from liquid to the gaseous. A face appeared,
well, not with features, and it really had no form
or depth. A presence, then, a voice. Well, not a voice.
The presence washed and in its wash was seen and felt
and heard in tones or rather images, but again, these
motives merged. The presence flashed in sounds and sights—
at once—a pure communication. The sign and all it signified
were instantaneous. At one. Shamshiel. It was close and
brushed my head. Shamshiel. It swept black the other way.
Shamshiel. The Angel of Paradise. Violets swept pink
across my brow. Shamshiel. I was lifted of all tension.
Shamshiel. I moved now as the presence moved, no longer
walking, just arriving. We approached a sea of airy color
which framed a set of soft-edged zones, and as we swept,
arrived, pulled near, there was a porous sense that each
was made of fluid stone. Yet, all were air. Waves of stony
air. Shamshiel kept sweeping me along. Vision was reason.
Concept was song. There was no need of form. At first, a
zone of silver, for those who starve their acquiescence,
the next, a wash of gold, for those who love often
with no need of names, the third, a cloud of ruby,
for those who shape their want to another's need,
and on through a coral scent that shone like pearl,
for builders of a life that welcomes all, then behind
or below or in the same place, I can't be sure, a thick
warm flow of copper, for the giving sons of selfish men.
It flashed and peeled to a marbled sheet all webbed
with brown, for those who fill the earth. Then we spun
or lifted through a rust-toned air, a teak, for those
who sing their knives as tools, and on we burst like
waves through dominions of blue where thirst was just
a topaz mist, for those who honor birds and shells
and unprotected forms. I spun. Shamshiel. I wanted

every one. They were safe, forever warm. Then out
or in, away or to, a maze of quartz that seemed
to breathe, for those who endure and never hate
the storm. Shamshiel. Speak to me. We swept higher,
lower, further, and landed like an atmosphere
with no thought of forming clouds
and there, a spring of loving water
which took on the feel of honey, and then
turned white as milk—the past, the present—
and now a brook of wine—the future—it mixed.
We merged and I wished never to reform. Shamshiel.
Shamshiel. Sweetly. Sweetly. Open-ended dying.

*Michelangelo has a flash of dizziness while working overhead. It stirs his*
*passion for otherness, then makes him ill as he sees pinpricks in the air and*
*starts to swerve.*

MICHELANGELO:
In one instant the eye is ribbed
with every sort of beauty that exists!
And nothing gives such pain as failing to seize it!
And failing, one must think on death, must relax the senses
to be what we have never been. And failing, the head grows
stubborn like an onion with its yellow tail growing
out the top. Failing, the mind softens, to accept—
the soul while in the body cannot see. And
failing, the mind dwells on being peeled
till the juice leaves the stem to burn the eyes
and stain the hands. And a cold man's hands
smell in the dark of something that can't
be cleansed. It's on the plates I carry to the sink,
on the belt I hang on the stair, on the yawn of light
that loops my brain, this quest turned death, sciatic!
And irksome moments flow among a thousand proofs! O!
What would I see, if I could hunt without suspicion?
It's been a day of stops and starts. I feel dispersed,
the whites of my eyes sore and all rehearsed.

I never should have bothered. My voice squirms
like a hornet in a jar.

*Moses looks out on the desert and remembers Aaron and Miriam accusing*
*him of abusing Sepporah, his wife, and how in his grief he conceived but*
*never shared, "Arnon And The Parable Of Intimacy."*

MOSES:

I knew when they entered. There was an undercurrent, an anger
and Miriam paced, "Why don't you sleep with her anymore?"
I was embarrassed. Aaron was more calm, but still
indicting, "She's seen it all since Sinai."
Sepporah just kept knitting. It didn't feel right,
them circling and nibbling. They thought
I was showing off how holy, how determined,
how wed to God. I really couldn't explain.
And to do this before her, after all the trials
and separations. The look in her wedded eyes
almost tore my sense of God in two. But God
had shown me what's above, what's below,
what's before, what's behind, what's in water,
what's in earth, and what will be in air.
And I've told you, it's hard to remember.

All this must remain clear. I want the touch,
to touch, to wake unknotted and soft of mind.
No principle in it, just fear and sense
that she will be a soporific, and all I've endured
will knot, a thicket of dark speeches. They continued.
I said nothing. Then she wept and dropped her knitting.
When they left, I sat cross-legged, staring through
the desert floor, my white hair down my shoulders.
She curled within my wingspan, her head nestled to my bone.
We could hear each other breathe, and I felt
the mask of fire that had seared all my perception
a burn away from all the living. I hadn't been
what she most wanted, out of sight when she most

needed, roaming for Your shadows, drinking up Your awe.
I really could say nothing and when she fell asleep,
I walked far into the desert to where my solitude
tends to cure me of my loneliness, and there
I tried but couldn't weep for the life
I couldn't give her, too obsessed to really feel
what she was going through. You've left no room
other than for making, for receiving, and for stoking
all Your fires. I hung my head, not wanting You near,
but the peace of all You'd shown me kept me on target
and away from my emotions. You could have let me weep
behind the dunes. We never talked about it
and after Aaron's death, we travelled slower
through the valleys, through a stark one called Arnon,
enclosed by two mountains, so close above
those on the summit could converse. But in
passing from mountain to mountain, like soul to soul,
one had to hike across the valley over jags and rocks
and through abandoned caves, only to climb the other's
rutted way. Arnon, where long-time lovers roam. Atop,
they doze and talk and survey the world, but wanting
to touch, they must retreat, alone, descending first
their own steepest side, then the valley
in between, and up the other's caves. And early on,
one works along and then returns, then
the other meets halfway, but has to wait
for her lover's trapped or injured
near the base. And after years the one
tries to leap and does, but the other's afraid
and so it goes, the valley, peaks, the caves—
they map their lands and share the maps
and plan to meet and separate
and mark the way with leaves.

*As he paints the fiery serpents green, the sculptor complains of a recurring
dream where he is an old wooden dome in which all he wants of Beauty is
trapped like a motherly bird.*

MICHELANGELO: I hunch inward like a cage,
  and like a bird with one good wing,
  she flutters half-way up, the bars all dark,
  no way out, no perch, no bottom.
  No cross-beams. The sad issue
  learns to know: I can support nothing.
  I feel intense heat like pressure
  from her flapping, forcing me
  to heal myself. Self-love
  deceives all men. The air
  beneath my dome is rare
  like the palate of a saint.
  Have confidence in no one.
  How the mood curves without breaking
  like ideas that never meet. The hub
  where all ribs merge keeps her from soaring,
  keeps her falling through my imagination,
  through the secret of my belonging
  till she spins the thought of perishing
  into an endless, spineless
  devout pain.


*Moses slightly tires, again wants more time for living, and remembers the
thirst they met at Marah, while Michelangelo makes the flesh of those bitten
lilac-grey to bring out the effect of the venom.*


MOSES: Honor pursues him who tries to escape it.
  How often in this desert have I escaped my self-attention,
  drinking from the people, drowning in their mirrors,
  their darkly breaded mirrors of the world.

  I've learned to shed the self
  as prime perceiver, which has made me
  old and crafty in working things around me
  to have God appear, and only then, when a dish
  of non-perception, without any theme or preference,

only when open like the ridge of desert crumbling,
only then has God spoken through the length of heat
to me, and only me. Through a clear tube of holy fire,
He's infused me with prophetic gifts, for which
my speech has sharply been impaired.

God always gives a pause, ripe time to grasp
what has been shaken, a flesh or two, which in sand
could be years, and this is when the life darkens
into schemes. Like now. Dead things come before me
casting shadows I still don't understand. Just
long enough, let's wait, right here. I want to see
the difference between the thirst for thirst
and the dizziness of drowning. Can one drown
in revelation, the way men scorch their lives,
believing they are never loved?

This is what it was at Marah,
more want than thirst, more
emptying than dehydration.
I sensed this in the throngs
swallowing their tongues,
sucking at their palates.
How acute a truth You showed me
when the lives began to perish,
to be thrust in bare positions
which they'd hidden all along.

Real death is always stunning
in a way that slows perceiving
till the drift of things stops forming
and the truth stuck in the living
as a cramp makes rock of muscle
is the dread not in death
but in dying, the pain
not in loss, but in losing.

To perish is to leave a place
and never leave it.

MICHELANGELO:
They make you sleep with your eyes open.
They're always dusting up the morning,
red voices out of view.
And I don't have the patience,
no more concentration.
It's ended now with Haman.
I get lost and stare at brushes
till I'm there, then here, then nowhere
till I love the space and then it pins me.
I hold the brush like a candle
and squeeze until it lights!
Tinder to a holy fire!
Only smoke.
I've got to wait it out.
They've formed a hive about me
with Gates of Canes!
As if the Ceiling's honey.
Only smoke.
Even God has left this place.


*Moses wants to return to the living, then recalls, after retrieving the Tablets*
*the second time, his trouble with God's instructions how to make the candle-*
*stick holy.*

MOSES:
It seems odd: the things I remember most
are circumstances of my deep forgetting.
When the Tabernacle was near completion,
I climbed the mount for Your instructions.
You were quite specific. You even showed me
how to hold, how to bless, how to maintain.
I focused on every flash of light
You washed across my brain.

But as I walked back down the mountain,
as I saw the people milling, as I heard
them discuss their problems, their squabbles
of whose children were aging better,
whose parents acted younger,
whose lovers were more loving
in more imaginative ways—
I forgot how to build.
I stopped and cleared things out,
certain it would all re-enter.
Nothing. Blank. Gone. I was enraged.
I couldn't pull a corner of its image.
The carrier was barren. I had no choice.
I stomped around, kept on stalling,
but finally started up again.
This time You went more slowly.
I repeated each part deeply,
put every other issue of my life in the basin.
I descended to the world again, repeating Your instructions
to the rhythm of my descending. I made it to the marketplace
where a young woman was washing clothes.
The sun enlarged her bosom
and splashed her arms yellow.
I found her sudden and alluring.
I carried on and heard her clothes
slosh against the stone. And then,
I shut my sense, and let her go
to nothing. But she had rinsed
all Your instructions.
Again, I was just empty.
I rushed back to find her.
Of course, she'd vanished.
I calmed, tried not to panic,
closed my eyes, began to imagine the slow descending,
the deep repeating. Not a trace! Twice more,
for different reasons, the same thing happened.

No matter what I tried, it escaped me.
I couldn't properly seize the idea,
could not form a clear conception.

There are only two conclusions:
the thing remembered will choose itself
its channel of remembering.
The light will choose the day,
the heart will choose the special words
or warmth with which they're said.
But some things defy construction,
defy being anchored in the world:
the light refuses to be carried,
the flame itself is brilliant
when using up the stick.

*The Ceiling dries and bleeds, unfinished, and Julius, unable to stay away, threatens Michelangelo.*

MICHELANGELO:
There is no pretense now. He's coming up.
I can feel the tension. I'm tired of it,
of the damp curve, the silly paints,
the splinters from the scaffold.
It's all gone. Opaque. Empty.
To Love God's Likeness is Not Loving
God. I'm a wet fuse. He's here.

"You've put me off enough.
Anyone but you, and I'd have you hung."
His eyes are flint, his nostrils flared.

"When?!"
"When I Am Able!"

He raises his hand, stops, turns,
comes close enough that I can see his gums,
"Do you want me to throw you off this scaffold?!"

He's incensed. I'm beaten, riled, my vision blurry.
They don't realize how much Blood It Costs!
Here we go. The lion and the hawk.
I watch his eyes simmer and glow.

I peer through his reckless skull
to the runway of my Ceiling.
Just burnmarks of some unknown fire.
Back to him. Perhaps he'll—"No!
Unbridled Souls Admit No Guide!"

*Moses reaches the summit and, beyond his last resistance, yields as God kisses his soul.*

MOSES:
Shamshiel. Shamshiel. Sweetly. Sweetly.
No. Yes. Let me never Resist. Resist.
Open my fisted heart releasing
All the lights encrusted.
O my entire head and more
feels all the colors throbbing.
My eyes dissolve into all the languages conceived.
My mouth, what was my mouth, begins in all directions
to wash the sights and sounds of every blessed thing
that ever was and Will Not Be . .

*Michelangelo, head pounding, heart raging, eyes slits, in clothes he's slept in, rattles the scaffold. Decides it's done. As Is. He storms down, throws his brushes cross the Chapel, stops once, twice, takes one last look and raves*

MICHELANGELO:
What Now?! What's There?! The Uncreated Spheres!
The Merciable Fount where All Things Flow!
EH!! What I feel and seek, what leads me on,
comes Not From Me! How can I tell?!
Where burns the Fire Without Witness?!

All Forms Arise!! And Shun,
like shattered bark, the Storm, and Flee!
Who feeds on death never dies!
What is the use of so much promised light?

# APPENDICES

*The sources here and throughout the headnotes, as well as in the Michelangelo chronology, spray back through most of the canon of Michelangelo literature, especially Brandes, Hartt, Hibbard, Papini, Seymour and Symonds. Each note is identified by page and line number. Where Roman and Italian antiquity are concerned, I rely heavily on Alta Macadam's* Blue Guides *(Benn/ Norton, 1984). For mythical information, I depend on* Bulfinch's Mythology *(Avenal Books, 1978). With regard to the Biblical notes, the Old and New Testaments and George M. Alexander's* Handbook of Biblical Personalities *(Seabury Press, 1962) have been invaluable sources from which I cite histories extensively. When possible, the meanings of Biblical names are given, for as Alexander remarks, "Hebrew names often express a thought in a simple sentence, and sometimes the thought is expressed indirectly when the words form a striking phrase or question."*

## I. ZECHARIAH

13, Headnote. *Fresco.* Italian word for fresh. According to Hartt, a painting made on wet plaster with pigments suspended in water so that the plaster absorbs the colors and the painting becomes part of the wall. Before fresco painting can be applied to a wall, the wall must receive a ground or mortar consisting of coarse sand and white plaster or lime, trowelled to even the surface. Over this rough coating, called arriccio, comes a thin finish coat or wash of lime and fine sand. While this is still damp and soft, the drawing or cartoon is transferred to the wall. In the 12th and 13th centuries, this is done by pricking the outline of the drawing with small holes over which a powder is dusted. In Michelangelo's time, this is done by tracing the outline with a stylus which leaves an incised line on the wet plaster.

Then, the painting proceeds with pigments mixed with lime water. The painter does as much as he can in a day's time, and the next day the unused finished coat is scraped away, to make room for a fresh coat on which the painter continues.

The painter cannot make revisions, for the pigments become chemically bonded to the plaster the very same day. He must have his composition fully planned and execute it with unfailing precision. If he wants to change anything, he must scrape away the old and start afresh.

14, l. 2. *Donato Bramante (1444–1514).* One of the great Renaissance architects, an influential advisor to Pope Julius II, who treats him as an intimate. At odds with Michelangelo, Bramante is known as Il Rovinante, "the ruiner," for his untrustworthiness, and for the callousness with which he dismantles the old St. Peter's. Michelangelo writes, "All the dissensions between Pope Julius and me arose from the envy of Bramante and Raffaello da Urbino, and this was the cause of my not finishing the Tomb in his lifetime. They wanted to ruin me."

14, l. 9. *Lorenzo Medici (1448–1492).* Lorenzo the Magnificent, patron of the famous Medici Garden in Florence, a forum of geniuses of the day, rivalling the great forums of Athens. He is a spiritual father to Michelangelo, taking him into the Garden and into his household when the sculptor is just 14. The Medici Circle includes Alberti, Pico, Poliziano, Pulci, and Ficino. Here Bertoldo, the aging student of Donatello, runs his school of sculpture into which Michelangelo is ushered.

14, l. 21. *Leonardo da Vinci (1452–1519).* The Renaissance genius, Michelangelo's elder by 23 years. Legend has it that when in Rome in 1513, he refuses to compete with Michelangelo and Raphael, spending his time instead inventing shellac, and grafting the wings of birds to the backs of live lizards and letting them roam his rooms so he could sketch what dragons would look like.

14, l. 21. *Raffaello da Urbino (1483–1520).* The young master painter Raphael, student of Perugino and admirer of Michelangelo, though the sculptor has no use for Raphael. They are opposites in personality. While Raphael paints his School of Athens, surrounded by friends and colleagues, Michelangelo broods alone in the Chapel, at work on the Ceiling. Raphael calls Buonarroti "the lonely hangman" and Michelangelo calls the painter "the provost." Years after Raphael's death, Michelangelo says, in bitterness, "All he had of art he owed to me."

14, l. 22. *Zechariah.* No less then 32 Biblical men bear this name, which ranges in spelling from Zachariah to Zacharias to Zechariah. Zechariah, the prophet of Judah, is the son of Berechiah, son of Iddo. His activities date from 520 B.C. His prophecy seems pale and mitigated, neither as robust in his hope as Ezekiel, nor as unwavering in his doom as Jeremiah. The Book of Zechariah also contains material later than the prophet's life. Chapters 9–14 contain "Oracles" from the Greek rather than the Persian period, including harbingers of Jesus and his entry into Jerusalem.

14, l. 24. *Darius.* Darius the Mede, probably modeled on the Persian king Darius the Great (522–486 B.C.). Darius is the third king to lord

over Daniel. And while Daniel and Zechariah appear to be contempo-
raries, there is no evidence that they ever cross paths, either in person or
reputation.

15, l. 25–26. *Stroke on stroke from out the living rock.* This is the first
line in a passage I have formed of Michelangelo's own phrases, using his
language as the palette. A line from that passage is placed in each section,
originating in the voice of each Ceiling persona. Then throughout the
last section, "The Brazen Serpent," these lines start to appear through
Michelangelo, as if he alone has been moved to speak them, and the poem
ends with Michelangelo ranting his own words entirely, rooted beyond
his awareness in their subliminal expression building across the book
from the other side.

15, l. 26–27. *Giuliano da Sangallo (1443–1516).* Architect and engraver,
Michelangelo's friend and elder. Responsible for having Julius bring Mi-
chelangelo to Rome in 1505.

17, l. 14–15. *Carrara.* The premier marble quarry, north of Pisa along
the Italian coast, known for its hard white stone. A special place for
Michelangelo. Where the stone for The Pieta is quarried.

17, l. 18. *Pier Matteo d'Amelia (1450–1508).* Commissioned in 1483 by
Pope Sixtus IV to cover the vault of The Sistine Ceiling when it is new
with gold stars on a blue sky.

17, l. 21. *Julius II (1443–1513).* Giuliano della Rovere, elected Pope
Julius II (1503–1513). Chief patron and antagonist of Michelangelo, from
whom he commissions his own Tomb, the bronze statue of himself done
in Bologna, and The Sistine Ceiling.

18, l. 8. *Marble.* A metamorphic rock, chiefly limestone, often irreg-
ularly colored by impurities. Typically, it evolves in the breakdown,
compression and recrystallization of calcium over extended periods into
a very hard stone. For example, ancient sea life from a warm sea, cast up
by volcanic action, compresses over centuries into marble.

18, l. 12. *Apuanes.* A mountain range along the western Italian coast,
north of Pisa, where the major marble quarries lie, such as Carrara, Ser-
avezza, and Pietra Santa.


## II. JUDITH AND THE HEAD OF HOLOFERNES

21, Headnote. *Spandrel.* The surface between two arches or the trian-
gular space on either side of an arch. It constitutes the leftover space in
each upper corner of The Sistine Chapel. They are difficult areas to fill.
The Ceiling has four spandrels, in which Michelangelo paints Judith and
the Head of Holofernes, David Slaying Goliath, The Punishment of Ha-
man, and The Brazen Serpent.

22, l. 19–21. *Santo Spirito.* The church in Florence where Michelangelo dissects cadavers to study anatomy.

24, l. 8. *Tophet.* A place near Gehenna, during the time of Jeremiah, where human sacrifices are made; a place where children are burned; from the Hebrew meaning "burning altar."

25, l. 1. *Ozias.* Ruler of the Jews in the time of Judith, when Holofernes lays siege to the town of Bethulia.

25, l. 17. *pigment.* Any coloring matter; in Renaissance painting, pigments are derived from mineral and vegetable sources ground to an appropriate fineness.

## III. DAVID SLAYING GOLIATH

30, l. 16–17. David is the youngest of eight brothers including Eliab, Abinadab, and his closest brother, Samma.

30, l. 16–17. *Samuel.* His name means "Name of God," "Heard of God." Born to Hannah and Elkanah, Samuel is devoted by his mother to the Lord, in the care of Eli the priest at Shiloh. Samuel becomes the grand old man among the judges. Both judge and priest, he tries to hold Israel to the ancient ways, to prevent the development of a monarchy. Finally, he yields to popular pressure and, still protesting, discovers and anoints Saul as Israel's first king. For a time he is an elder statesman to Saul, but the king, growing more popular and powerful, diminishes Samuel's influence. Samuel, not surprisingly, becomes dissatisfied with Saul, and, acting on an oracle of God, fills his horn with oil and goes to Jesse the Bethlehemite, demanding to see his sons. Having seen them all except the youngest, he has Jesse summon David. When David arrives, God instructs Samuel, "Arise and anoint him, for this is he," the man to be king in Saul's place.

31, l. 11–12. *Pieta.* The Italian word meaning both pity and piety. Has come to refer to the depiction of the Virgin Mary holding her dead son, Christ, in her arms. It is a particular form of art that surfaces as early as the 12th century. And Michelangelo evolves, at the age of 25, as the master of the form; primarily with the famous Rome Pieta (1500) mentioned here, but also later with the Nicodemus Pieta (1552), and the unfinished Rondanini Pieta (1563–1564) which he works until his death.

33, l. 1. *Buonarroto.* Michelangelo's elder and closest brother, a merchant and prior. From eldest to youngest the brothers are Buonarroto, Michelangelo, Lionardo, Giovansimone and Gismondo.

33, l. 16–17. *Saul.* His name means "Asked," "Inquired of." The first

King of Judah, anointed by Samuel. The story of Saul's anointment begins when his father, the wealthy Benjamite Kish, sends him to search the hill country of Ephraim for a herd of lost asses. His search brings him to a city in the land of Zeph where "a man of God" is known to be. There he finds Samuel, who has anticipated his arrival through a vision. When Saul appears, God instructs Samuel, "Here is the man who shall rule over my people." And Samuel anoints Saul, who then joins a band of prophets at Gibeah in an ecstatic experience.

34, l. 9–10. *Pier, the other Lorenzo.* Lorenzo di Pier Francesco (1463–1507) belongs to the younger branch of the Medici family. He is Lorenzo the Magnificent's cousin.

34, l. 27. *Baldassare del Milanese.* An art dealer in Rome, to whom Michelangelo misrepresents his sleeping cupid as an antique.

34, l. 27. *Cardinal Riario* of Rome, who purchases Michelangelo's sleeping cupid for 200 ducats, believing it to be an antique uncovered in a vineyard. Riario has the young sculptor brought to Rome, where he commissions him to carve The Bacchus.

36, l. 32. *Jacopo Galli.* The Roman banker who, as sponsor and intermediary, arranges for the elderly French Bishop Jean Bilheres de Lagraulas to commission Michelangelo to sculpt his famous Pieta. On August 27, 1498, Michelangelo signs the formal contract for The Pieta, which promises "the most beautiful work in marble which exists today in Rome."

36, l. 33. *San Lorenzo.* The church in Florence intimately connected with the Medici family, and the burial place of all its principal members, after they commission Brunelleschi to rebuild it.

37, l. 5. *Philistines.* The word means "Immigrants." A people, Aryan in origin, possibly from Crete, who are the chief opponents of the Israelites as they begin to consolidate their position in the land of Canaan. The Philistines eventually give their name to the land, Palestine. Occupying the coastal plains and being a seafaring people, they offer Israel an everpresent threat, even to the days of David and Solomon, who keep them in bounds but never subdue them completely. David, who slays the Philistine Goliath, and who, as a king, is often involved in guerilla warfare with the Philistines, is also befriended by them during his outlaw days.

37, l. 19. *Greaves.* Leg armor worn below the knee.

39, l. 1. *scrip.* A small pouch-like satchel or bag, like the one in which David puts the stones he intends to use against Goliath.

39, l. 22. *Goliath of Geth.* His name means "An Exile," "A Soothsayer." The famous giant (nine feet tall) and champion of the Philistines whom David slays.

45, Headnote. *The Intoxication of Noah.* When Noah gets drunk, he lies naked in his tent where Ham, his troubled son, views him boldly in his nakedness. Ham then tells his brothers, Sem and Japheth, who take a robe and, laying it on their shoulders, inch backwards, their faces turned away, to cover their father's nakedness. When Noah is awakened, he oddly curses Ham's son, Canaan, for the shame of seeing him naked: "Meanest of slaves shall he be to his brethren!" It is unclear where nakedness derives this shameful connotation beyond the traditional expulsion of Adam and Eve from Eden.

46, l. 9–20. *Moses and the burning bush.* It is in the wilderness of Madian, tending Jethro's flocks, that Moses encounters on Mount Sinai the bush which burns and will not be consumed. After that he persuades his brother, Aaron, to join him and they wrestle with Ramses for the freedom of the Jews.

46, l. 22–34. *Buddha.* Sometime between 600–500 B.C., Siddhattha Gautama grows up an aristocrat in a small tribal community in the north of Bengal. He passes from gratification to gratification unsatisfied, feeling that the reality of life is evading him. At 29 he experiences four omens with his charioteer, Channa, and in the night after the birth of his first son, he awakes in a great agony of spirit, "like a man who's told his house is on fire." He and Channa steal away, severing all ties, to begin his new life.

47, l. 26–28 *Mani.* Founder of Manichaeism, a religious attempt to sort the teachings of Moses, Zoroaster, Buddha, and Christ by explaining the perplexities and contradictions of life as a conflict of light and darkness. Born in 216 in Ecbatana, the old Median capital, Mani begins his teaching in 242. He travels and preaches widely throughout Iran, Turkestan, into India, and over the passes into China. By 270 he returns to Ctesiphon with a strong following and becomes, much like Jesus, a threat to the religious order. In 277 the Persian monarch has him crucified, and his body flayed. His adherents, like the early Christians, are fiercely persecuted.

47, l. 32ff. *Muhammad, Also Mohammed (570–632).* Prophet and founder of Islam. Born in considerable poverty, it is doubtful he ever learns to write. At 25, Muhammad marries Kadija, the widow of a rich merchant. Fifteen years later he begins preaching the unity of all peoples under one God, Allah, and is quickly at odds with local polytheistic traditions. The next 20 years become a host of intrigues and failures and triumphs and attempts on his life. During this time he fathers a son, Ibrahim, with Mary the Egyptian but the beloved boy dies as a child. By 629 Muhammad comes to Mecca as its master, and by his death in 632 he is the master of all Arabia.

48, l. 4–9. *Marco Polo (1254–1324)*. Venetian explorer who travels to the court of Kublai Khan. He is young and clever and masters the Tartar tongue so thoroughly, he pleases the Great Khan. He returns to Venice about 1295, looking so strange to his kin they refuse him entry to his own house. Among other things he brings back diamonds and coal. He is mocked for his accounts of China and given the nickname Il Milione because he is always talking about the millions of people and the millions of ducats.

48, l. 19. *Lodovico Buonarroti (1444–1534)* is Michelangelo's whining, timid, diffident father who serves as a professional mayor of sorts. Early on he tries to dissuade his son from Art and, in fact, is terse and demanding when he hands the boy over to Lorenzo the Magnificent. Nonetheless, as Michelangelo becomes prominent, he supports his father and his brothers throughout their lives.

48, l. 31. *Giovansimone*. Michelangelo's second younger brother, who devotes himself to poetry and licentiousness.

## VI. THE DELPHIC SIBYL

51, Headnote. *The Delphic Sibyl*. Until the fourth century B.C., there is only one sibyl, Cumae. Thereafter the number varies, but Varro cites as many as ten. According to Hartt, sibyls are Greek and Roman prophetesses who foretell the coming of Christ. Michelangelo enthrones five sibyls on the central part of the Ceiling (Delphica, Eritrea, Cumae, Persica, Libica) to balance his five central prophets (Joel, Isaiah, Ezekiel, Daniel, Jeremiah), mounting Zechariah and Jonah at each end of the vault. It is unknown if the Delphic Sibyl is associated with the Delphic Oracle or just the region. Delphi is the ancient town of central Greece on the southern slope of Mount Parnassus and is the seat of the Delphic Oracle, the Oracle of Apollo. In this temple of Apollo, the Adytum, where the oracle is delivered, lies in the southwest part. It is supposed to be the center of the earth, and the exact spot is marked by a stone called the omphalos (navel). Questions are put to the Pythia or priestess by a male prophet, who interprets the answers.

53, l. 14–15. *the casting of Julius*. Difficulties with Julius over the building of his tomb cause Michelangelo to flee from Rome to Florence in 1506. After months of anxiety and three Papal Briefs, he leaves for Bologna to submit himself to the powerful Julius, who exacts penance from the sculptor in the form of a bronze statue of himself, which takes Michelangelo until the early months of 1508 to complete.

53, l. 21. *Lapo*. The Florentine foundryman who fails to assist Michelangelo in the casting of the bronze statue of Julius in Bologna.

53, l. 28. *Bernardino di Antonio del Ponte.* A superior Florentine foundryman who assists Michelangelo in the casting of the bronze statue of Julius when Lapo fails. Even he has trouble, as the casting weighs an estimated 18,000 pounds.

54, l. 3–5. Ever driven, Michelangelo says, "I already have a wife who is too much for me; one who keeps me unceasingly struggling on. It is my art, and my works are my children."

54, l. 9. *San Petronio.* The church in Bologna where Michelangelo's bronze statue of Julius is placed in 1508.

## VII. THE FLOOD

58, l. 3. *Ham.* His name means "Swarthy," "Hot." He is one of Noah's three sons, along with Sem and Japheth. It is believed the African peoples descend from Ham. Ham's son Cush fathers the Ethiopians. Cush's son Nimrod fathers the Assyrians. Ham's son Egypt is father of the Egyptians. And Ham's son Canaan, whom Noah curses, is father of the early inhabitants of Palestine, the Canaanites.

59, l. 8. *Tiber, Arno, Sieve.* The major rivers of northern and central Italy. The Sieve starts along with the Arno, the river running through Florence, and the Tiber, the river running north and south through Rome, in the mountains east of Florence and north of Rome. It is with the autumn rains in these mountains that the floods of northern and central Italy traditionally begin—as many as 130 in the last 50 years. Florence has been hit the hardest with the legendary floods of 1333, 1557, 1844 and, most recently, 1966; the worst in its history, ruining countless Renaissance treasures and posting a high-water mark of 16 feet 2 inches above the Arno's normal tide.

61, l. 16. *spinet.* A small, compact upright piano, or a small harpsichord with a single keyboard.

61, l. 16. *cittern.* A 16th century guitar with a pear-shaped body, also called a "cither" or a "cithern."

## VIII. THE ERITREAN SIBYL

65, Headnote. *The Eritrean Sibyl.* A prophetess of Eritrea, a northern region of Ethiopia bordering the Red Sea.

66, l. 5. *lunette.* A semi-circular space in a vault or ceiling, or above a door or window, often decorated with a painting or relief. In The Sistine Ceiling the lunettes are the triangular spaces above the eight windows in The Sistine Chapel, in which Michelangelo portrays the Ancestors of Christ.

68, l. 23. *florin.* The Florentine unit of money used during the Renaissance; roughly equivalent to the Roman ducat and worth at most about 50 dollars.

## IX. THE SACRIFICE OF NOAH

72, l. 16. *Avena.* The small town where Michelangelo arranges for cartloads of marble he has quarried at Carrara to be shipped to Rome in 1505.

72, l. 21. *the General Julius.* Julius is commonly known as the Warrior-Pope, due to his thirst for conquest and his military skill.

74, l. 16-17. *Francesca di Neri di Miniato del Sera.* Michelangelo's mother, who dies in 1481 at the age of 26.

## X. ISAIAH

81, l. 23-24. *cartoon.* From *cartone,* meaning large sheet of paper. A full-size preparatory drawing for a painting or fresco. Vasari describes how the large sheets are made: "Sheets of paper, I mean square sheets, are fastened together with paste made of flour and water cooked on the fire. They are attached to the wall by this paste, which is spread two fingers' breadth all round on the side next the wall, and are damped all over by sprinkling cold water on them. In this moist state they are stretched so that the creases are smoothed out in the drying. Then when they are dry the artist proceeds."

Symonds describes Michelangelo's cartoon process, regarding The Sistine Ceiling: "He first made a small-scale sketch of the composition, sometimes including a variety of figures. Then he went to the living models, and studied portions of the whole design in careful transcripts from Nature, using black and red chalk, pen, and sometimes bistre. Finally, returning to the first composition, he repeated as much as could be transferred to a single sheet, on the exact scale of the intended fresco. These enlarged drawings were applied to the wet surface of the plaster. When we reflect upon the extent of the Sistine vault (it is estimated at more than 10,000 square feet of surface), and the difficulties presented by its curves, lunettes, and spandrels . . . we (are amazed) that this enormous space is alive with 343 figures in every conceivable attitude, some of them 12 feet in height, those seated as prophets and sibyls measuring nearly 18 feet when upright—and all, animated with extraordinary vigour."

84, l. 3. *Dante Alighieri (1265-1321).* The great Italian poet whose *Divine Comedy* is the first major work written in Italian and not Latin.

Dante is a strong influence on Michelangelo, who never learns Latin. One of the sculptor's first works, at the age of 15, is The Battle of the Centaurs, a relief prompted by Dante's reference to the rape of Dejanira. The sculptor becomes well-versed in Dante's work and, in one famous incident, chides Leonardo for misquoting him.

84, l. 8. *Duomo.* Italian for cathedral. Here, the cathedral dedicated to the Madonna of Florence, also known as Santa Maria del Fiore. Brunelleschi's construction of its dome is one of the chief architectural feats of the Renaissance, and is often seen as the beginning of the Renaissance.

84, l. 14. *Tantalus.* In Greek mythology, a king who for his crimes is condemned in Hades to stand in water that recedes when he tries to drink, with fruit hanging above him that recedes when he tries to eat. Michelangelo, in trying to temper and control his hypersensitive nature, must have felt like a Tantalus. Ramsden remarks: "He knew it to be essential for the preservation of his equilibrium, both as an artist and a man, to maintain a certain measure of isolation, not because he was a misanthrope and a recluse, as everyone has always contended, but because he was exactly the reverse, being all too prone to love not wisely but too well." And Michelangelo, himself, says: "Whenever I see someone who is good at something, who shows some power of mind, who can do or say something better than the others, I am compelled to fall in love with him, and give myself to him as booty, so that I am no longer my own, but all of his."

89, l. 1. *Gismondo.* Michelangelo's youngest brother, who becomes a farmer at Settignano.

89, l. 12–13. *Charles VIII.* King of France from 1483–1498.

89, l. 17. *Girolamo Savonarola (1452–1498).* The Dominican monk who, in 1489, is appointed Prior of San Marco in Florence. His evangelical fervor and his political adroitness enable him to become, for a short time, the virtual dictator of the Florentine Republic. One of the most chilling and affecting orators of his day, he condemns the humanism of the time in favor of an austere bareness of prayer. He disturbs everyone and converts many, including Michelangelo's younger brother, Lionardo, who becomes a Dominican monk. Pico says "the mere sound of the monk's voice is like a clap of doom." And Botticelli, as a gesture of reform, burns some of his work at Savonarola's behest. On May 23rd, 1498, Savonarola is burned at a stake in the piazza in front of the Palazzo Vecchio in Florence.

89, l. 23. *Angelo Poliziano (1454–1494).* The most eminent of the Medici Circle after Alberti. Also known as Politian. Poliziano is a poet-philosopher who translates the writers of antiquity. Among the Greeks he

prefers Aristotle; among the Romans, Quintilius. He is a close intimate
of Lorenzo, and in fact saves his life during the Pazzi Conspiracy of
1478. He has a tremendous influence on Michelangelo, and also tutors
Lorenzo's children.

## XI. THE FALL OF MAN AND HIS EXPULSION
## FROM PARADISE

94, l. 1. *Eve.* Her name means "Life," "Life-Giving," "Mother of All
Living." Most references to Eve in the Old Testament, especially given
that she is the "Mother of All Living," are unsatisfactory. Everything
seems too man-centered, much as the universe is too earth-centered be-
fore Galileo. A more potent correlation exists between Eve and Gaea,
the goddess of the earth in Greek Mythology, who bore the Titans, the
Furies and the Cyclopes; especially when we consider that Gaea comes
from the Greek, Gaia, meaning "personification of earth."

94, l. 12. In accordance with a male-biased tradition, Michelangelo
depicts the Temptor as female.

96, l. 9. Note how D.H. Lawrence views the Temptation: "When Adam
went and took Eve, after the apple, he didn't do any more than he had
done many a time before, in act. But in consciousness he did something
very different. So did Eve. Each of them kept an eye on what they were
doing, they watched what was happening to them. They wanted to
KNOW. And that was the birth of sin. Not doing it, but KNOWING
about it. Before the apple, they had shut their eyes and their minds had
gone dark. Now, they peeped and pried and imagined. They watched
themselves. And they felt uncomfortable after. They felt self-conscious.
So they said, 'The act is sin. Let's hide. We've sinned.' "

## XII. EZEKIEL

100, l. 1. *Ezekiel,* whose name means "God is Strong," is a priest-
prophet among the exiles who live by the river Chobar in Chaldea, an
ancient region in southern Babylonia along the Euphrates river and the
Persian Gulf. He is the son of Buzi, who was a priest of Jerusalem.
Ezekiel, born in that city during the time of Jeremiah the prophet, is
carried into captivity when Nebuchadnezzar captures Jerusalem in 586
B.C. In Babylon, Ezekiel has a wife and the privilege of a house of his
own, together with religious freedom. About five years after the captivity
begins, he is called to his prophetic ministry by a vision of four seraphim.

His early prophecies are apocalyptic, while his later visions are full of hope and restoration. Jeremiah, Ezekiel, and Daniel appear to overlap in three successive generations, spanning roughly from 640–522 B.C.

101, l. 2. The eating of the scroll serves as an archetype for the mystery of communion, though it remains unclear why Ezekiel ingests God's word. Is it to internalize God or to hide and preserve the Godly moment against an unwilling world?

101, l. 13. *Palazzo Vecchio.* The town hall of Florence, built on the site of a Roman theatre. There the conspirators in the Pazzi Conspiracy are hung in 1478, and in the Piazza outside, Savonarola is burned to death in 1498, and Michelangelo's David is originally placed in 1504. The main hall is where Leonardo, in 1505, works his Battle of Anghiari, while Michelangelo, on the opposite wall, works his Battle of Cascina. And the Cancelleria is where Machiavelli has an office, from 1498 to 1512, as government secretary.

102, l. 16. *Agostino Duccio (1418-1481).* The Florentine sculptor who in 1464 ruins an enormous block of pure Carrara marble. Considered cut beyond salvage, the block becomes known as the Duccio stone, and is idle for 37 years. Even Sansovino says he would only work it if he could add marble to it. It is the Duccio stone that Michelangelo turns into David.

102, l. 17. *Andrea Sansovino (1470-1529).* A well-known sculptor and architect who is in competition with Michelangelo and Leonardo for the Duccio stone.

107, l. 4–5. *Ohola and Oholiba.* The women in Ezekiel's tale of sisters (Ezekiel, 23). The names appear to be symbolic. The first, standing for Samaria, may be read as meaning "her own tent." The latter, standing for Jerusalem, means "my tent is in her." The references could refer to the schismatic temple and cult of the Lord in Samaria, as opposed to their authentic counterpart in Jerusalem.

111, l. 2. *Campanile.* A bell-tower, often detached from the building to which it belongs. The campanile referred to here belongs to the Duomo in Florence.

111, l. 3. *Ghiberti's doors.* Lorenzo Ghiberti's (1378-1455) north and east bronze doors of the Baptistery of San Giovanni, one of Florence's oldest and most revered buildings. The north door depicts scenes from the life of Christ, the Evangelists, and the Doctors of the Church. The more celebrated east door contains ten scenes from the Old Testament, in which breathing figures seem dipped in gold. Michelangelo, in awe, calls them "the Gates of Paradise."

111, l. 19. *Piero Soderini.* Appointed Gonfalonier of Justice for Florence in March 1501. A powerful ally of Michelangelo, he appears to be instrumental in securing the Duccio stone for Michelangelo's sculpture of David.

111, l. 26. *the commission of 30.* Much to Michelangelo's dismay, a commission of 30 is convened to decide where to place his unprecedented David. The members include Leonardo, Botticelli, Rosselli, Sansovino, and Ghirlandaio, whom the sculptor apprenticed with before entering the Medici Garden.

112, l. 2. *Cosimo Rosselli (1439–1507).* A member of the commission of 30, Rosselli favors placing David at the Duomo. Rosselli is among the first, along with Botticelli, to paint the side walls of The Sistine Chapel when it is bare and new in 1483.

112, l. 4. *Sandro Botticelli (1444–1510).* The Florentine master whose best-known works include the allegories Primavera and Birth of Venus. He also executes a famous series of illustrations for Dante's *Divine Comedy.*

## XIII. THE CREATION OF EVE

119, Headnote. *The Creation of Eve.* The Old Testament contains two versions of the creation of Eve. The first indicates a simultaneous and equal creation of both Adam and Eve: "So God created man in His own image, in the image of God created He him; male and female created He them." The second issues the more traditional view that God created Eve from Adam's rib: "And the Lord God caused a deep sleep to fall upon Adam, and he slept: and He took one of his ribs, and closed up the flesh instead thereof; And the rib, which the Lord God had taken from man, made He a woman, and brought her unto the man. And Adam said, This is now bone of my bones, and flesh of my flesh: she shall be called Woman, because she was taken out of Man."

The traditional male-oriented interpretation views the first as a more general view, followed by the specific method of creation. The feminist interpretation gives priority to the more equitable first version, believing, as Biblical scholars have noted, that the differing versions are probably the result of two authors, eventually merged by yet another into the Genesis we have today. It is no surprise Michelangelo's version has God pulling Eve mysteriously from a sleeping Adam.

119, Headnote. David, whose name means "Beloved," remains one of the most ambiguous of Biblical figures. After slaying Goliath, stories of David's success and anointment spread, causing Saul to become jealous and suspicious. He becomes obsessed with the boy, and sends David into battle unnecessarily, hoping to have him slain. Each foray, however, establishes David's legend further till Saul drives him into exile, and tries to hunt him down. Eventually, Saul is slain by the Philistines and David returns to be anointed king. After years of internal strife David drives the Philistines out and storms Jerusalem, and calls it Zion, the city of David. Judah's power grows to the point that lesser princes submit to David's rule without a fight. Peace and prosperity settle. And while ruling his forces from home, David becomes entangled in his illicit affair with Bethsabee, more commonly known as Bathsheba.

120, l. 16. *Urias the Hethite.* Urias means "God is Light," "My Light or Flame" and Hethite means "Sons of Heth," Heth meaning "Terrible." An interesting genesis: Light out of Dark; Flame, Son of Terrible. The Hethites are a non-Semitic people whom the patriarchs meet in Canaan, and who are met again as the Israelites force their way into Canaan after the deliverance from Egypt. In the days of Moses, the Hethites defeat an army of Ramses II, but fail to follow up the victory. Some think the Egyptians learn the use of iron-tipped weapons, chariots, and laminated bows from their experiences with the Hethites, who are also known, in later times, as expert horse breeders.

121, l. 5. *Joab.* When David first meets Bethsabee, her husband, Urias, is under Joab's command. Joab, whose name means "God is Father," is David's brilliant field general, who, in the early years of David's career, is loyal almost to a fault.

124, l. 18. *Nathan,* whose name means "Giver," "Gift," is a fearless prophet of high integrity who is both friend and critic of David. It is Nathan who anoints Solomon as king.

125, l. 29. *Solomon,* whose name means "Peace," "Peaceable," is David's son by Bethsabee. He is the successor to David as the King of Judah.

## XV. THE CREATION OF ADAM

145, l. 12–13. *Cain,* whose name means "Possession," "Smith," "Artificer," is the first son born to Adam and Eve, conceived in Eden, born in the world. He is the first farmer, the first to be guilty of fratricide, the first fugitive from the consequence of murder, the first builder of a city; another enigmatic prototype for the race. After killing Abel, he flees to the land of Nod, where he builds the city of Enoch, which he names after his first son.

145, l. 12–13. *Abel* is the second son of Adam and Eve, who becomes a herdsman and whose sacrifice to God is preferred over that of his brother Cain, the farmer. Abel sacrifices the firstlings of his flock, a costly and carefully prepared offering, while Cain's offering is cheap and casual. The difference is, of course, known to God and finally to Cain, who, through his own psychological maneuvering, becomes estranged and kills Abel and becomes an outcast.

149, l. 13. *Seth,* whose name means "Appointed," is the third child of Adam and Eve. Adam, who lives to be 930, is 130 when he sires Seth.

## XVI. THE PERSIAN SIBYL

151, Headnote. *Cumae's books.* Cumae, too deeply stirred by love like a knife, comes to Italy to sell her books of prophecy to Tarquin, an early Roman king. The books are kept in the Capitol by a college of priests, consulted only by order of the Senate. They are believed destroyed by fire in 83 B.C. A new unauthorized collection is assembled and preserved until 405 when it is burned. However, Persica, at Cumae's request, has harbored the originals.

154, l. 19–20. *Nicholas Copernicus (1473–1543).* The Polish astronomer who begins to enunciate the principle of a sun-centered universe. He comes to Italy in 1496 and lives in Bologna. In 1500 he comes to Rome for a year and, shortly after his arrival, begins giving informal lectures on mathematics and astronomy.

155, l. 15. *Cristoforo Solari.* Called the Gobbo of Milan, mistakenly identified by drunkards in a crowd as the sculptor of The Pieta.

## XVII. GOD SEPARATES THE WATERS ON EARTH
## AND BLESSES HIS WORK

168, above l. 1. *Gianfrancesco Aldrovandi.* The Customs Officer in Bologna who takes Michelangelo in as a guest during the sculptor's flight from Florence in 1494.

168, l. 9. *Cardiere.* A musician in the Medici Garden with Michelangelo at the time of Lorenzo's death.

168, l. 13. *Francesco Granacci (1469–1541).* The Florentine painter who is Michelangelo's oldest friend. They apprentice with Ghirlandaio together, and are both brought into the Medici Garden at the same time, along with Giuliano Bugiardini (1475–1554).

169, below l. 28. At the corners of the nine panels of creation across the center of the Ceiling, Michelangelo paints his ignudi or nude figures. They are positioned in pairs and each pair holds aloft a bronze medallion which depicts a scene from the Old Testament in miniature, such as the Death of Urias, Nathan and David, the Death of Absalom, and Elias on the Chariot of Fire. The medallions frame every other panel and they appear to be held aloft by open robes used as slings.

170, l. 12. *Francesco Petrarch (1304–1374).* The Italian poet and scholar famous as a founder of humanism, though his contemporary reputation rests on his Latin scholarship. Among his works is *Africa,* a self-analysis in the form of a dialogue between himself and St. Augustine.

170, l. 12. *Giovanni Boccaccio (1313–1375).* The Italian writer and humanist who writes *Filostrato,* the story of Troilus and Cressida, on which both Chaucer and Shakespeare draw. His masterpiece, *The Decameron,* written about 1348, at the time of the Great Plague, is a series of prose tales which gives a broad view of the human comedy.

## XVIII. DANIEL

173, Headnote. *Nebuchadnezzar.* The King (605–562 B.C.) of Babylon who defeats Pharoah Necho, extending his empire into Egypt. A great military man and a good administrator, who is responsible for the grandeur of ancient Babylon.

173, Headnote. *Belteshazzar* means "Bel Protect His Life," Bel being a major Babylonian god.

174, l. 1. *Daniel.* Though I have focused on Daniel's relationship with Nebuchadnezzar, Belshazzar, who is actually a crown prince given royal authority, succeeds Nebuchadnezzar. As king, he has a banquet in which the plundered silver and gold vessels taken from the Temple in Jerusalem are used. And as the guests celebrate and praise their gods of gold and silver, the fingers of a hand appear, writing on the plaster wall. Terrified, Belshazzar calls on Daniel to read what has been written. Daniel says, "This is the writing inscribed: MENE, TEKEL, and PERES. These words mean: MENE, God has numbered your kingdom and put an end to it; TEKEL, you have been weighed on the scales and found wanting; PERES, your kingdom has been divided." This story yields the declaration "I can see the writing on the wall."

Darius becomes the third king Daniel encounters. His famous experience in the lions' den comes when Daniel's popularity spawns jealousies and intrigues to which Darius succumbs. In the appendix to the Book of Daniel, the story of Bel and the Dragon is related, which involves Daniel with yet a fourth king, Cyrus, whose name means "Sun," "An Heir." This is probably Cyrus I, King of Persia (c. 539 B.C.), who questions why Daniel does not pray to Bel, and Daniel says because it is not

a living God. Brief encounters ensue and Daniel's shrewdness foils Cyrus
in such a way that the people begin to accuse Cyrus of being a Jew. As
pressure mounts, he sends Daniel to the lions' den. This is a second
rendering of the lions' den, different from when Darius sends him.

174, l. 8. *Caltazzar the Chaldean.* A magician-astronomer in the court
of Nebuchadnezzar, adept at charting the future by a process of casting
rings and interpreting their patterns in relation to the stars.

178, l. 15. *Giovanni Balducci.* The banker in Rome, from whom Michelangelo has to borrow 250 ducats to pay for the marble that has arrived from Carrara in 1506, when Julius refuses to spend any more money
on his Tomb.

178, l. 28. *God's impetus.* Michelangelo is often called "terribilita,"
Italian for "terrible," "awful," "full of awe." It signifies the torrential
magnificence and horror, the double edge of being infused with creation.
He is a paradox: on fire and drowning.

181, l. 9. *Susanna.* Though I intend a different psychology for the story
of Susanna, whose name means "Lily," the original can be found in the
appendix to the Book of Daniel, first appearing in the Greek. There,
Susanna, a woman of "great refinement and beauty," is the virtuous wife
of a prominent Jew in Babylon. Two elders, coming often to his house,
catch her bathing in the garden and threaten to accuse her of adultery
with a young man if she doesn't give herself to them. She refuses and
they bring her before the Babylonian Assembly, in which they serve
among the judges. As it appears that Susanna will be put to death, the
Spirit moves young Daniel to cry out for justice, for further examination.
He presses the accusers and, questioning them separately, uncovers different versions of accusation. Susanna is vindicated and Daniel's reputation spreads quickly among the people.

185, l. 10. *Eban.* A messenger in the court of Nebuchadnezzar loyal
to Daniel.

185, l. 24-25. *Martin Luther (1483-1546).* The German monk who
founds Protestantism and writes the famous *Theses of Wittenberg* in 1517.
Luther comes to Rome in 1510 to ask the Pope for two concessions,
neither of which he obtains.

186, l. 3. *St. Peter's.* The Basilica of St. Peter's in Rome, the central
church of the Roman Catholic faith. Originally an oratory built around
90 over the bones of Peter, near where he's martyred in Nero's Circus.
The original basilica is built by Constantine (319-322). By the middle of
the 15th century, the church shows signs of collapse and Nicholas V
entrusts its repair to Alberti, Rossellino, and Giuliano da Sangallo. At
the death of Nicholas, all work stops, until Julius II in 1505 decides on

a complete reconstruction. Julius and his Architect, Bramante, break ground for the new St. Peter's on April 18th, 1506. Bramante dismantles the old church ruthlessly. At Bramante's death, Raphael becomes the Architect. When Raphael dies, work ceases until Paul III (1534–1549) installs Antonio da Sangallo (1483–1546) as Architect. At his death, Michelangelo, at the age of 72, becomes the Architect of St. Peter's and designs the cupola. And under Bernini the enormous piazza and portico, and vast interior, are brought into being.

188, l. 16. *Bel* which means "Lord," "Owner," "Possessor" is the Babylonian form which Daniel encounters of the fertility god Baal. Baal is the generic name for the local deities the Israelites encounter in their wanderings.

199, l. 5. *Brief.* As in Papal Brief, a Papal letter pertaining to matters of discipline. An instrument of Papal demand, command, or reprimand.

200, l. 9. *Biagio Bonaccorsi.* An associate of Machiavelli who entrusts Michelangelo with money for the politician when the sculptor is enroute to Bologna to submit himself to Julius late in 1506.

200, l. 17–18. The inevitable opening and restructuring of one's life by crisis is profoundly perceived by Yeats when he says, "Genius is a crisis which joins the buried self, for brief moments, to the daily mind."

## XIX. GOD CREATES THE SUN AND MOON
## AND PLANTS ON EARTH

211, l. 15. *Friar Bene.* An ancestor of Michelangelo who is a contemporary of Dante. In 1283 Bene enters the monastery of Santa Maria Novella, which Dante frequents, and remains there as an ironworker until his death in 1343.

212, l. 22–23. *Giovanni Pico della Mirandola (1463–1494)* is a leading member of the Medici Garden. He has a tremendous influence on Michelangelo. Pico is said to speak 22 languages at the age of 18. It is said once he reads a page three times, he can recite it from memory forward or backward. His philosophical disposition is founded on his simultaneous absorption with Greek and Hebrew. He loves both Plato and the Cabbala, a theosophy of rabbinical origin widely transmitted in medieval Europe and based on a mystical interpretation of the Hebrew Scriptures. Pico continues to master the ancient tongues in an effort to fuse all the known religions into one unified philosophy. The result is his *900 Theses,* a treatise to be delivered in Rome in 1486. Thirteen of the 900 are declared heretical, so they are all banned and never made public. Pico dies eight years later, at the age of 31, two years after Columbus sails. It is a death which wounds the young Michelangelo, who is 19 at the time. The Theses are lost, save the introduction, which is ultimately published by itself as an *Oration on the Dignity of Man.*

## XX. JEREMIAH

220, below l. 26. *Baruch,* whose name means "Blessed," is the son of Neriah. He is secretary and scribe for the prophet Jeremiah. Barred from the Temple area prior to the fall of Jerusalem, Jeremiah calls on Baruch to record the messages he is receiving from the Lord and to read them to those gathered in the Temple area on the day of fasting.

220, below l. 26. *Zedekiah,* whose name means "God is Might," is the youngest son of Josiah. He is appointed King of Judah under Nebuchadnezzar in 597 B.C. Originally his name is Mattaniah. Nebuchadnezzar seems to be involved in the change of names as well. Zedekiah takes an oath of obedience to Babylon, but joins a coalition of Moab, Ammon, and Tyre against Nebuchadnezzar after considerable hesitation and vacillation. In 588 B.C. there is an open revolt. Egypt promises assistance, an important factor in the decision to rebel. Babylon lays siege to Jerusalem, but the siege is lifted when word comes that Egypt is involved. Two years later Babylon renews the attack and takes Jerusalem.

## XXI. GOD SEPARATES LIGHT AND DARK

229, above l. 1. *Pazzi Conspiracy.* A conspiracy, hatched by Girolamo Riario, Jacopo de Pazzi, and his nephew, Francesco Pazzi, to murder Lorenzo Medici and his popular and beloved younger brother Giuliano (1453–1478). Riario, who is not a Pazzi, is the nephew of Pope Sixtus IV (1471–1484) who has The Sistine Chapel built (1473–1483) and who is, as well, the uncle of Pope Julius II. The Pazzi, a distinguished Florentine banking family of ancient lineage, are rising to prominence in Florence, becoming rivals of the Medici.

230, l. 5–9. When Giuliano is found, he is pierced by 19 wounds.

230, l. 29–33. Baroncelli is hung as well. Leonardo da Vinci, who is 25 at the time, is among the crowd and sketches Baroncelli hanging. See illustration, p. 231. Lorenzo also has the hangings immortalized by Botticelli, but the frescos are destroyed when Lorenzo's son, Piero, is expelled from Florence in 1494.

230, l. 34–36. After the burial of Jacopo de Pazzi in hallowed ground, Florence is drenched by rain for days. The people decide it's because the wicked old man is buried in sacred soil. They dig him up and finally hurl him into the Arno, after which the rain stops.

232, l. 2. *Leone Battista Alberti (1404–1472).* The immense and leading genius of the Medici Garden is considered to be a predecessor of Leonardo da Vinci. He is a painter, architect, philosopher, poet, and engineer. He invents a surveying instrument and a method for raising an ancient ship from the bottom of Lake Nemi. In 1491 his book *Ecantonfila*, dealing with the art of loving and being loved, is published in Venice. Though he dies three years before Michelangelo is born, his influence on the young sculptor is great. Consider what Alberti says in *Della Pittura* (1435): "And if you would like to reproduce some work because you have more feeling towards that than towards live things, I would prefer to copy a mediocre sculpture than a fine painting. From a painting, nothing is acquired other than a knowledge of copying; but from a sculptured piece, one learns to copy and also acquaints himself with the copying and knowledge of (ilumi) light."

232, l. 2. *Falconry.* The art of training a swift, bright, wild animal to hunt on command. When locked up, the falcon is of no use. Yet each time it is sent out, there is a real possibility it will turn on its trainer or declare itself unattached and never return.

235, l. 15–16. In the early 1490's, Italy is not a unified country, but a collection of provinces, usually at odds with each other. The mainland has as many as ten. Rome is the hub of the Papal States, while Florence is the center of the Republic of Florence. Among those to the north are the Republic of Venice, the Duchy of Milan, the Duchy of Ferrara, the Republic of Genoa, and the Duchy of Savoy. Between Florence and Rome is the Republic of Siena, and to the south, the Kingdom of Naples. Here, the Republic of Florence endures a threat from King Charles VIII (1483–1498) of France.

244, l. 25. *scupper.* A small semi-eliptical hole carved into a ship's rail to allow water which comes on deck to drain back into the sea.

## XXII. THE LIBYAN SIBYL

247, Headnote. *Libica.* The Libyan Sibyl is the daughter of Zeus and the sorceress Lamia, who herself is the daughter of Poseidon. She is a prophetess of Libya; originally the Greek name for the continent of Africa.

250, l. 2. *Tiresias.* The blind soothsayer in Greek mythology who is half-man and half-woman. When Zeus and Hera argue over who receives more pleasure during intercourse, Hera claims it is man, while Zeus says it is woman. They resolve to ask Tiresias, since he is both sexes. He sides with Zeus, and Hera, in a rage, blinds him, which Zeus cannot undo. But as compensation, Zeus makes Tiresias immortal and capable of seeing into the future.

252, above l. 1. *Giuliano de Medici (1479-1516)* is Lorenzo's third son, also known as the Duke of Nemours, probably named after Lorenzo's murdered brother. He is the one son whom Lorenzo regards as good at heart, but Giuliano, long after his father's death, becomes taut and skewed and obsessed with his sexuality and with the garnering of mystical powers.

# XXIII. JONAH

266, l. 1. *Hadrian's Rotunda.* Hadrian's Tomb or Mausoleum, situated on the Tiber just east of the Vatican, known also as Castel Sant' Angelo. An enormous circular structure begun by Hadrian in 130 as a sepulchre for himself and his family. It is completed in 139, a year after his death. In the early Middle Ages, the Tomb is surrounded with ramparts and becomes the citadel of Rome.

268, l. 7-8. *The Battle of Cascina* is a massive cartoon which Michelangelo prepares between 1504 and 1505 for a fresco to be done in the Palazzo Vecchio in Florence. The cartoon embodies his exhaustive exploration of the naked human form in motion. Engaged on the opposite wall is Leonardo, working on his Battle of Anghiari. See Michelangelo Chronology, 1504, p. 395.

268, l. 20. *braccia.* Plural for braccio, Italian for arm. A unit of measurement, between 20 and 25 inches.

277, l. 32. *Pietro Perugino (1446-1523).* The aging master, with whom Raphael studies, is opposite in temperament and aesthetic from Michelangelo. His fresco of The Assumption is the original painting on the altar wall of The Sistine Chapel, which has to be torn down for Michelangelo's Last Judgment.

278, l. 21. *Rovere.* The surname of Pope Julius II, Giuliano della Rovere.

283, l. 22-23. *Sangallo the Younger.* Giuliano da Sangallo's son, Francesco, whom Michelangelo encounters during his stay with Sangallo, when brought to Rome by Julius in 1505. Sangallo is a prevalent name during the Renaissance. And as Francesco does not distinguish himself in the arts, Antonio da Sangallo (1483-1546), who is unrelated, is the more notable Sangallo the Younger in Renaissance Art. Antonio is an architect who submits plans for Julius' Tomb as well.

*283, l. 22–23. Baldassare Peruzzi (1481–1537).* An architect and painter who competes with Michelangelo for the Tomb of Julius.

## XXIV. THE PUNISHMENT OF HAMAN

*293, Headnote. Esther.* Though I pursue a different Esther, the Esther of the Old Testament, whose name means "Star," is, indeed, solicited for the pool of virgins. Her uncle Mordecai is constantly at the Gate on her behalf, and while there, overhears a plot to kill the king. When Esther is chosen as the next queen, Mordecai reveals the plot to her. She saves the king in Mordecai's name and Mordecai is rewarded. Up till now, Esther has not revealed she is a Jew. The powerful Prince Haman has an altercation with Mordecai, out of which he issues a decree to annihilate the Jews. Esther prompts Ahasuerus to invite Haman to a private banquet. Haman by now has prepared gallows for Mordecai and the Jews. At the banquet Esther manages to turn the tables on Haman, so he is hanged on the gallows he has constructed.

The occasion of the turning of the tables is the alleged origin of the Feast of Purim. In keeping the Feast each year, Jews remember and honor the beautiful and courageous Esther, who offered herself for the safety of her people.

The Book of Esther is not verifiable. Records do not show a queen named Esther or a Jewish queen by any name at the court of Ahasuerus, who is also known as Xerxes, the Persian King (476–465 B.C.). The name Ahasuerus means "Mighty Eye." It is thought that the Book of Esther is written around 125 B.C. The real Xerxes is murdered in his palace in 465 B.C.

Michelangelo strays from the Biblical version and portrays Haman's tortured body as nailed to a tree, a rendering that might derive from Dante's reference in *The Purgatorio* to Haman as crucified. Haman is placed dramatically in the center of the fresco, surrounded by a surreal collection of scenes leading to his punishment.

*293, Headnote. Vashti.* When Vashti refuses to submit totally to her husband's commands, Ahasuerus issues a decree, tantamount to the first Biblical evidence of male chauvinism: " 'And let this be published through all the provinces, and let all wives, as well of the greater as of the lesser, give honor to their husbands.' And he sent letters to all the provinces of his kingdom, as every nation could hear and read, in diverse languages and characters, that the husbands should be rulers and masters of their houses: and that this should be published to every people." The decree is enacted and Vashti is put away, that "another, that is better than her, be made queen in her place."

339, Headnote. *Moses.* The name means "Drawn from the Water," possibly derived from an Egyptian word meaning "Son," "Child." He is the legendary leader who shepherds the Jews from Egypt through their 40 years wandering to Palestine, during which he retrieves the Ten Commandments. Eventually Moses—deliverer, leader, lawgiver, judge, prophet and father to his people—leads them to the borders of a new land, but is not himself allowed to enter.

340, l. 16–17. *Torah.* The first five books of the Bible (Genesis, Exodus, Leviticus, Numbers, and Deuteronomy) as well as the scroll of parchment or leather on which the books are written.

341, l. 23. *Aaron.* The brother of Moses, the spiritual conduit between Moses and the people.

343, l. 7–8. *Joseph.* The son of Jacob and Rachel, whose name means "May He Add," "He Shall Add," "Increaser." Through him the Jews come to settle in Egypt. It is "Joseph's tribes" that populate and threaten the Egyptian culture to the point that Ramses orders all Hebrew males killed at birth and thus the stage is set for Moses. Legend has it that before Moses can lead the Jews out of Egypt, he must take Joseph's bones with him.

343, l. 15. *Antechamber of Egyptian Kings.* An edifice most likely built by Ramses II (1301–1234 B.C.) who is pharoah during the Exodus of the Jews under Moses.

344, l. 11. *Isis.* The Egyptian god, identified by the Greeks with Demeter and Hera. Her popularity is such that she absorbs the qualities of all the goddesses, but originally she is the protective deity of the Nile Delta. Wed to Osiris, they bear a son, Horus; all three form an Egyptian trinity. The cow is sacred to Isis, who possesses the magic knot "Tat," called "The Knot of Isis." She is normally represented as a woman who bears a throne on her head.

344, l. 11. *Khnum.* The Egyptian god of the region of the Cataracts. Portrayed as a ram-headed man with long wavy horns, he is a god of fecundity and creation. He presides over the formation of children in the womb.

344, l. 12. *onyx bird.* Perhaps the Egyptian god Bennu; a lapwing or a heron, worshipped as the soul of Osiris.

345, l. 23. *Benjamites.* One of the 12 tribes of Israel; a small but powerful warlike tribe, descendent from Benjamin. Saul, the first King of Judah, is a Benjamite; and the Benjamites are faithful to him and his heirs. They support David and Solomon. Saul of Tarsus, who becomes Paul the Apostle, is a Benjamite.

345, l. 23. *Judeans.* Another of the 12 tribes of Israel, the descendants of Judah, the fourth son of Leah. The name Judah means "May God be Praised." It is Judah who hates Joseph, who suggests, after Reuben refuses to let Joseph be killed, that he be sold into slavery. The tribe of Judah becomes a dominant one, largely by absorbing Simeon and by adding the Kenites and the Calebites and, eventually, the Benjamites. When the kingdom is divided after the death of Solomon, the kingdom of Israel is in the north with Samaria as its capital, and it includes ten of the tribes. The kingdom of Judah is in the south with Jerusalem as its capital, and it is comprised of the Judeans and the Benjamites. The closer we get to the Age of Christ, the more interchangeable Judah and Israel become.

350, l. 5. *parasong.* A unit of measurement in Hell.

352, below l. 32. *Laocoon.* An overwhelming Greek statue from the first century B.C., believed to be done by Agesandrus and his sons, Polydorus and Atendorus. It portrays Laocoon, the priest of ancient Troy, and his sons being swept down by serpents, as they try to warn their people about the Trojan Horse. Michelangelo witnesses its excavation in Rome in 1506, and it influences him profoundly.

357, l. 2–3. *Miriam.* The sister of Aaron and Moses, thought to be the eldest of the three. Her name means "Fat," "Thick," "Strong," "Bitter." It might be Miriam who stands guard over the child Moses hidden in the rushes and who, when he is discovered by the servant of pharoah's daughter, offers to call a nurse for him. It is Miriam who stands in protest with Aaron to Moses' marriage to a Cushite woman, Sepporah. They begin to question his authority, reminding each other that they, too, have the power of prophecy. As tension mounts, God calls them into the tent and describes the difference between them, by saying that He speaks "mouth to mouth" with Moses, to them only in visions.

359, l. 21–22. *Marah.* The bitter oasis in the desert from which the Jews cannot drink, and where some die of thirst, until God points out a piece of wood, and when Moses throws it in the water, the water becomes fresh.

361, l. 24. *Tabernacle.* The portable sanctuary in which the Jews carry the Ark of the Covenant through the desert.

*In providing a chronology useful to the poem, I have fused E.H. Ramsden's chronology of Michelangelo's entire life, which can be found in* The Letters of Michelangelo, Volumes I & II *(Stanford University Press, 1963), with Charles Seymour's chronology of The Sistine Ceiling, from* Michelangelo, The Sistine Chapel Ceiling *(Norton & Co., 1972). Using that as a frame, I've added dates and details crucial to the poem, and have commented freely throughout. The numbers in parentheses denote the sculptor's age. And Michelangelo's sonnet regarding his toils at the Ceiling is my version of John Addington Symonds' translation. It helps to begin with Berenson's remark, "He passed most of his life in the midst of tragic disasters. In his most creative years he found himself alone, perhaps the greatest but, alas, also the last of the giants born so plentifully during the 15th century."*

*March 6, 1475: Caprese.* Michelangelo Buonarroti is born to Francesca di Neri di Miniato del Sera at Caprese in the Casentino where his father, Lodovico, is Podesta.

*1481 (6): Florence.* Death of Michelangelo's mother, Francesca, at the age of 26.

*1485 (10):* Marriage of Lodovico to Lucrezia Ubaldini, his second wife. Michelangelo attends the school of Francesco da Urbino.

*1488 (13):* Michelangelo is apprenticed to Domenico and David Ghirlandaio, April 1st.

*1489 (14):* Enters the sculpture school in the Medici Garden under the aging Bertoldo di Giovanni, a pupil of Donatello. Francesco Granacci, his boyhood friend, is also taken into the Garden after apprenticing with Ghirlandaio.

*1490 (15):* Received into the household of Lorenzo the Magnificent. There he works his early statues: *The Faun, The Madonna of the Stairs, The Battle of the Centaurs,* and *Hercules.*

*1492 (17):* Death of Lorenzo the Magnificent, April 8th. During this time, he carves a wooden *Crucifix for San Spirito,* where he studies anatomy in rooms provided by the Prior.

*1494 (19): Florence, Bologna, Venice, Bologna.* Flight to Bologna and Venice in October with Granacci and Cardiere, the Garden musician. Returns to Bologna and lives in the house of Gianfrancesco Aldrovandi. Piero de' Medici, Lorenzo's eldest, is expelled from Florence on November 9th. At the same time, the Friar Savonarola is rising to power. While in Bologna with Aldrovandi, Michelangelo works *The Kneeling Angel* as one of three statues done for the church of San Domenico.

*1495 (20): Bologna, Florence.* Michelangelo returns to Florence, where he works a statue of *St. John*, and a *Sleeping Cupid*, which is sold to Baldassare in Rome as an antique.

*1496 (21): Florence, Rome.* Michelangelo arrives for the first time in Rome on June 25th. He is commissioned by Cardinal Riario to sculpt *The Bacchus.*

*1497 (22): Rome, Carrara.* Death of Michelangelo's stepmother Lucrezia in July. Now living with the banker Galli, he is commissioned to sculpt *The Pieta.* Travels in November for the first time to Carrara, where he quarries the marble for The Pieta.

*1498 (23): Carrara, Rome.* In Carrara at least until April. Hard at work on The Pieta. On May 22nd, Savonarola is burned at the stake in the piazza before the Palazzo Vecchio in Florence. By August Michelangelo is in Rome for the formal contract for The Pieta. Signed on the 27th, it promises "the most beautiful work in marble which exists today."

*1499 (24): Rome.* Spends the year at work on The Pieta. According to Charles Rich, "It must have been inspired, because how could a boy, 24 years old, create a work like that? You can't imagine how. It was a special grace from God. It is true, he had to be an artist, but art alone could not have made The Pieta. The Pieta transforms you inwardly . . . The spiritual and the artistic have never been so perfectly blended. One is inseparable from the other; and the fact that both reached the same degree of depth and intensity and mastery in one person, that is the essence which makes Michelangelo unique."

*1500 (25): Rome.* No records exist of what Michelangelo is working on in this year. Though there is no definitive date, The Pieta is completed during this period. The fall brings the great flood of 1500 to Rome. And during this time the young Polish astronomer, Copernicus, is lecturing in Rome.

*1501 (26): Rome, Florence.* Michelangelo returns to Florence, and is contracted, on May 22nd, for 15 figures for the Piccolomini Chapel in Siena, which he abandons once securing his commission to do *The David*, on August 16th.

*1502 (27): Florence.* Contracted on August 12th to do a bronze David, which is eventually completed by Benedetto da Rovezzano in 1508.

*1503 (28): Florence.* While working on David, he paints *The Doni Tondo*, and contracts to sculpt the 12 Apostles for Santa Maria del Fiore, a commitment he never fulfills. On September 22nd, the aged and ailing Francesco Piccolomini is elected Pope Pius III, only to die 26 days later on October 19th. And on November 1st, Giuliano della Rovere is elected Pope Julius II.

*1504 (29): Florence.* Michelangelo completes The David in April. And in October he is commissioned to execute a fresco, *The Battle of Cascina*, for the Sala del Consiglio in the Palazzo Vecchio. This marks the only time that Michelangelo and Leonardo face each other artistically. On one wall Leonardo, who is 52, paints *The Battle of Anghiari*, a skirmish among mounted troops, enabling him to explore his mastery of horses. On the opposite wall Michelangelo, freshly off his David, is eager to pursue his gift for human anatomy and chooses to render The Battle of Cascina, an ancient clash with Pisa which had taken place on July 31, 1364. In those days, Pisa had recruited a band of English mercenaries led by John Hawkwood. The Florentines were camped six miles north of Pisa at Cascina, and Hawkwood planned to surprise them while bathing in the Arno. But the Florentines were ready, because an old salt, Manno Donati, had called a false alarm the day before while the men were bathing themselves of the heat. Michelangelo chooses the instant Donati calls out as the moment of his drawing, offering himself an opportunity to create a burst of naked men in every contortion possible.

The size of these projects is enormous. The supplies for Leonardo's Cartoon alone consist of one ream and 29 quires, or about 288 square feet of royal folio paper, the mere pasting of which necessitates 88 pounds of flour.

Neither Cascina nor Anghiari survive. Leonardo, with the aid of a passage in Pliny, tries to fathom the secret of how the ancients had prepared wax pigments. He lights fires to harden the surface of his fresco. This melts the wax in the lower portions of the paste, and the colors run as his paints blister off the wall. And Michelangelo is summoned to Rome by Julius in March 1505 to execute his Tomb. Michelangelo's Cartoon, near completion, is eventually handled and neglected until only fragments remain. We only know what both may have looked like by a copy of Anghiari done by Rubens, and a copy of Cascina done by Aristotile da Sangallo.

Of the originals, Cellini writes: "Michelangelo portrayed a number of foot-soldiers, who, the season being summer, had gone to bathe in the Arno. He drew them at the very moment the alarm is sounded, and the men all naked run to arms; so splendid is their action, that nothing survives of ancient or modern art which touches the same lofty point of excellence; and, as I have already said, the design of the great Leonardo was itself most admirably beautiful. These two Cartoons stood, one in the palace of the Medici, the other in the hall of the Pope. So long as they remained intact, they were the school of the world. Though the divine Michelangelo in later life finished that great chapel of Pope Julius (the Sistine), he never rose halfway to the same pitch of power; his genius never afterwards attained the same force of those first studies."

*1505 (30): Florence, Rome, Carrara.* In March Michelangelo is summoned to Rome and commissioned to execute *The Tomb of Julius.* In April he goes to Carrara to quarry marble for The Tomb, returning to Rome in December.

*1506 (31): Rome, Florence, Bologna.* On January 14th Michelangelo witnesses an extraordinary excavation of The Laocoon, an ancient Greek sculpture believed to have been done by Agesandrus and his sons, Polydorus and Atendorus, during the middle of the first century B.C. It is unearthed in Rome, in the vineyard of de Freddis above the ruins of the Baths of Titus, and it influences Michelangelo tremendously.

On April 17th, after difficulties with Julius, Michelangelo flees from Rome to Florence. On April 18th, with Bramante at his side, Julius breaks ground for the new St. Peter's. After months of anxiety and three Papal Briefs, Michelangelo leaves for Bologna on November 28th to submit himself to Julius, who exacts penance from the sculptor in the form of a bronze statue of himself.

*1507 (32): Bologna.* At work on *The Bronze Statue of Julius.*

*1508 (33): Bologna, Florence, Rome.* On February 13 he completes the statue of Julius and returns to Florence by mid-March. By the end of March or the beginning of April Michelangelo is called to Rome to work on *The Sistine Ceiling.*

In 1473, Pope Sixtus IV, who was Julius' uncle, began building a ceremonial Chapel next to the Vatican, which had only recently become the permanent Papal residence. One of the functions of the Chapel was to house the Cardinals during the conclave which elected a new Pope. As author of the project, Sixtus had the Chapel named after himself (Sixtine/Sistine) and built according to the proportions of Solomon's Temple, as described in the Book of Kings ("the length is twice its height and three times its width"). All the surfaces that Solomon had covered in cedar and gold were to be painted.

In 1483 Giovannino dei Dolci finished The Sistine Chapel. Its flattened barrel-vault was painted by Pier Matteo d'Amelia with gold stars on a blue background, following an ancient tradition where the vault is considered to be the image of the sky. And Sixtus had assembled a renowned group of painters to line the south side of the Chapel with scenes from the life of Moses, and the north with scenes from the life of Christ; including Botticelli, Signorelli, Perugino, Rosselli, and Ghirlandaio. The Chapel was dedicated to Mary Assunta and Perugino painted a fresco of *The Assumption* on the altar wall, which Michelangelo would cover as well in due time with *The Last Judgment.*

*May 10, 1508: Rome.* Contract for the Ceiling is signed in Rome: "On this May 10, 1508, I, Michelangelo, sculptor, have received on account from our Holy Lord Pope Julius II 500 papal ducats toward the painting of the ceiling of the papal Sistine Chapel, on which I am beginning to work today according to those conditions and agreements which appear in the contract written by the most reverend Monsignor of Pavia (Francesco Alidosi, a close friend of Julius) and signed by me." According to De Tolnay, the actual painting does not begin until January 1509, the interim being spent on preparatory work.

*May 13, 1508:* Orders pigments from Florence from Father Jacopo of the Order of the Gesuati: "As I have to supervise certain things to be painted here, or rather, I must myself paint them, I have to inform you that I need a certain quantity of first-quality blue pigment. See that you send whatever you may have of first quality."

*June 10, 1508:* Scaffolding being worked on during the Vespers of the Vigil of the Pentecost, as reported by Paris de Grassis, Master of Ceremonies at the Papal Court: "In the upper portions of the Chapel, the scaffolding was being constructed causing a lot of dust, and the carpenters did not stop as I ordered. The Cardinals complained of this. Moreover, when I had reproved them several times and they did not stop, I went to the Pope who was angry with me. The work continued without permission even though the Pope sent two of his chamberlains who ordered the work stopped, which was finally done with difficulty."

*July 27, 1508:* Scaffolding probably in place, as the Ceiling is being prepared to be painted.

*August 7, 1508:* Contemplates hiring assistants. Granacci responds from Florence: "The others are talking about finishing off their work first before going to Rome and that it is not possible to do anything else until Easter. At best Giuliano (Bugiardini) and Jacopo (di Sandro), though wanting to do so sooner, cannot get off because of pledges they have given for other work. Jacopo would clearly like to know what he is to be paid. I have not spoken with others, but it seems to me Agnolo di Donnino is handy for fresco work. If you need more help let me know; I will do nothing more until you reply. Something may come up so I might get away anyway, if necessary, I alone and Bastiano (Aristotile da Sangallo)."

*September 2, 1508:* Pigments sent from Florence.

*October 7, 1508:* Assistants, known as the Florentine Expedition, arrive in Rome including: Granacci, his boyhood friend; Jacopo Indaco, a fellow student in Ghirlandaio's school; Giuliano Bugiardini, who also had joined the Garden school of Bertoldo back in 1489; Aristotile da Sangallo, the nephew of Giuliano da Sangallo, who had been a disciple of Perugino, but who joined Michelangelo on seeing The Battle of Cascina (It is his copy of Cascina that survives today); three other painters; and Jacopo di Sandro, who is dismissed at once.

*January 27, 1509 (34):* By the end of January Michelangelo has dismissed all his assistants and is working alone. Work is going badly. Vasari reports that during the winter spots of mold appear on the Ceiling, and Condivi mentions that Michelangelo consults Giuliano da Sangallo about the problem.

*June 3, 1509:* Sometime prior to this date Albertini, author of a famous Roman guide-book, sees part of the Ceiling.

*June, 1509:* Michelangelo is ill.

*September 15, 1509:* Michelangelo receives a payment from the Pope.

*1510 (35):* Michelangelo writes to Giovanni da Pistoia, sending him a sonnet about working the barrel vault:

ON PAINTING THE SISTINE CHAPEL

I've grown a goiter from squatting
in this den. It rubs the belly with the chin.
As cats in stagnant Lombard streams, my beard
drips to Heaven, my nape falls in.
Fixed on my spine, my cage bends like a harp
and brush-drops slick my face.
My loins into my paunch like levers grind.
My buttock like a crupper bears my weight.
In front my skin hangs loose,
crosswise I strain, all false
and quaint, a Syrian bow: I know
bad fruit of squinting brain.
Come then, Giovanni, try,
try to succor my dead
pictures and my fame,
for painting is my shame.

Your Michelangelo,
Sculptor in Rome

Sometime in the fall (1510), the scaffolding is taken down to be moved. De Tolnay maintains that only the first half of the vault, up to and including *The Creation of Eve,* is done at this point.

I o gia facto ungozo inquesto stento
chome fa lacqua agacti inlonbardia
ouer daltro paese chessi chesisia
cha forza luentre apicha soctolmeto

La barba alcielo ellamemoria sento
insullo scrignio elpecto fo darpia
elpennel sopraluiso tuctauia
melfa gocciando un riccho pauimeto

E lobi entrati miso nella peccia
e fo delcul p chotrapeso groppa
epassi seza ghochi muouo inuano

Dinazi misallunga lachorteccia
ep piegarsi adietro siragroppa
e tedomi comarcho soriano

po fallace escrano
surgie iludicio che lamete porta
ch mal sispra p cerboctana torta

lamia pictura morta
disendi orma giouanni elmio onore
no sedo flosg bo ne io pictore

*Manuscript of the Sonnet to Giovanni da Pistoia*

*1511 (36):* Michelangelo undergoes a series of altercations with an impatient Julius, including being struck by a stick and threatened. With only touches of tempera missing, both ultramarine and gold, Michelangelo declares the vault complete. On August 14th or 15th the vault is unveiled. For De Tolnay, this means everything is complete except the lunettes. By early October Michelangelo begins the lunettes.

*1512 (37):* In July the Duke of Ferrara, who is in Rome to regain Julius' favor after skirmishes of alliance, visits Michelangelo, as Grossino, a minor diplomat at the Court, reports: "The Duke came to the Vatican Palace with his attendants and they dined in the Papal Chamber. His Excellency wished very much to see the ceiling of the large Chapel which Michelangelo was painting, and Federico (the Duke's nephew) arranged to ask the Pope's permission. The Duke went up to the ceiling with several people who one by one came down, while the Duke stayed above with Michelangelo and could not look enough at those figures. These pleased him so much that his Excellency wished to have Michelangelo paint him a picture and talked with him, offered him money, and had him promise he would paint for him. After the Duke came down from the scaffold, I wanted him to see the Papal Stanze which Raphael was painting, but he did not want to go."

This is the same Duke who, in recapturing Bologna the year before (1511), had Michelangelo's bronze statue of Julius melted in his cannon foundry and made into a gun to use against Julius.

By early October the lunettes are done. By the end of the month the entire Ceiling is unveiled. Condivi records the toll of such effort: "At the conclusion of this work, Michelangelo, because he had painted so long with his eyes turned upward toward the vault, could hardly see anything when looking down. When he had to read a letter or look at a small object, it was necessary for him to hold it over his head."

*1513 (38): Rome.* On February 20th Julius lays ill in bed and sets the program for the carnival season, then gives instructions for his interment. As a last effort to save him, he is given molten gold to drink. On the 21st Pope Julius dies. Erasmus had said of him: "He wages war, wins victories and plays the role of Caesar to perfection." On March 11th Giovanni de' Medici, Lorenzo's second son, at 37, is elected Pope Leo X. On May 6th Michelangelo signs the first contract for The Tomb of Julius with the della Rovere heirs. From this time through the next four years he works on *Moses,* and *The Captives.*

*1514 (39): Rome, Florence.* Contracted on June 14th for *The Risen Christ.*

*1515 (40): Rome, Florence, Carrara.* In April he visits Florence briefly, and in September goes to Carrara for marble for The Tomb, which continues to plague him.

*1516 (41): Rome, Florence, Carrara.* On July 8th he signs the second contract for The Tomb of Julius. He spends the summer in Florence, and the fall in Carrara, and leaves for Rome in December to see the Medici Pope, Leo X, in connection with the proposed *Facade of San Lorenzo,* the Medici family church in Florence.

*1517 (42): Carrara, Florence.* In January he returns to Carrara and stays engaged in the quarries until August, when he returns to Florence to prepare a model of The Facade.

*1518 (43)–1520 (45): Rome, Carrara, Florence, Pietra Santa.* On January 19th, 1518 he signs a contract with Leo X for The Facade of San Lorenzo, and wastes much of these years at Pietra Santa, where he is forced to open a new marble quarry. And on March 10th, 1520 the contract for The Facade is cancelled.

*1521 (46): Florence, Carrara.* In Rome on December 1st Leo X, only 45, dies.

*1522 (47): Florence.* In Rome on January 9th Adrian Dedel of Utrecht is elected Pope Adrian VI. Adrian, who was formerly a professor in Louvain, arrives in August. He is austere and monkish and takes deep offense to the nude figures in Michelangelo's Sistine Ceiling. He even covers his face when standing before the much-admired Laocoon group. In Florence Michelangelo begins to work on *The Medici Tombs.*

*1523 (48): Florence, Rome.* Adrian VI dies on September 14th, and Giulio de' Medici is elected Pope Clement VII.

*1524 (49): Florence.* In January he accepts a monthly salary of 50 ducats from Pope Clement. He is occupied on models for The Medici Tombs, and on designs for *The New Sacristy,* and for *The Laurentian Library.*

*1525 (50): Florence.* In June he appoints Francesco Fattucci as his attorney in the negotiations for yet another contract for The Tomb of Julius.

*1526 (51): Florence.* At work on The Medici Tombs, The New Sacristy, and The Laurentian Library.

*1527 (52): Florence.* On May 6th while in Florence Rome is sacked by a large Hispano-German army riding under Charles of Bourbon. Gold and silver to the value of ten million is carried away. The rich are forced to ransom themselves. Campfires are kindled on the mosaic floors of the Vatican, and stain-glass windows are smashed to get the lead mullions. The public statuary is broken with a savagery matched only by the Vandals, and the churches and madonnas are badly mauled. On May 17th the Medici are expelled from Florence. On November 29th Michelangelo is appointed to superintend the fortifications at Bologna. He doesn't go. On December 9th Pope Clement escapes to Orvieto.

*1528 (53): Florence.* On July 2nd Michelangelo's closest brother, Buonarroto, dies of tuberculosis.

*1529 (54): Florence, Pisa, Leghorn, Ferrara.* In April he is appointed Governor General of Tuscan fortifications, and throughout the summer he inspects fortifications at Pisa, Leghorn, and Ferrara. On September 21st, as Florence is under siege, Michelangelo flees to Venice. From Venice he writes: "I left home without saying a word to any of my friends and in great confusion; you know that I wanted to go to France, and often asked to leave, but did not get it. Nevertheless, I was quite resolved, and without fear, to see the end of the war out first. But on Tuesday morning, September 21st, a certain person came out by the gate at San Niccolo, where I was attending the bastions, and whispered in my ear that if I meant to save my life I must not stay in Florence. He accompanied me home, dined there, brought me horses, and never left my side until he got me outside the city, declaring this was my only salvation. Whether God or the devil was the man, I do not know."

*1531 (56): Florence.* Michelangelo's father, Lodovico, dies. In September Michelangelo completes *Dawn* and *Night* for The Medici Tombs, but experiences a serious nervous breakdown, complicated by inflammation of the head and eyes. On September 29th G.B. Mini writes, "It is a long time since I have seen Michelangelo, he has been confined to his house for a week . . . he seems very thin and shrunken to me . . . I have spoken about him in confidence to Bugiardini and Antonio Mini and we all fear that he will not live long unless some measures are taken for his health. He works very hard, eats little and poorly, and sleeps less. For a month or more he has been strongly afflicted with headaches and dizziness." On November 21st he receives a Papal Brief forbidding him to work for anyone save the Pope.

*1532 (57): Florence, Rome.* Maneuvers back and forth between Florence and Rome, unable to find peace in either place, but does meet Tommaso del Cavaliere in Rome, a man who becomes a life-long friend. In the winter he writes as part of a sonnet (Girardi 66), "without other guide, my soul has fallen, that was once worthy . . . so near to death and yet so far from God." In April the third contract for The Tomb of Julius is signed.

*1534 (59): Rome, Florence, Rome.* In May he returns to Florence for the last time, and in September moves to Rome permanently and doesn't venture from the city for the rest of his days. On September 25th Pope Clement dies. On October 13th Alessandro Farnese is elected Pope Paul III.

*1535 (60): Rome.* Begins preparatory work for *The Last Judgment,* the painting of the altar wall in The Sistine Chapel. On April 16th the joiner Perino del Capitano receives 25 florins for the erection of a scaffold. On September 1st Pope Paul III appoints Michelangelo as Supreme Sculptor, Painter, and Architect to the Vatican at a salary of 1200 scudi a year. On December 7th the scaffolding for The Last Judgment is fully paid for.

*1536 (61):* From January to April the altar wall is being prepared. This includes tearing down three frescos by Perugino (The Assumption on the altar wall, a fresco of St. Peter, and a fresco of Jesus), as well as tearing down two of his own lunettes, painted as part of the Ceiling over 20 years before. Two windows are walled up. Michelangelo orders the wall itself to be inclined forward about half an ell toward the top, hoping to protect his work against the accumulation of dust. Sebastiano del Piombo persuades the Pope that the painting will look best in oil, and the wall is prepared to receive oil pigments. This delays the beginning of the work, as Michelangelo declares oil-painting an effeminate art and insists on painting al fresco, as he had done with the Ceiling. The wall surface has to be done over, and Michelangelo severs ties with Sebastiano.

In May Michelangelo begins work on The Last Judgment. During the year he is introduced to Vittoria Colonna, Marchesa di Pescara, whom he befriends quickly and deeply. On November 17th Paul issues a motu proprio exempting Michelangelo from legal penalties consequent upon his non-fulfillment of the contract of 1532 for The Tomb of Julius.

*1537 (62)–1539 (64):* At work on The Last Judgment, which takes on the same exhaustive exploration of the naked human form as his lost Battle of Cascina: souls ascending from the grave, the damned tumbling into Hell, the martyrs writhing toward Heaven, the elect turning, yearning toward Christ; all naked, even Mary, and the risen Christ with no robe or beard. It seems profoundly simple: what need of clothes when called from the grave?

*1540 (65):* On December 15th payment is made for lowering the scaffold.

*1541 (66):* Michelangelo falls from the scaffold and severely injures his leg. He is found on the Chapel floor, unable to move, enraged. He orders himself delivered home. Once there he orders the doors locked and that he be left alone. Within a few days the physician Baccio Rontini forces his way into the sculptor's home to help him. The Last Judgment is completed and uncovered on October 31st. On November 19 Nino Sernini writes to Cardinal Gonzaga: "There is no lack of condemnation; the most reverend hypocrites are the first to say that nudity should not appear in such a place . . . and the beardless face of Christ is too young." According to Symonds, "The Last Judgment remains a stupendous miracle. The note is of sustained menace and terror . . . a sense-deafening solo on trombone." The public unveiling is reserved for Christmas day.

*1542 (67):* He signs the fourth and last contract for The Tomb of Julius on August 20th.

*1544 (69):* In July Michelangelo is taken seriously ill and is nursed by Luigi del Riccio. On New Year's eve there is a fire on the roof of The Sistine Chapel.

*1545 (70):* In February he at last completes The Tomb of Julius, and in July completes the fresco of *The Conversion of St. Paul.* In December the Council of Trent opens session. Michelangelo again takes ill and is again nursed by Luigi del Riccio.

*1546 (71):* At work on the fresco, *The Martyrdom of St. Peter.* On March 20th he receives the honor of Roman citizenship. On August 3rd Antonio da Sangallo, the Architect of St. Peter's, dies, and in September Luigi del Riccio dies.

*1547 (72):* On January 1st he is appointed Architect of St. Peter's in succession to Antonio da Sangallo. On February 25th his intimate, Vittoria Colonna, dies. In the spring Benedetto Varchi delivers a discourse on Michelangelo's sonnets to The Florentine Academy. In June Sebastiano del Piombo dies.

*1548 (73):* On January 9th his brother Giovansimone dies.

*1549 (74):* March finds him ill with a severe attack of the stone. On October 11th he is given supreme powers as Architect of St. Peter's. In October Pope Paul views the almost completed fresco of The Martyrdom of St. Peter, and on November 10th Pope Paul III dies.

*1550 (75)–1552 (77):* In 1550 Gianmaria del Monte is elected Pope Julius III, Vasari publishes his famous *Lives of the Artists,* and Michelangelo completes The Martyrdom of St. Peter.

During this period (1550–1552) Michelangelo is deeply involved with *The Nicodemus Pieta,* which he intends for his own tomb, and in which the figure of Nicodemus is believed to be a self-portrait. More than half-finished, the sculptor grows frustrated, loses patience, and strikes the statue repeatedly until stopped by his servant Antonio. The damage is severe. The left arm of Christ is broken at the shoulder, carrying with it the Virgin's left hand and a small area of Christ's breast around the nipple. Michelangelo is unsettled, embarrassed, and unresolved. Vasari visits him at night and finds him working on the broken Pieta and, to prevent Vasari from seeing it, the sculptor lets the lantern fall. He ushers Vasari through the dark saying, "I am so old that often death pulls me by the cloak to go with him."

It is revealing that Michelangelo should choose Nicodemus as his own likeness. Nicodemus means "Champion of the People." He was a Pharisee and ruler of the Jews who wanted to know more of Jesus, but was afraid to be associated with him openly. He therefore sought Jesus by night to discuss various matters of importance.

*1553 (78):* July sees the publication of *The Life of Michelangelo Buonarroti* by his young friend Ascanio Condivi. It is generally regarded as a dictated autobiography, and seems to have been generated as a reaction to Vasari's version of his life.

The French traveler Vigenere visits Michelangelo and writes: "I saw Michelangelo at work when he was over 60, and though he was not very strong, he struck more chips off the defiant marble block in a quarter-hour than three or four young stone masons could have done in three or four times as long—which may sound incredible, unless one saw it. So zealous was he that I was sure the work must break in pieces. With a single blow he struck off pieces three or four fingers thick, and he struck the marked point so precisely that the whole would have been destroyed, had only a little more marble split off."

*1555 (80):* Michelangelo's brother Sigismondo dies.

*1557 (82):* Ludovico Dolce writes to Gaspero Ballini complaining about the nudity in The Last Judgment: "No one can convince me that it is not possible to demonstrate great talent in painting without displaying those parts of the human body which were intended by nature to be concealed. Michelangelo is beyond the limit of decency; his work is flagrantly obscene."

*1560 (85):* He completes the model of *The Cupola of St. Peter's.*

*1561 (86):* Michelangelo has a seizure but recovers quickly. On September 6 the theologian Saurolo writes to St. Charles Borromeo reproaching the nudity in The Last Judgment: "It was greatly displeasing to Paul III, of blessed memory, and if he had lived longer he would have done something about it; this was told to me by Cardinal Santacroce, and I also remember that Cardinal Alessandrino told me that Paul IV also wanted to make changes, having in mind to enlarge the Chapel by pushing back the rear wall. I argued with everyone about this. I also know that in the last year of the reign of Paul IV, Michelangelo was heard to say that he desired in every way to cover the nudity of the painting because it was on his conscience to leave such a picture."

*1564 (89):* On January 12 the Congregation of the Council, upon the advice and full consent of Pope Pius IV, decrees that the nude bodies in The Last Judgment be covered. The repainting of the nude bodies is commissioned to Michelangelo's devoted pupil, Daniele da Volterra. After

Volterra's death it is continued by Girolamo da Fano. Other painters cover more of the original under Popes Sixtus VI and Clement VII. And still more garments are drawn into the fresco under Popes Gregory XIII and Clement VIII.

In his last days Michelangelo works on yet another Pieta, despite suffering from a fever. Volterra writes that on February 12th, "Michelangelo worked all the Saturday of the Sunday of Carnival and he worked standing up, studying on that body of The Pieta."

On February 14th Tiberio Calcagni writes, "When I went out in Rome today, I heard from many sides that Michelangelo is ill. I went to visit him at his house and though it was raining found him about to go out. I told him I thought it unwise for him to go out in such weather. 'What would you have me do?' he replied. 'I am ill and cannot find rest anywhere.' His uncertain speech and his look and complexion made me afraid for his life."

On the 15th Volterra writes, "I then left him a little after eight in full possession of his senses and in a quiet mood, but plagued with constant drowsiness. This so irritated him that in the afternoon between three and four he tried to go out for a ride as he did every evening in good weather. But the cold weather and the weakness in his head and legs prevented him. He returned to his fireplace and seated himself in his armchair, which he prefers to his bed."

On the 16th he goes to bed. On the 17th, in the presence of two physicians, he dictates his will in three clauses, leaving his soul to God, his body to the earth, his belongings to his nearest relatives. He requests that his coffin be taken to Florence in secret.

On the 18th he dies in the presence of Daniele da Volterra, Antonio del Francese, Diomede Leoni, two doctors, and his dear friend, Tommaso del Cavalieri. Only a few marble works and three cartoons are found among his possessions. He had burned his drawings. And in the year of his death both Galileo and Shakespeare are born.